Consuming public services

Consuming public services

Edited by

Nicholas Deakin

and

Anthony Wright

R

Routledge
London and New York

First published 1990
by Routledge
11 New Fetter Lane, London EC4P 4EE

Simultaneously published in the USA and Canada
by Routledge
a division of Routledge, Chapman and Hall, Inc.
29 West 35th Street, New York, NY 10001

Typeset in 10/11 Times by LaserScript Limited, Mitcham, Surrey
Printed in Great Britain by TJ Press (Padstow) Limited, Padstow, Cornwall

British Library Cataloguing in Publication Data

Consuming public services.
1. Great Britain. Public Services. Administration
I. Deakin, Nicholas II. Wright, Anthony
363'.068
ISBN 0-415-03208-3   344328

Library of Congress Cataloging in Publication Data

Consuming public services / edited by Nicholas Deakin and Anthony Wright.
p. cm.
Includes index.

1. Decentralization in government–Great Britain.
2. Administrative agencies–Great Britain–Evaluation. 3. Consumer
satisfaction–Great Britain. 4. Political participation–Great Britain. I. Deakin,
Nicholas. II. Wright, Anthony.
JN329.D43C66 1989
354.4107'3–dc20   89-33921

Contents

Preface

The original impetus for this book came from discussions between the two editors, arising out of an earlier collaboration on the decentralization of public services. The opportunity to pursue some of the lines of thinking opened up then came when the Fabian Society received a donation of funds designed to support examination of current policy issues. A successful application to the Dartmouth Street Trust for support under the scheme enabled us to bring together a group of contributors with special interests and expertise in various areas of public service to explore the applications of the concept of user control in these areas.

The funding for the project was sufficient to enable us to call the group together for a seminar on the main policy issues. This was held in September 1987; we owe thanks not only to our collaborators for taking part in this event but also to a number of other people with special interests in the field who joined our discussions and helped us to clear our thoughts on the major priorities: John Stewart, Colin Ward, and Geoffrey Hulme. Fircroft College acted as hosts and we are grateful to Pam Davies for helping with the arrangements.

In Birmingham University, Mary Knox looked after the administration of the project with her customary efficiency; at the Fabian Society, John Willman kept a benevolent eye on the progress of the project. Our thanks to both of them.

Finally, and most important, we would like to record our gratitude to our contributors. Although we should set down the usual formal disclaimer, to the effect that they take no collective responsibility for the views expressed in our conclusions, their active participation and lively interest in the whole project made it (for us, at least) an unusually agreeable editorial experience.

Nicholas Deakin
Anthony Wright
Birmingham, December 1988

Contributors

Marian Barnes worked for several years in research and development posts in social services departments. She has also been a shop steward and Nalgo branch president. She is currently a Research Fellow in the Department of Social Policy and Social Work at the University of Birmingham and has recently jointly completed a major piece of research into the implementation of the Mental Health Act, 1983.

David Clapham is Assistant Director of the Centre for Housing Research at the University of Glasgow. He has carried out research into a wide range of housing issues including the organization and effectiveness of housing management and the structure and role of housing co-operatives.

Nicholas Deakin has been Professor of Social Policy and Administration at the University of Birmingham since 1980. Before that he worked in local government and in an independent research organization. His most recent book is *The Politics of Welfare* (London: Methuen, 1987).

William Hampton is a Professor in the Division of Continuing Education, University of Sheffield. His research interests are centred on the ways in which local government can contribute to a participatory democracy. His recent books include *Public Participation in Local Services* (co-authored with N. Boaden, M. Goldsmith, and P. Stringer: Longman, 1982) and *Local Government and Urban Politics* (London: Longman, 1987).

Christine Hogg has worked for many years in the health field both in the UK and overseas, including a period with a community health council. She now works part-time at the Relief and Development Institute, London, and as a freelance writer and researcher, mainly on health and social service issues.

Rod Morgan is director of the Bristol and Bath Centre for Criminal Justice and co-editor of *Policing and Society*, an international journal and *Coming to Terms with Policing* (London: Routledge, 1989). He is currently engaged on research into the implementation of the Police and Criminal Evidence Act, 1984.

David Prior trained and worked in manufacturing industry before undertaking academic social policy research. He has subsequently held research, planning, and development posts in social services departments and a health authority, and is currently head of the planning unit at Birmingham Social Services Department.

Stewart Ranson is Professor of Education, and chair of the Centre for Education Management and Policy Studies, at the University of Birmingham. He has researched and written widely on the government of education and public-sector management and is the author of *The Politics of Reorganising Schools* (London: Unwin Hyman, forthcoming).

Neil Thomas is a Senior Lecturer in the Department of Social Policy and Social Work, University of Birmingham. His investigations, over twenty years, into how services respond to people with special needs have always included a user perspective and he has tried to use the insights gained to inform his teaching of service managers. He edits the journal *Social Services Research*.

Enid Wistrich is a Lecturer in Public Administration at Middlesex Polytechnic. She has served on a London borough council and on the Greater London Council, where she was vice-chair of the Transport Committee. She is the author of *The Politics of Transport* (London: Longman, 1983).

Anthony Wright is Senior Lecturer in Political Studies in the School of Continuing Studies, University of Birmingham. He is a former chair of a community health council and organizes training courses for school governors. His publications include *G.D.H. Cole and Socialist Democracy* (Oxford: Oxford University Press, 1979), *Socialisms: Theories and Practices* (Oxford: Oxford University Press, 1986), and *R. H. Tawney* (Manchester: Manchester University Press, 1987).

Introduction

Nicholas Deakin and Anthony Wright

The public services are now at the centre of political debate in Britain. That, at least, is to be welcomed. So far, the initiative in this debate has come overwhelmingly from the political Right and, in deliberately cracking the post-war consensus on the issue, this has had the positive effect of raising questions about the appropriate role of the state in the provision of services and about the efficiency of the organization and delivery of such services. Rather, it could have had this positive effect if the spirit of the approach were not so unremittingly negative and ideological.

Instead of a drive for better public services, the Right has launched a drive for fewer public services. In justification, it has simply relied on an Orwellian incantation of 'public bad, private good'. Instead of seeking ways to extend choice, improve quality, and strengthen accountability within public services for all, it has preferred to find ways to give more choice to some and even (as with the opt-out provisions for schools) more opportunities for some to exit altogether. Behind the 'power to the people' rhetoric of the prospectus that launched the third Thatcher government, there was the barely concealed reality of a programme which promised more power to some people, notably to those who were already in possession of a disproportionately generous share of that commodity. Moreover, in its preoccupation with the economy and efficiency of public services, the Right has altogether evaded the further and fundamental question of the effectiveness of such services (in other words, the extent to which they succeed in doing the things that they are supposed to be doing). For all these reasons, then, the debate about public services is 'not yet a reasoned one, if only because its terms are still confused' (Plowden 1987).

However, the fact remains that the Right has found it possible to launch a major ideological assault on the public provision of services and to cut, deregulate, privatize, and market them in the vocabulary of a populist rhetoric. It has been possible to appeal to, and nourish, an image of public services as bleak, unresponsive, and inefficient bureaucracies and to contrast them unfavourably with the private sector in these respects. Of course, neither the image nor the antithesis is accurate (for example, a MORI survey for the National Consumer Council recently revealed that the service with which the public was most dissatisfied was the privatized British Telecom), but it does undeniably have some public resonance. It demands a response.

Defining the problem

Unfortunately, the Left has found it difficult to respond effectively or imaginatively to the assault on public services. It has resisted cuts and urged the need for more resources. It has reaffirmed principles of equity and access. Above all, it has defended jobs. These are, of course, entirely proper concerns. Yet they are not, of themselves, enough. The defence of the *principle* of public services has tended to become a defence of the existing *form* of public services. This position was never adequate or satisfactory; it has now become untenable. The choice for the Left is clear: either to take seriously the task of addressing issues of quality, responsiveness, and accountability in relation to the whole range of public services or to watch the steady erosion of these services at the hands of people who equate the value of services with their cost and have no commitment to the principles of equity and communal provision which they represent.

It is not difficult to identify some of the reasons (both good and bad) why the Left's approach to public services has remained so inadequate and undeveloped. Attention given to the needs of producer groups (fortified, in the case of the Labour Party, by an institutional attachment) has not been matched by an equivalent concern for the needs of consumers. The belief in collective provision has tended to become a belief in uniform provision. Defining needs has become confused with meeting them. Provision has too often become paternalism. Excessive dependence on using the state, centrally and locally, as the means for service delivery has fostered an administrative, 'top-down' version of socialism. The language of producerism, collectivism, statism, centralism, and municipalism is, of course, shorthand; but it does at least identify the difficult inheritance of attitudes and practices that the Left brings to its present task.

The traditional socialist assault on 'monopoly' now has to accommodate the fact that in many crucial areas of their lives the monopolies that people experience daily are public ones: housing departments, social services, the DHSS, the National Health Service, and the rest. It also has to accommodate the fact that the traditional relationship between producers and consumers now looks rather different in many of these public services: '"Trade Union" used to mean the organised workers fighting the rich bosses. In many places today it means the public service unions: organised producers fighting consumers of the public services they provide – consumers poorer and less effectively organised than themselves' (Donnison 1987). Further, it involves a recognition of the fact that public services have traditionally paid too little attention to the views and needs of their consumers and too much to the views and needs of their providers. This has cost the Left dear, and merely to be the defender of public services is no longer enough. Martin Smith makes the essential point:

> In order to combat the radical Right, socialists will need to be able to present an entirely new model of a regulated, socially-owned public utility which is less monolithic and more responsive – to workers and consumers alike – than anything British socialists have yet constructed.

> (Smith 1986: 18)

That is also our starting point here.

In one sense, at least, we have been here before. It was not long ago, in the late 1960s and early 1970s, that the demand for more 'participation' in services seemed to be carrying all before it. Starting with planning, and building on the proposals contained in the Skeffington Report (1969), which appeared to give official blessing to the spirit of the times, the movement spread rapidly to other services. The Seebohm Report on the future of social services (1968) had endorsed public participation as a goal for the new local authority social service departments and suggested mechanisms for implementing it. The community development projects, also launched at the end of the 1960s, had the explicit objective of involving local people in the regeneration of their own areas (Higgins *et al.* 1983).

It should also be recalled that this pressure for greater public involvement in the planning and delivery of public services came overwhelmingly from the Left, whose dissatisfaction with bureaucratic modes of service delivery found expression in such contemporary developments as the squatting campaigns. The word 'libertarian' was much in vogue to describe this rejection of rigid structures and their replacement by alternative forms of popular power. This concern tapped a number of important, if usually minority, traditions within the ranks of the Left which had gone into eclipse during the period of consolidation of the Attlee government's welfare state reforms (Lapping and Radice 1968; Robson and Crick 1970; Hatch 1973; Wright, Deakin, and Stewart 1984; Landry *et al.* 1985). It is worth disinterring this buried history, if only as a necessary reminder that the search for new models of responsive public service has its origins on the Left, rather than the Right.

However, these initiatives failed, and left little behind them by way of durable changes in the nature of service provision. Their real effect was largely symbolic and literary – one bibliographical review of public participation in Britain ran to nearly 200 pages (Barker 1979). In one sense this was scarcely surprising, since the essence of the project was to achieve a lasting transfer of power and those engaged upon it both underestimated the scale of the task and misconstrued its character. So Boaden and his colleagues could conclude that: 'Little has been achieved by way of a fundamental shift in power, a shift which implicitly underlay the ideas of radical proponents of participation in the late 1960s' (Boaden *et al.* 1982: 179). Yet enough has been learned about the problems and possibilities of greater participation to make it possible now to build upon the experience of the late 1960s and early 1970s rather than having to learn it all over again. As one writer on the subject nicely puts it, this is a 'delightful discovery' (Richardson 1983: 123).

But it is a discovery that needs to be set in context. One reason why the earlier attempts at greater participation failed lies in the economic setbacks of the middle and late 1970s. The great frost that descended on the public sector after the IMF deal of 1976 blighted the few tender shoots that had taken root in the local government sector. Public participation, widely associated (not altogether justly) with unnecessary delays in implementation and incontinent demands for more resources, became a luxury that public services could not afford to be seen to indulge in. At the same time, the reductions in public spending from 1976 onwards furthered the process of run-down in the services. This in turn progressively reinforced the image of poor-quality, insensitive, inflexible, and undiscriminating provision which formed a key element in the Conservative opposition's successful assault on the Callaghan government during this crucial period.

By this point, of course, the neo-liberal counter-revolution had taken firm hold and a very different kind of Conservative Party took power in 1979, committed to drastic reductions in the role of the state. The appropriation of many of the Left's earlier criticisms of the inadequacies of the public sector, including elements of its vocabulary ('libertarian' and 'radical' are only two examples of terms that have crossed the floor of the house), created an entirely new climate – one in which the traditional Left found itself profoundly ill at ease.

Yet it is of fundamental importance not to take the neo-liberal rhetoric, with all its borrowed plumage, at face value. Behind the Conservative government's professions of more sensitivity to consumer needs, more openness, and enhanced accountability, its actual record over the past decade reveals a very different reality. What has been truly remarkable about this period has been the unchecked growth of unaccountable state power. The basis of local democracy has been steadily eroded, as more functions are allocated to institutions like the Training Agency (née MSC), while urban development corporations have been created to take over responsibility for large areas of major cities from elected local authorities. The abolition of the GLC and metropolitan counties accelerated that process, spawning a myriad of anonymous residuary bodies and further exposing the lack of any form of real democratic control over a range of services, including of course the police. Public bodies of all kinds have been subjected to a plague of patronage and packed with appointees who have passed the political loyalty test. Behind these developments lies the steady extension of Treasury control and the imposition of the objectives of government economic policy across the whole public sector (Ham 1985).

This form of reinforced central control requires new instruments for its implementation. Hence the solution of privatization or, when some residual public body is permitted to remain in place, the compulsory contracting out of services previously provided within the public domain. Alternatively, the responsibilities are transferred to individuals, who are provided with incentives to reach their own solutions to the provision of services. Empowered with cash subsidies, former users of the public services can now house themselves as owner occupiers, educate their children in schools that have opted out of the local education system, and provide their own health care through private insurance schemes. In all these processes, they can look for support to their families and to voluntary associations (of a strictly non-political character), and for remedies for any failings in the new mechanisms to the majestic impartiality of the law.

In practice, this image of 'post-socialist man' is still only half formed, although it has come a great deal nearer realization than anyone outside the right-wing think tanks could have believed possible a decade ago. However, other changes have taken place too; and by no means all of them work against positive developments in public services. Closer scrutiny of the performance of the public-sector bureaucracies has led to the publication of more information. The establishment of the Audit Commission has not produced the kind of witless pillorying of the public sector that some critics feared. The creation of ombudsmen for local government and the Health Service, though their services are grossly underused, has opened up new channels for redress. The community health councils, hardy survivors of the previous wave of consumerism, soldier on, under-resourced but still able to take advantage of new opportunities opened up by the Griffiths Report (1983), with its emphasis on sensitivity to user needs and quality of service.

Elsewhere, in local government, the deeply engrained paternalism of the system of management of the public housing stock has been successfully challenged; and the powers and responsibilities of social workers and the ways in which they are exercised has come under scrutiny in a succession of reports (Barclay 1985). The reconstruction of school governing bodies has opened up real prospects of greater power for parents, although practice has so far fallen short of theory (Kogan 1984). More ambitiously, many local authorities have launched decentralization initiatives linking different service areas, in an attempt to make those services more accessible and responsive to need (Stoker 1988). By no means all these new developments were promoted by central government. Some of them owe their origins to recent legislation; but the main driving force behind the move to change practice in local government has come from its former critics on the Left, who now control the authorities they once fought (Gyford 1985).

There is, therefore, much in the contemporary scene that is unclear and ambiguous. Initiatives that promise to strengthen the position of the users of services are met by others that work in a directly contrary direction. Choice rapidly becomes a synonym for exit from the system. A consumerist rhetoric can be used to conceal a reality of diminished funding and eroded accountability. A new emphasis on financial accountability has not been paralleled by an equivalent attention to political accountability. Further confusion is generated by failure to draw on relevant experience – not just lessons from the immediate past, or other comparable societies, but also the outcome of parallel experiments in different service areas. Many of the techniques and devices now being applied in education and social services are already familiar from experience in the planning field (intensive consultation exercises, community forums, outreach workers attached to user groups). Statutory–voluntary sector collaboration has advanced at different speeds in parallel service areas with little or no attempt at exchange of ideas on good – or bad – practice.

It is against this confused – and confusing – background, full of hazards and opportunities, that we set out to develop a new approach to public services, which reaffirms their status as *public* services while also seeking to enhance the quality of the *service* they provide.

Finding new approaches

Faced with these issues, there has been a renewed attempt to find an approach to public services that responds to the situation in which they now find themselves.

Rethinking public service

One approach has been to stress the first side of the equation – to try to revive public services and the concept of public service as such. This approach begins with an attempt to isolate what is distinctive about such services: the fact that they have different forms of accountability, that their budgetary procedures are unlike those of private-sector companies (though they may impose constraints just as rigid as the notorious 'bottom line'), and that decision-taking takes place as part of a process that is open to political developments both inside and outside the system and to the activities of pressure groups pursuing particular interests (Stewart and Ranson 1988). Others would add that the public sector is peculiarly open to the pressures that can be brought to bear by professional groups and organized labour; that users of the service often have a variety of relationships to it (that is, they may be providers as well as recipients, or funding the service as well as benefiting from it); and, finally, that users may have no legal redress against it (Pollitt 1986).

Against this distinctive background, a systematic attempt has recently been launched to revive the concept of public service. In a series of papers, Clarke and Stewart (1986, 1987) have suggested that a public service can easily become service *to* the public rather than *for* the public and recommend as an antidote the adoption of a 'public service orientation'. They define what this approach would involve for a local authority:

- closeness to the customer and citizen
- listening to the public
- access for the public
- seeing service from the public's point of view
- seeking out views, suggestions, and complaints
- the public's right to know
- quality of service
- the public as the test of quality.

This approach proposes a different attitude towards the public, founded on a willingness to take customer attitudes seriously, encouraging the expression of views and responding constructively to them. But ultimately, it is suggested, change in the approach of an authority to its public and its attitudes towards them can best be achieved by a 'demonstration of commitment and willingness to change by those in authority' (Local Government Training Board 1987: 85).

This may seem straightforward enough in principle, but in practice implementation is far from easy, since changes of the kind being advocated involve a fundamental shift in traditional attitudes and practices in local government. This approach is mirrored by similar developments taking place within the Health Service, designed to make it more consumer-sensitive and quality-conscious. It is perhaps worth remarking that these developments are taking place simultaneously despite the different organizational basis of the two bodies. This, in turn, suggests that it is unwise to regard elected bodies as automatically being in a better position to be responsive to their consumers – a conclusion supported by recent research findings (Day and Klein 1987), to which we shall return later.

An example of the attempt to define 'quality' in health care is the one suggested by Robert Maxwell of the King's Fund (Maxwell 1984). Six ingredients of health care quality are identified:

- access to services
- relevance to need (for the whole community)
- effectiveness (for individual patients)
- equity (fairness)
- social acceptability
- efficiency and economy.

The purpose here is not to discuss the scheme (which has been widely used and cited in discussions of these issues) but to note that, like the local government approach to public service, it emphasizes managerial needs and change originating within the organization. Sir Roy Griffiths, in a recent essay commenting on changes in the NHS since his first report – and enquiring 'Does the public service serve?' – observes that 'one cannot do justice to the consumer dimension by a few superficial statements or by asking employees to wear the fixed smiles of Arctic winter towards the customer' (Griffiths 1988: 196). Managerial in their emphasis, such approaches fail to assimilate into their definitions of quality in services aspects such as the obligation to respect human dignity or to provide information on performance, which a more consumer-orientated definition would include. More important still, they do not consider sufficiently whether a quality public service should not be one that has constructed effective mechanisms by which users can define their own needs and criteria of acceptability.

Consumers first?

This might suggest an alternative approach that would be 'bottom-up' in its focus, addressing the needs of consumers of public services in their own terms. Although this might appear to be a simpler approach, it will not necessarily be wholly straightforward in its applications. First of all, it is clear that there are many criteria that consumers will want to apply in considering the performance and organization of any particular service. This was well illustrated in a recent report from the National Consumer Council on consumer assessment of local authority services (see Figure 1).

Figure 1 Consumer criteria for service evaluation

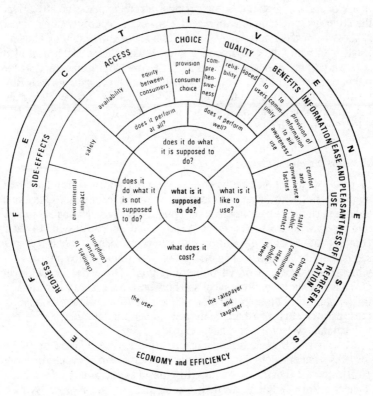

Source: National Consumer Council (1986)

The great merit of this approach is that it integrates questions about the status of consumers within public services with questions about performance and provision. At the same time, many public services, of which the Health Service is one leading example, exist to meet general needs, not merely to respond to the demands of individual consumers. Indeed, the language of consumerism, with its focus on the position of individuals in a market-place of goods and services, has obvious limitations in relation to services which are essentially organized on the basis of collective provision for common needs and not as responses to individual consumer demands and power in the market.

There is also the problem that 'consumers' are not a monolithic category with clearly defined common interests, but may well have sharp disagreements of interest, which they will articulate with varying degrees of effectiveness. In addition, a current group of consumers may not have the same interests as future or potential consumers – which raises questions about the former taking decisions that crucially affect the latter, as for example with recent legislation to permit opting out of schools from the state system or the transfer of ownership of housing estates. So while the consumerist approach has much to offer, it is also necessary to travel beyond consumerism to find appropriate models for public services. If we do not, we may find ourselves asking, with Roy Griffiths: 'Does one have the sinking feeling that we may be talking the language of consumerism without tackling the central realities?' (Griffiths 1988: 200).

Towards a synthesis

In practice, the choice between a managerial and a consumer-based approach is by no means as clear-cut as we have implied. Questions about the status of consumers within public services can and should be integrated with questions about performance and provision, to their common advantage. Too often, as has been seen, these issues are separated. The advocacy of 'participation' can often fail to connect with wider considerations of what participation is intended to achieve. Discussions about 'performance' and how best to measure it can equally fail to connect with consideration of the role of consumers in making these assessments. Too many of the arguments and initiatives simply fail to meet, and wither in consequence.

The air is full of assorted, separate initiatives in relation to public services (under such flags as audit, consumerism, decentralization, public service orientation, quality assurance, and performance measurement). What is needed, we suggest, is an approach which combines a model of an effective and user-friendly service with a strengthening of the means by which this might be achieved and sustained. In particular, this involves paying attention not merely to the responsibilities of the providers of such services, but also to the powers and opportunities that are to be made available to the users.

In other words, our dual proposition is that a concern with the position of the user should form an integral part of all discussions about the quality and performance of public services, and that to strengthen the position of the user is to make an essential contribution to the achievement of these service objectives. A good public service will ensure an effective role for the user; and an effective role for the user will do much to ensure a good public service. Efficiency and responsiveness are not in opposition, but two sides of the same coin.

Significantly, this was one of the major conclusions of the National Consumer Council study referred to on p. 9. Although that study's main emphasis was on the development of performance indicators for public services, and associated methods of evaluation, it soon became clear that the role of the consumer was central, not marginal, to the achievement of real progress towards these objectives:

> As our work progressed, we became more convinced of the value of consumer involvement in performance evaluation. If local government is to become truly consumer-responsive, real people must continually put over real problems and real points of view to the service providers, and not rely entirely on authorities' willingness to assess their own performance.

> (NCC 1986: xix)

Here is a powerful endorsement of the need to strengthen the position of the consumer, which is all the more powerful because it originates with a concern to improve performance and evaluation. Thus 'user control' is not peripheral, still less inimical, to these objectives, but integral to their achievement.

But there is still one further step that we need to take. Our concern must be not just with current performance and present outcomes, but with long-term policies and their consequences – or, in the familiar distinction, with the *effectiveness* of public services in meeting collective needs. Hence our argument cannot be for public services in which users and managers alone share responsibility for control; a third actor has to be introduced: the citizen.

Indeed, it should not be forgotten (although it frequently is) that 'the difference between citizens and consumers is all important' (Klein 1984: 20). The general body of citizens has views and interests, as non-users, or 'contingent users' (as Klein terms them), or simply as taxpayers or ratepayers. These may diverge from those of the immediate users of the service. Hence the case for wider participation is not the same as the case for more power for the users of specific services or facilities. The attempt to increase the accountability of a public service to the general citizen body is not the same as the attempt to increase accountability to particular bodies of consumers. It may well be right to think of moving simultaneously on both these fronts (as we do); but this makes it all the more important to recognize that the directions in which we will need to move are not only not the same, but may diverge quite sharply. If we prefer 'user' to 'consumer' as a term (although they are used interchangeably here), it is because the former seems less exclusive and easier to integrate with a larger conception of citizenship.

So it is with these considerations in mind that we approach the question of increasing user control of public services. Our concern is with both the user as a consumer of a specific service and with the user (or non-user) as citizen. We believe that it is necessary to strengthen the position of both in the public services, without pretending that they are always necessarily the same. Nor should the role of the user-as-worker be overlooked. A good public service pays attention to that, too, even while insisting that the primary obligation of a public service is always to provide the best service to the public. Citizen, user, worker: all have a large – and enlargeable – role to play in bringing this about.

Criteria for user control

Against this background, we now seek to identify the main criteria that would need to be satisfied in any public service in which the position of the user, as both consumer and citizen, is fully recognized and strengthened. These criteria should, we suggest, be as follows:

(i) *Accountability:* Are there effective (not merely formal) ways in which the providers of the service are made accountable to the users of the service and the community it serves?

(ii) *Representation and participation*: Are there effective means by which representatives of the whole citizen body and users of the service can take an appropriate share of responsibility for the service by participating in discussion and decision-making on policy and practice?

(iii) *Information*: Is there a regular free flow of information, in accessible form, about the availability, operation, organization, and performance of the service, available on demand to all those with a legitimate interest in the service?

(iv) *Access*: Is the service readily available and easy to use? Is this true for everyone who wants or needs to use it? Can new facilities be made available to meet new needs, as they are identified?

(v) *Choice*: Does the service make provision for consumers to make choices freely, and if so how and of what kind?

(vi) *Redress*: Are there readily accessible channels through which complaints about the service can be pursued without disproportionate cost or delay, and redress obtained?

These criteria, which are developed from earlier consumer review exercises, are not intended to be exhaustive. Rather, they are meant to give some substantial content to generalizations about 'user control in public services', by focusing on the powers and opportunities available to the users themselves, and the range of legitimate expectations open to them, rather than on the duties and obligations of service providers. This explains why the approach here differs from (but also complements) the attempts to evolve a 'public-service orientation' discussed above. There, the perspective is properly managerial; here, it is rooted firmly in the position of the users.

This means that, while providers and users may well share a commitment to a high-quality service, its achievement should not be made to depend on the actions and evaluations of service providers alone. Service users should have the means to define their own needs and objectives, just as they should also be involved in the process of setting standards and assessing performance. For example, it is valuable that some local authorities and health authorities are now undertaking consumer surveys to discover how their services are viewed by those who use them and pay for them; but this is not a substitute for giving users a direct voice of their own. Indeed, such initiatives are more likely to bear fruit in terms of better and more responsible public services if they are linked to a strengthening of the position of the users of these services. The user control criteria outlined on p. 12 need to be seen as an integral element in initiatives concerned with improving quality, measuring performance, or emphasizing service.

There is a further relevant point here. It is always useful to ask of any organization exactly what the pressures are (for example, financial stringency or the professional culture) which make it work in the way that it does, including those pressures that promote organizational change. There are many such pressures on public services: but in general effectively marshalled consumer demands have not been among the most significant. Our argument is that they should be; and that there should be effective mechanisms by which the consumers of public services may exercise continuous influence on their delivery. Users should be a constant point of reference and source of pressure.

Hence, the user control criteria should be seen as a means of measuring how far initiatives aimed at improving quality, measuring performance, or increasing responsiveness are actually doing so in a form which is consistent with the users' own perception of what is required. In this way, user and citizen control can become an integral part of the process.

Down to cases

The approach adopted here is not presented as a rigid model, more as a set of questions which any public service should be called upon to answer. It is already clear that the attempt to strengthen the position of the public-service user confronts problems of both principle and practice, and these must be squarely faced. What is also clear is that the kind of approach described and advocated here will need to be developed through many different kinds of initiatives, various in both type and scope. For example, some will focus on the general accountability of a service as a whole, while others will concentrate on initiatives to enhance the role of users in relation to particular aspects of a service. Some initiatives will seek to strengthen the position of users in formal ways, others will cultivate more informal arrangements. There will be organizational, fiscal, and rights-based kinds of consumerism (Clode *et al.* 1987). There will be much scope for experiment, diversity and shared learning.

Yet it should not be forgotten (to return to our beginning) that the context in which these matters are now discussed is sharply political. Public services are under sustained ideological attack from the Right, which uses genuine dissatisfactions with unresponsive bureaucracies to further its project of undermining the principles of equity and communal provision on which such services are based. New forms of unaccountable public power are invented, while existing provisions for accountability, participation, and redress across the whole spread of public administration look increasingly inadequate. The context, then, is one in which there are 'serious deficiencies in the manner in which our governmental institutions operate from the point of view of consumer service and satisfaction, and from the point of view of democratic involvement of the public they serve' (Birkinshaw 1985: 13), but also one in which these deficiencies are being relentlessly exploited to undermine and dismantle public services and the principles upon which they are based. Our argument here is that, for those who believe in these principles, it is neither an adequate nor an effective response simply to defend public services as they are. A new kind of public service is required, where a commitment to quality is rooted in a strengthening of the position of service users.

Our approach, reflected in the criteria outlined on p. 12, is deliberately broad enough to encompass a wide range of actual service developments. We have eschewed any neat demarcation between a 'consumerist' and a 'collectivist' approach (cf. Hoggett and Hambleton 1987) in favour of an approach which acknowledges that the empowerment of public-service users will come through a package of provisions which draw upon a variety of perspectives. Furthermore, any discussion of these matters needs to be sensitive to the particular character and circumstances of different public services. That is why we have sought to explore our general theme through a consideration of a number of public services which differ widely in character and organization. Our contributors were asked to consider how user control could be strengthened in these services. Their common commitment is to the principles of a public service, to a public service in which user control is strengthened, and to a realistic radicalism in confronting the issues involved. We return, in our conclusion, to some of the larger themes in the light of these particular studies.

References

Barker, A. (1979) *Public Participation in Britain: a Classified Bibliography*, London: Bedford Square Press.

Birkinshaw, P. (1985) *Grievances, Remedies and the State*, London: Sweet & Maxwell.

Boaden, N., Goldsmith, M., Hampton, W., and Stringer, P. (1982) *Public Participation in Local Services*, London: Longman.

Clarke, M. and Stewart, J. (1986) *The Public Service Orientation – Developing the Approach*, Luton: Local Government Training Board.

——(1987) 'The public service orientation: issues and dilemmas', *Public Administration* 65 (2).

Clode, D., Parker, C., and Etherington, S. (eds) (1987) *Towards the Sensitive Bureaucracy: Consumers, Welfare and the New Pluralism*, London: Gower.

Day, P. and Klein, R. (1987) *Accountabilities: Five Public Services*, London: Tavistock.

Donnison, D. (1987) 'New drama for a crisis', *Guardian*, 11 May.

Griffiths, R. (1988) 'Does the public service serve?: The consumer dimension', *Public Administration* 66 (2).

Gyford, J. (1985) *The Politics of Local Socialism*, London: Allen & Unwin.

Ham, A. (1985) *Treasury Rules: Recurrent Themes in British Economic Policy*, London: Quartet.

Hatch, S. (ed.) (1973) *Towards Participation in Local Services*, London: Fabian Society.

Higgins, J., Deakin, N., Edward, J., and Wicks, M., (1983) *Government and Urban Poverty*, Oxford: Basil Blackwell.

Hoggett, P. and Hambleton, R (eds) (1987) *Decentralisation and Democracy: Localising Public Services*, Occasional Paper 28, Bristol: School for Advanced Urban Studies, University of Bristol.

Klein, R. (1984) 'The politics of participation', in R. Maxwell and N. Weaver (eds) *Public Participation in Health*, London: King's Fund.

Kogan, M. (ed.) (1984) *School Governing Bodies*, London: Heinemann.

Landry, C. *et al*, (1985) *What a Way to Run a Railroad*, London: Comedia.

Lapping, B. and Radice, G. (eds) (1968) *More Power to the People*, London: Longman/Fabian Society.

Local Government Training Board (1987) *Getting Closer to the Public*, London.

Maxwell, R. (1984) 'Quality assessment in health', *British Medical Journal* 288, 12 May.

National Consumer Council (1986) *Measuring Up: Consumer Assessment of Local Authority Services*, London.

Plowden, W. (1987) 'The battles of ideology that ill serve the public', *Independent*, 24 June.

Pollitt, C. (1986) 'Democracy and bureaucracy', in D. Held and C. Pollitt (eds) *New Forms of Democracy*, London: Sage.

Richardson, A. (1983) *Participation*, London: Routledge & Kegan Paul.

Robson, W. and Crick, B. (eds) (1970) *Protest and Discontent*, Harmondsworth: Penguin.

Seebohm Report (1968) *Report of the Committee on Local Authority and Allied Personal Services*, London: HMSO.

Skeffington Report (1969) *People and Planning: Report of the Committee on Public Participation in Planning*, London: HMSO.

Smith, M. (1986) *The Consumer Case for Socialism*, London: Fabian Society.

Stewart, J. and Ranson, S. (1988) 'Management in the public domain', *Public Money*, Spring-Summer.

Stoker, G. (1988) *The Politics of Local Government*, London: Macmillan.

Wright, A., Deakin, N., and Stewart, J. (1984) *Socialism and Decentralisation*, London: Fabian Society.

2

Planning

William Hampton

For a few years in the 1970s the phrases 'public participation' and 'planning' went together as easily as 'fish and chips'. Now the emphasis in discussions of citizen involvement is changing: the concept of 'participation' is being replaced by 'decentralization' and 'user control'. Attitudes towards planning itself have also changed. There is less confidence in the ability of planners to produce blueprints for developments stretching far into the future: there is more emphasis on the importance of unplanned market forces. It is timely, therefore, to reassess the role of public participation in relation to planning; and to consider the implications of the experience of this local service for a general discussion of user control.

The nature of planning

Land use or town planning is essentially a regulatory activity: a process not a product. The intention is to impose order on anarchic social reality and to influence developments towards agreed objectives. These objectives may be very broad and general in content. In introducing in 1909 the first legislation to include the term 'town planning', the President of the Local Government Board remarked: 'The Bill aims in broad outline at, and hopes to secure, the home healthy, the house beautiful, the town pleasant, the city dignified and the suburb salubrious' (quoted in Cullingworth 1985: 2).

In less elegant language, local authorities were advised in 1974 to produce structure (i.e. strategic) plans which might include as 'key issues':

a. The location and scale of employment
b. The location and scale of housing ...
c. The transportation system ...
d. The extent of conservation of the character of the area ...
e. The extent of provision for recreation and tourism

f. The location and scale of shopping centres and

g. The location and scale of land reclamation.

(Department of the Environment 1974: 2–3)

Two points of interest in the present context emerge from these broad descriptions of the content of planning. First, it is essentially a political rather than a technical activity. That is, it is concerned with matters containing considerations of policies or values – what we want or what ought to happen – as well as practical proposals and regulations to achieve agreed policies. Moreover, the practical issues themselves involve political choices. The tension between policies for employment or transportation on the one hand and housing or conservation on the other is a regular source of conflict between planning authorities and the public. Less obvious is the conflict that can arise within a particular policy area. The cost of conservation, for example, may be the 'gentrification' of the neighbourhood with a consequent loss of low-cost housing for existing residents. Professional planners may obscure the political choices to be made by a concentration on the sophisticated analysis of large collections of data, but the public and politicians are well advised to keep their eyes on the classic political questions: 'who gets what, when and how?' There is more to planning than the provision of plans!

Second, as planning is concerned with the development and implementation of policies affecting the future, it is difficult to separate specific 'users' from the mass of the general public. The user of the education service is the individual parent or child, the user of the health service is the patient, but who is the user of planning? This metaphysical question causes considerable difficulties when plans for large-scale future developments are discussed. The development of new towns, for example, was often opposed by the existing populations of the areas involved: the planners claimed to be working for the benefit of the future inhabitants who obviously could not be identified. More generally, there is a rhetoric of 'planning for the future of our children' who are either not born or too young to contribute their view of the society in which they would wish to live.

The identification of the user of planning becomes no easier when we turn to matters of development control. Consider, for example, the case where Mr X seeks planning permission for an extension to his house. His neighbours raise various planning objections to the extension. The planning authority decides whether or not to grant consent. Who is the 'user' of the service provided by the planning authority? Is it Mr X or his neighbours?

A discussion of user control in planning is likely to involve, in summary, a consideration of the extension of collective democracy together with an extension of the consumer rights of individuals. Planning is part of an interventionist approach to the political process. As such, the 'users' are *all* citizens: user control in planning involves a move to a more open, participatory stance in the overall political process. User control is not, however, the same as public participation and a certain amount of confusion can result if the two concepts are conflated. When user control is discussed in the case, for example, of a tenant co-operative, the tenants (users) are not participating in a process dominated by other people: 'They do not need to share the decision-making process with anyone else besides their peers' (Richardson 1983: 23). The concept of public participation, on the other hand, implies an involvement in a process already entered by another. In the case of planning this other will be a statutory authority such as a local or central government department which ultimately controls both the content and the process of the participation.

As planning affects people both as consumers and as citizens, it can be discussed in the light of the criteria and characteristics outlined on p. 12. The position of the users of any service can be recognized and strengthened by considering the service within a framework containing the following concepts: access, information, participation, accountability, representation, redress, and choice. We may easily place planning within such a context. For example, as *consumers* of planning, when applying for planning consent or when affected by proposed developments, individuals should have ready *access* to the department or decision-making process involved. They should also receive the *information* necessary to present their case. On the other hand, as *citizens*, people should have adequate opportunities to *participate* in discussions about the development of plans affecting their area. In both cases, for consumers and citizens, *accountability* and *representation* can be enhanced by the providers of planning – whether councillors, local government officers, or civil servants – showing a readiness to conduct the process in an open manner. Discussions should take place at the most localized level possible for the scale of planning being undertaken. As a last resort, the rights of *redress* through both local or national ombudsmen and the courts must be retained.

Choice is the only characteristic identified in the discussion on p. 12 which is not appropriate to planning. As a regulatory activity, the planning process must result either in a plan or in a decision not to plan: the concept of a planning process resulting in a number of plans for an area, among which an individual is free to choose, is a nonsense.

The experience of planning will now be considered in the context of this general discussion, and a few general themes will be identified as a guide for future policy.

The development of public participation in planning

The Town and Country Planning Act, 1968, introduced a distinction between the structure plans which formulate policy and provide general proposals for a county area, and local plans which implement, in various ways, the broad policies contained in the structure plan. Following local government reorganization in 1974, structure planning became the responsibility of the county councils, with local planning mainly undertaken by the districts. The abolition of the metropolitan counties in 1986 unified these two aspects of planning at the district level in the major urban areas. But it also meant the removal of the only local authorities capable of planning for the conurbations as a whole (Hampton 1987: 198–201).

The introduction of the 1968 legislation must be seen in the context of rapid changes in the urban environment and a growing demand from the public for a right to be heard on planning matters affecting their property. It had taken fourteen years for all authorities to submit their plans after the 1947 planning legislation. The rapid growth in private transport and the proposals for town-centre redevelopment after 1960 required a rather faster planning response. Furthermore, the centralization of the planning process caused by ministerial involvement proved 'to be quite unwieldy. During the 1960s there was an annual average of more than 11,000 local planning inquiries' (Boaden *et al.* 1982: 56). These local inquiries gave individuals an opportunity to contest refusals to grant planning permission: they did not give a general right to the public to express their views except in certain 'bad neighbour' developments of such facilities as public conveniences, slaughterhouses, and the like.

The 1968 Act separated the policy aspects of planning from its detailed application. The Minister continued to have the duty to approve the broad policy (structure) plans but withdrew from involvement in the local plans based upon them. The statutory provisions for greater public involvement were in part a counterbalance to the distancing of the Minister from the planning process and in part an attempt to reduce the flood of contested decisions once plans were adopted.

Provisions were included in the Act which made possible the development of participatory planning, although the word 'participation' is not used in the legislation. With appropriate adjustments the provisions apply to both structure and local planning. Planning authorities are required to secure:

(a) That adequate publicity is given in their area to the report of the survey under section 1 above and to the matters which they propose to include in the plan;

(b) That persons who may be expected to desire an opportunity of making representations to the authority with respect to those matters are made aware that they are entitled to an opportunity of doing so; and

(c) That such persons are given an adequate opportunity of making such representations; and the authority shall consider any representations made to them within the prescribed period.

(Section 3(1), Town and Country Planning Act, 1968)

Before considering a structure plan submitted for his approval, the Secretary of State for the Environment must satisfy himself of the adequacy of the local authority's compliance with the provisions of Section 3 (1) of the Act.

To assist local authorities in understanding their new responsibilities for involving the public, a committee was established with Mr Arthur Skeffington in the chair. The committee was charged 'to consider and report on the best methods, including publicity, of securing the participation of the public at the formative stage in the making of development plans for their area' (Skeffington Report 1969: 1). The Skeffington Report took a broad view of both the nature of participation and the people who were to be involved. Participation was understood 'to be the act of sharing in the formulation of policies and proposals'. It 'involves doing as well as talking and there will be full participation only where the public are able to take an active part throughout the plan-making process'. The public were regarded 'as an aggregate comprising all individuals and groups within it without limitation' (ibid.: 1).

In its enthusiasm for public participation the Skeffington Report went beyond the letter of the 1968 Act. Indeed, it went beyond what the Department of the Environment was willing to recommend as good practice. The report included detailed proposals for holding public meetings, arranging exhibitions, and involving the local news media. The public were to be encouraged to participate by helping with surveys and other activities as well as by making comments. Local authorities were also to consider both the convening of meetings with a view to setting up community forums and the appointment of community development officers to secure the involvement of people who do not join organizations. These last two recommendations received only a luke-warm reception from the Secretary of State (Department of the Environment 1972: 7). In more recent years the Conservative governments of the 1980s have retracted much of the official support for even a moderate interpretation of the Skeffington approach. Local authorities have been given discretion in extending public participation. At a time of financial constraint, many local authorities have adopted minimal interpretations of the legislation.

The experience of the 1970s

During the 1970s, the county planning authorities began to produce their structure plans. Their commitment to public participation naturally varied but all were obliged to make some effort to fulfil their statutory responsibilities. To monitor progress and promote good practice, the Department of the Environment established a research project to report on the public participation exercises associated with five structure plans.

The Linked Research Project into Public Participation in Structure Planning (henceforth LRP) developed an organizing framework for their material based on traditional schemes for analysing communication patterns: who is the communicator?; what is to be communicated?; with whom do we communicate?; and how do we communicate? (Boaden *et al*. 1980: 18–20; cf. Hampton 1977: 30–2). Each of these questions raises issues which need to be considered in discussions of public participation and user control.

First, who is the communicator or official face of the elected representative institution? In most cases the LRP found it was the planning officers rather than councillors who accepted this role. As a result, public participation in planning

> has tended to be planner orientated. The planning department ... compose the publicity ... and disseminate it through channels over which they have control.... Understandably they do this in the hope of improving their planning process.... As professionals they cannot accept reinterpretations of their plans nor plans drawn up by unqualified people.
>
> (Boaden *et al*. 1982: 67)

Second, what is to be communicated? A planning authority might distribute information once the important decisions had been taken, leaving the public to discuss the details; or it might conduct its planning in the full glare of open government; or it might opt for an intermediate position. South Yorkshire, for example, made it clear that a decision in favour of a low-fare policy for public transport was at the heart of its structure plan, but encouraged widespread discussion of both this policy and other issues where the options were more open. The leader of the council said: 'we want people to be involved and interested in what we do' but 'Labour group policy will not be compromised by the structure plan process which demands public participation' (quoted in Darke 1979).

Third, with whom do we communicate? The Skeffington definition of the public is more useful as an exhortation than as a practical guide to action. How would we involve 'all individuals and groups ... without limitation'? A discussion of this point is crucial when considering who are the users of planning in the context of user control.

The LRP 'adopted a three-fold classification of the public into major élites, minor élites, and individual members of the public ... the use of the term "élites" [implied] a selection of sectional interests rather than an appeal to the general public' (Boaden *et al.* 1980: 19). This classification produced an interesting analysis. Planners are obviously more at home with the major élites who comprise neighbouring local authorities, commercial and industrial concerns, nationalized industries, and other public bodies. Without their co-operation and advice, the planning authority will find it difficult, or even impossible, to construct and implement a plan. The major élites are a part of the urban political process even if they are not within the responsibility or control of the local authority. 'Consultation' with such bodies is thus distinguished from 'participation' in the perception of many planners; and consultation becomes, somewhat unusually, the stronger term. In some cases, certain major élites have a statutory right to be consulted during the planning process.

The minor élites comprise the host of voluntary organizations that occur in any area. The problem is how to approach such a heterogeneous collection of groups which can number several thousand in most structure plan areas. Even those planning authorities who made determined efforts to involve local groups in the planning process only succeeded in gaining a response from a few hundred. Those who were most likely to respond were environmental groups who identified their aims with the purposes of planning. Political groups and tenants' associations were less well represented and the response from commercial or employee organizations, including trade unions, was even lower. The lack of interest expressed by the trade unions may have been due to the difficulties of relating their organizational structure to a participatory exercise for which it was never intended. It may also have been a realistic assessment of the significance of the exercise. From the trade unions' point of view, the planning authorities might deliberate employment issues, but major industrial concerns such as ICI or British Steel would decide. Whatever the reasons, the greater involvement of environmental groups compared with other voluntary associations caused the approach to minor élites to be biased in favour of these organizations (Boaden *et al.* 1980: 89–91; cf. Woodcock 1986).

When considering communication with the third group within the classification framework, the mass of the public as individuals, we are really concerned with publicity rather than participation. No planning authority has ever managed to involve more than a small minority of the public in discussions about planning matters.

Finally, the LRP considered how planning authorities attempted to communicate with the public. The methods and techniques adopted obviously related to the purposes of the planning authorities. The LRP analysed the methods according to whether they were concerned with giving information, receiving information, or promoting interaction between the public and the planning authority. Giving information is obviously crucial for any extension of popular involvement in decision-making. Indeed, one political theorist has claimed 'that maximisation of participation is a false hope to pursue in the name of democracy, compared to, for a prospect of real change, a maximisation of communication and publicity' (Crick 1971: 157). The giving of information, is not however, the same as ensuring that people receive it. The publicity methods adopted can ensure that particular sections of the public may be more or less likely to receive the messages being transmitted (Boaden *et al.* 1980: ch. 5), thus raising the possibility of mobilizing a sectional political bias.

Many planners view a more open planning process as an opportunity to produce better plans based on more accurate information about public needs and attitudes. Within participatory exercises, therefore, they use methods such as sample surveys which enable them to receive this information. The consultation process also enables information to be gathered from major élites, and similar if less regular and systematic approaches may be made to minor élites. Whether such information gathering becomes relevant in a discussion of public participation depends on the willingness of the planners to accept and process whatever information the public offers. It is clear, however, that control of the information remains in the hands of the planning authority (ibid.: ch. 6).

When 'information-giving and information-collection are interwoven in a process of interaction between the local authority and the public' (ibid.: 72), we approach the proper meaning of public participation. Where local authorities have begun to move in this direction they have relied heavily on the two techniques recommended by Skeffington but received with caution by the Department of the Environment: community workers and community forums. South Yorkshire used part-time community workers to approach the minor élites in an effort to improve the breadth of their response (ibid.: 80) and the Department of the Environment sponsored an experimental appointment of Environmental Liaison Officers to local Councils of Voluntary Service in Loughborough and Birmingham (Hampton 1978). The experience gained by these officers was never followed up once their appointments ended. More generally, community workers have played an active part in promoting public participation in planning matters at both a structure plan and a local level. They have sometimes been employed by voluntary organizations and sometimes by local authority departments other than planning. The experience has not always been harmonious. The underlying concern about public participation which is felt by both councillors, who fear a threat to their representative authority, and officers, who fear a threat to their professional status, has been aggravated by the intervention of full-time *animateurs*.

The term 'community forum' can cover a number of meanings ranging from 'elected representational bodies' to 'formal opportunities for consultation'. The following three examples, drawn from local rather than structure planning, show both the difficulties and the possibilities of the use of community forums in the present context. When planning the redevelopment of Covent Garden, the Greater London Council sponsored a forum 'elected by popular ballot and consisting of 30 members drawn from the following categories: 9 residents, 9 business interests, 9 "service" interests (e.g. theatres, crafts, welfare and education) and three owners of property in the area' (Hain 1980: 104). After a detailed and critical analysis of the forum's activities, Peter Hain suggested that it 'was able to influence, in some significant respects, the "paper" content of the plan. But it is very doubtful whether ... the Forum's influence will prove to have been very great' (Hain 1980: 167). A later assessment concluded:

> the popular plan which began as opposition to major commercial and public sector redevelopment, only gained ascendancy after 1973 when the property boom collapsed. Although a popular plan was eventually agreed for the area, it is questionable whether it would have occurred in more buoyant market conditions.
>
> (Brindley *et al.* 1986: 21–2)

In Birmingham, the Community Forum co-ordinated communications between the residents' groups in the Urban Renewal Areas and acted as a representative body which could present residents' views on urban renewal policy in meetings with the local authority. It was serviced by the Environmental Liaison Officer (referred to on p. 24) for part of its existence and many of its most active members were full-time community workers attached to other projects. The forum had difficulty in retaining the support of some residents' associations and lost the confidence of councillors after a change in political control (Hampton 1978: 3–15). The difficulty was its lack of political authority suspended as it was between the grassroots support of the residents' associations and the electoral legitimacy of the councillors.

The third example of a community forum is more recent and was quite clearly defined within the overall procedures of the local planning department. During the preparation of the city centre plan in Sheffield in 1986 the approach developed by the Linked Research Project in Structure Planning was adopted within a programme which identified three main elements: publicity, information collection, and discussion/debate (Alty and Darke 1987). In addition to the more usual techniques of publicity, public meetings, and contacts with various interest groups, twelve advisory groups were formed to represent different perspectives on city centre issues and proposals. The advisory groups – or community forums – were representative of women, elderly people, parents with young children, young people, the low-paid and trade unionists, people with disabilities, environmental and transport groups, ethnic minority communities, property agents, and commercial and industrial interests. Each group met on a number of occasions before having an opportunity to present their views to a small panel of councillors. The groups were serviced by planning officers and received a small grant to assist them in their work. In their evaluation of the exercise, Alty and Darke consider the outcome as providing a considerable amount of useful information to the planners as well as developing a positive relationship with key groups in the city. The weakness of the approach lay in the small number and self-selecting nature of the people involved and the difficulty of developing interaction between the various sectional perspectives represented by the different groups. The final meeting, when all the groups came together to hear the response of the councillors to the issues raised by particular groups, was not very successful. The size and formality of this meeting contrasted sharply with the intimacy of the individual groups.

In discussing community workers and community forums, we have begun to move away from the experience of structure planning into that of local planning. At first sight the local scale of much planning at this level would appear more conducive to public involvement. Although this is true, the difficulty remains that the closer planning moves to the local scale within which people move and live, the further it is from policy decisions. Local participation is often about implementation – important in its own context – and seldom about policy. Nevertheless, the significance of these small-scale projects in maintaining or improving the quality of life for the individuals concerned should not be overlooked when considering broader political issues. There are many small-scale examples of successful and uncontentious user control over environmental improvements in General Improvement Areas and Housing Action Areas (Boaden *et al.* 1982: 98–9) and some examples of neighbourhood involvement in drawing up local plans.

The critique of planning and public participation in the development of plans

The optimism of the 1960s and early 1970s has given way to a quite different economic and political climate in the 1980s. These major economic and political changes, together with the ideological opposition to public agencies shown by Conservative governments (see Chapter 1) have affected attitudes towards planning. Urban planning styles now vary between prosperous and non-prosperous areas of the country but in both cases are influenced by economic realities. In the prosperous areas in the south of the country, planning is pushed by the growing demand for both development sites and housing for an increasing population. In the hard-hit urban areas in the Midlands and the north, planners and local authorities have sought to become developers themselves in attempts to retain or attract economic activity. Neither approach is conducive to public participation, or indeed to the type of environmental planning characterized by 'green belts' or restrictions of certain types of use in particular localities. In the prosperous areas the demand is for land to be released: in the derelict areas the need for jobs is often paramount. In these circumstances the planning system introduced in the early 1970s 'has effectively fragmented and sent planning off in a number of new directions' Brindley *et al.* 1986).

McAuslan has identified three competing ideologies as the basis of planning law:

> firstly, that the law exists and should be used to protect private property and its institutions.... Secondly, the law exists and should be used to advance the public interest.... Thirdly, the law exists and should be used to advance the cause of public participation against both the orthodox public administration approach to the public interest and the common law approach of the overriding importance of private property.
>
> (1980: 2)

Each of these ideologies has featured in the general critique of planning and public participation that has developed since the late 1970s. This critique has included contributions from both the Right and Left of the political spectrum and from academics.

First, the growing scope and pretensions of planning have been attacked from the Right as an interference with the ability of individuals to use private property in the most profitable manner. From this point of view, planning prevents 'user control' over individually owned resources! Nor is this seen purely from a selfish perspective. The argument goes on to describe economic regeneration as a consequence of individual initiative and free enterprise. In pursuit of this aim the Conservative government created Urban Development Corporations (UDC) in 1980 for the Liverpool and London Docklands. Further areas are now being treated in a similar manner. The UDCs operate as single-purpose agencies with special powers that place them outside the normal framework of local government and the planning process. Their membership includes business men and other prominent local people who do not hold elective office. They are removed, therefore, from any direct citizen involvement or control. The Enterprise Zones (EZ) now established in many urban areas are another example of this approach. The EZs attempt to encourage industry and commerce by the removal of certain taxes and the easing of planning controls. Once again, the possibility of citizen involvement in the making of planning policy either through elected representatives or by more direct methods is reduced or avoided altogether. This emphasis on free markets and the rights of property owners is also affecting the development control process and 'can only be seen as weakening the position of the public' (Mordey 1987: 199).

Second, the left-wing critique of public participation and planning challenges the notion of 'the public interest'. Such a concept implies a homogeneous 'public' and a consensual 'interest'. Neither assumption can be easily justified. Public participation exercises can, from this point of view, be seen as an attempt to incorporate potential dissent into the framework of orthodox policy-making. Cynthia Cockburn, for example, considers the Skeffington proposals as an attempt both 'to make *implementation* of plans easier by preparing the public in advance ... [and to] bring people into a friendlier acceptance of local authority' (Cockburn 1977: 104–5; her italics). In this way, she believes, the capitalist state will find it easier to pursue its essential purpose of profit and the accumulation of capital. The two aspects of public participation identified by Cockburn were undoubtedly present in the official justification for its introduction into planning. The essential purpose she points to is not, of course, acknowledged by people who do not share her political views.

There is much evidence which points to the success of particular participation exercises in reducing conflict within the planning process (Hain 1980: 189; Young 1984: 165). The disagreements around the left-wing critique occur over the question of whether incorporation is an inevitable outcome of public participation or whether opportunities are provided for opposition interests to gain strength. Most of the left-wing critics accept the ambiguous, or dialectical, nature of public participation which enables it to provide a focus for political struggle; but they are pessimistic about the chances of using public participation as a vehicle for major social change. Brindley *et al.* argue 'that for a popular plan to stand a chance, an area must be of marginal rather than mainstream interest to either private or public developers' (1986: 21).

Third, the academic evaluation in the 1970s pointed to the difficulties of implementing the ideology of public participation. This ideology, according to McAuslan, denies 'that the public interest can be identified and acted upon by public servants on the basis of their own views and assumptions as to what is right and wrong' (1980: 5). There is a need, therefore, for debate in which the general public can directly participate. But can the general public participate in this way? We considered earlier the difficulties that arose in interpreting the Skeffington definition of the public as 'all individuals and groups ... without limitation'. Boaden *et al.* in their discussion of the public participation exercises conducted in the preparation of structure plans point to their failure to broaden the social basis of popular involvement. They 'confirm the general picture of participants as being middle-class, owner-occupiers, long-term residents, the older, the better educated and the males' (Boaden *et al.* 1980: 87). In a later survey of public participation in a range of local services the same authors concluded: 'In the end, élite perspectives have won out, and participation has served the purposes of building up a consensus for the proposals of those in power, thereby legitimating them' (Boaden *et al.* 1982: 179). The reasons for the social bias in the characteristics of the participating public are well known. Participation of any kind depends on the motivation to become involved and on the possession of the resources and skills which make participation possible. These attributes are more likely to be present among the participants in Boaden *et al.*'s description (1980: 87). For example, property owners recognize an interest in planning matters which may affect the value of their property; they are thus motivated to participate. Communication skills and organizational sophistication are also more widely distributed among professional and managerial occupations than among other sections of the population. If participation exercises are not able to overcome the biases inherent in the existing social structure then the result will be to provide further opportunities for those who already have access to the policy-making process.

The way forward

Any proposals for the extension of user control in planning, in the user's role as either consumer or citizen, need to take full account of the critiques mentioned on pp. 27–9. There is a need to establish how far planning should, or indeed can, establish control over the physical development of the environment. We should neither pretend, like the courtiers of King Canute, to recognize a power that does not exist, nor exercise a paternalist control over the details of personal taste. But once these limits have been established, then the public should be enabled to become involved more closely as the users of the product of planning. This product, presumably, is the twofold one of encouraging economic prosperity through the regeneration of our urban areas and appropriate rural redevelopment, while at the same time maintaining a pleasant living environment. The tensions present in such a broad definition are obvious and provide the justification for the widest possible debate among the users of the policies to be adopted, that is the general public. The critique from the Left must be understood in this context. 'User control' of planning can only be fully achieved at the strategic level of major policy outcomes as part of a more general extension of social control over the economic direction of the country: in a word, socialism. Nevertheless, a way forward to this broader objective may be found through more openness in the planning of developments, both public and private, if account is taken of the lessons learnt in the 1970s.

These lessons may be summarized in a number of propositions. First, a simple commitment to 'public' participation in the policy process within a consensual view of politics is not sufficient. Positive action is needed to enable people to participate who are at present excluded. The GLC popular planning initiative and the Sheffield approach in drawing up a city centre plan both recognized the need for such positive action. There was an attempt to combine the radical policy directions of the local authority with the perceptions of specific local groups whether of local residents in the case of London Docklands (Brindley *et al.* 1986: 23) or of women, elderly people, people with disabilities, ethnic minorities, and so on in the case of Sheffield City Centre (Alty and Darke 1987).

Second, the public need assistance to participate in discussions about planning and the time-table must allow for the debate. The large-scale public inquiries that have taken place over some national planning issues have shown that environmental groups based on voluntary effort have found it difficult to match the resources of such giants as the Central Electricity Generating Board. There is a need for financial and professional help to be available for groups who wish to challenge the proposals of the developers. At the more local level, Sheffield in planning for the city centre provided a planner to assist the groups it established in an attempt to include people whose views are usually excluded from the planning process. At both the national and the local level technical support must of course be seen as enabling rather than manipulative. As such it may be more appropriate for the professionals concerned to be independent of the planning authorities as in the case of the experimental Environmental Liaison Officers in Birmingham and Loughborough (Hampton 1978) or in other forms of planning aid. There could also be a wider involvement by adult education in all forms of participation and user control (Groombridge *et al.* 1982). If such approaches became a regular feature of planning projects then both the methods of public participation and the public response could be expected to improve.

Third, a movement towards greater openness in development control obviously means a movement away from the ideology of private property and towards those of the public interest and public participation. The aim should be to make decisions upon the basis of open discussion rather than on the adversarial model of applicant for planning permission versus objectors. At least one local authority is already approaching matters in this way. Information about planning applications in Calderdale is made public through a weekly list displayed in public buildings and published in local newspapers. Any member of the public can arrange to discuss proposals with the officer dealing with the case. The applicant is encouraged to present written arguments in favour of the proposal which again are openly available. The subcommittee considering the application meets in the evening and is open to the public not merely as observers but as participants who comment on the application. The councillors make the final decision. A planning officer in Calderdale considers: 'Over the years, officers and councillors have come to show much greater awareness, understanding and respect for applicants' and objectors' interests' (Nicholson 1985: 26). Such a move towards greater openness should be accompanied by an extension of planning aid to assist both applicants and objectors without the personal resources to engage professional advice. Development control could then move away from a focus on individual property rights and play a 'role in interpreting the preferences of local people' (Mordey 1987: 212).

Finally, the introduction of some form of localized collective forum which could discuss planning matters would emphasize the distinction between the public interest approach embodied in our proposals and the individualistic approach inherent in the Conservative government's claim to be returning power to the people. Such a local forum might come from an introduction of parish councils into the larger urban areas. The introduction of such councils was considered in Birmingham in 1986 but was subsequently rejected (Hoggett and Hambleton 1987: 64; Stoker 1988: 49). Since 1974, parish councils (these exist mainly in rural areas and small towns) have enjoyed a statutory right to comment upon planning matters coming before local planning authorities. A study of Central Berkshire shows this right to have been exercised by all the parish councils in that area and we may assume those in other areas are likely to show a similar interest. The main interest among parish councils in Central Berkshire has been in development control matters rather than general policy. However, the authors of the study consider the powers enjoyed since 1974 have 'raised the planning consciousness of a few parish councils' (Short *et al.* 1986: 202) and this must contribute to public awareness.

Less formal approaches to a local participatory forum could take many forms. For instance there could be an extension of the Scottish concept of community councils (Boaden *et al.* 1982: 46–7) into the rest of Britain. Community councils are a cross between a parish council and a neighbourhood voluntary association. They have a statutory basis and an authority stemming from formal election, but no statutory functions. As such they fit easily into the limbo between representative and participatory democracy occupied by public participation and user control. Yet another attempt 'to try and establish a new form of local decision-making body which involves both elements of the existing council system and elements of direct democracy' has taken place in Islington (Hoggett and Hambleton 1987: 77). A number of neighbourhood forums have been established alongside the local authority's decentralized neighbourhood offices. Once again there has been a conscious effort to take positive action to ensure representation from sections of the population who usually play little part in public affairs. We cannot as yet be clear which approach to localized organization will be best for our purposes. Experience is only now being obtained. There is clearly much room for experimentation as we seek a broadening of the base of representative democracy.

Conclusion

The experience of public participation in planning offers several points of guidance in the growing discussion of user control of public services. First, there is the emphasis on openness rather than institutional titivation as the crucial factor in moving towards more responsive systems of government. Second, there is the need to be aware of the danger of simply opening the system to those who have already gained most influence through the conventional political process. Third, there is the need for technical advice and education to be available for those who wish to take advantage of the increased opportunities to participate or to obtain redress through existing mechanisms. Finally, we should be concerned to extend the concept of *public services* rather than *private privileges*. We seek a broader definition of citizenship which allows a greater measure of personal choice within areas of collective concern. The difficulties are enormous and not easily resolved within the existing structure of society; but through constant struggle to find better forms of control, the public should become increasingly aware of the advantages of collective action.

Note

I am grateful to Roy Darke and Gerry Stoker for commenting on an earlier draft and for drawing my attention to several useful sources.

References

Alty, R. and Darke, R. (1987) 'A city centre for people', *Planning, Practice and Research* 3, September.

Boaden, N., Goldsmith, M., Hampton, W., and Stringer, P. (1980) 'Planning and participation in practice', in P. Diamond and J. B. McLoughlin (eds) *Progress in Planning*, vol. 13, Oxford: Pergamon Press, pp. 1–102.

——(1982) *Public Participation in Local Services*, London: Longman.

Brindley, T., Rydin, Y., and Stoker, G. (1986) 'Urban planning in the 1980s', paper presented at the Annual Political Studies Conference, University of Nottingham. Cf. Brindley, T., Rydin, Y., and Stoker, G. (forthcoming), *Re-Making Planning*, London: Unwin Hyman.

Cockburn, C. (1977) *The Local State*, London: Pluto Press.

Crick, B. (1971) *Political Theory and Practice*, London: Allen Lane the Penguin Press.

Cullingworth, J. B. (1985) *Town and Country Planning in Britain*, 9th edn, London: Allen & Unwin.

Darke, R. (1979) 'Monitoring the structure planning process within a new metropolitan county council', final report to the SSRC of project HR3363.

Department of the Environment (1972) *Town and Country Planning Act 1971: Part II Development Plan Proposals: Publicity and Public Participation*, Circular 52/72, London: HMSO.

——(1974) *Structure Plans*, Circular 98/74, London: HMSO.

Groombridge, B., Durant, J., Hampton, W., Woodcock, G., and Wright, A. (1982) *Adult Education and Participation*, Sheffield: Universities' Council for Adult and Continuing Education (available from Division of Continuing Education, 85 Wilkinson Street, Sheffield, S10 2GJ).

Hain, P. (1980) *Neighbourhood Participation*, London: Temple Smith.

Hampton, W. (1977) 'Research into public participation in structure planning', in W. R. D. Sewell and J. T. Coppock (eds) *Public Participation in Planning*, Chichester: John Wiley & Sons.

——(1978) *Providing the Posh Words ...*, London: Department of the Environment.

——(1987) *Local Government and Urban Politics*, London: Longman.

Hoggett, P. and Hambleton, R. (eds) (1987) *Decentralisation and Democracy: Localising Public Services*, University of Bristol: School for Advanced Urban Studies.

McAuslan, P. (1980) *The Ideologies of Planning Law*, Oxford: Pergamon Press.

Mordey, R. (1987) 'Development control, public participation and the need for planning aid', in M. L. Harrison and R. Mordey (eds) *Planning Control: Philosophies, Prospects and Practice*, London: Croom Helm.

Nicholson, K. (1985) 'Access to information – the steps beyond' *The Planner* 71 (5): 25–6.

Planning Advisory Group (1965) *The Future of Development Plans*, London: HMSO.

Richardson, A. (1983) *Participation*, London: Routledge & Kegan Paul.

Short, J. R., Fleming, S., and Witt, S. J. G. (1986) *Housebuilding, Planning and Community Action*, London: Routledge & Kegan Paul.

Skeffington Report (1969) *People and Planning. Report of the Committee on Public Participation in Planning*, London: HMSO.

Stoker, G. (1988) *The Politics of Local Government*, London: Macmillan.

Woodcock, G. L. (1986) *Planning, Politics and Communications*, Aldershot: Gower.

Young, T. (1984) 'The politics of public participation in planning', unpublished M.Phil. Thesis, University of Sussex.

3

Transport

Enid Wistrich

Transport and the right of access

Everyone needs to be able to reach essential services in their daily lives. People have to get to work, children to school, the sick to hospital, and goods have to be delivered from factories to shops. Transport which supplies mobility is an essential part of living: thus it can be said that people are entitled to have access to the services they need through whatever transport is the most suitable for them.

The right to access has never been fully defined, nor has the point at which public services or assistance are an essential aid to it. There are certain indications of the standards which have to be observed for some public-service activities, and minimum requirements have been set out. For example, children walk to school but there are education authority rules which establish at what distance they are entitled to the free school bus service. The sick have to make their own way to doctors and hospitals, but there are free ambulance services for the acutely ill, the disabled, and the elderly. Local authority departments will provide access by bringing services to people (e.g. mobile libraries, playbuses, information units) or by taking people to services (e.g. day centres, youth club visits). Both central and local government recognize the general right of the elderly to access by subsidizing bus travel. In some areas, attempts have been made by local authorities to establish the need for access, and the standard of public transport service which therefore needs to be provided. These are described later.

However, there are many areas which need to be further examined. The right of the unemployed to access to work opportunities is one, the right of single-parent workers to access to nurseries is another. Moreover, the broader question of whether personal access to facilities can be substituted by modern telecommunications has never been explored. Telephone and television can help to bring services to the home, but they are not a substitute for the full right of personal access.

Access is affected by the availability of transport means, but also by decisions taken by business enterprises and by planning authorities. The decision by a developer and a planning authority to site a shopping centre well outside a town will affect some people's access to it. Similarly, decisions by an education authority to close a school, or by a health authority to build a hospital, will have important results for access to those services at the nearest available point. Decisions by planning and highway authorities also have significant results for access. A new highway may divide a community from services, or it may bring them nearer. A pedestrian precinct, a car park, a road crossing, the siting of bus stops and stations, all have important effects on access.

The right of access to services is one which applies to all individuals. But the individual has no absolute right to unrestricted use of whatever transport means suit his or her own convenience. The impact of transport affects both individuals and communities; individual transport use has to be subject to broad community rules. For example, cars and lorries are regulated for speed and noise, emissions and weight, and may be directed away from residential centres. The social, collective need for a good environment here imposes constraint on transport use. One person's car use may be the cause of another's reduced ability to walk or cycle with safety.

Transport, personal choice, and collective action

If transport is defined as a means of personal access – a person's movement from one destination to another – there is a variety of choices which an individual can make. These are between private methods of movement – walking, cycling, or the private car – or public transport – bus, train, or plane. Private transport is the most immediate and easy to use for the individual but is contingent on both individual resources (i.e. the cost of a car) and public decisions, for example petrol tax and car licence charges, the state of road repairs, street pavements, and lighting. The choice for an individual or family may well be a flexible one within their control. A household may use a car for one wage earner to commute to work, a bus for a second wage earner, a cycle for a third or for a teenager to go to school, and a walk to a shopping centre. Private decision-making will be governed by the purpose of the journey, the resources of the individuals, and the public services available. Control over the choices will be limited by these factors, but to the extent that the individual can use private transport means and trade them off against public ones, his or her choice is greater. Where a bus or train service appears to be failing, individuals can and do opt for exit from the public transport services. They use their choice as a method of user control (Hirschman 1970; Papadakis and Taylor-Gooby 1987). There are, however, circumstances and groups where exit to private transport is either not practical or not possible. Where a long journey has to be made, it may scarcely be practical to use a bicycle instead of a train. Where a short journey to a town centre has to be made, a car will not substitute for a bus if there is no available parking. A child cannot walk or cycle to school where main traffic arteries intervene. And any journey exceeding a few miles requires public transport for households which cannot afford a car, or for members of car-owning households who do not control its use. For all these people, exit to the private sector is not an option which increases control.

The alternative for these groups has to be to seek to influence the provision of public transport services, or the facilities which otherwise improve their access to services. Only in this way can they hope to exert greater user control. The method used is one of 'voice' (Hirschman 1970), seeking to exercise influence over the decisions which are made about transport provision and the factors which affect it. While an individual may start as a complainant, say about the poor reliability of a bus service, it is not long before a grouping of individuals is seen to be necessary. Collective action, the creation of a user or pressure group to present a common case, is the method. It is the solution of pressure politics in a pluralist society: through the process of consultation and participation, interested users seek to present their case to the transport operator or the public authorities who take the decisions and control the resources.

In the account which follows, the form and effectiveness of collective voice and pressure are considered. But as a method of control the collective voice may fail to persuade a bus company to run a service, and citizen opposition to a new motorway may not be effective. In such circumstances, the only way for a group to gain greater influence over policy decisions is to capture the decision-making process at the necessary level. That involves consideration of the relationships, and the powers and rules, of government at different levels, and the ways in which policy decisions can be changed.

It is also necessary to address the question of how a transport service is performed or delivered. The way in which a service is provided is of great importance to the user. Price is clearly one vital factor in public transport. Others are choice of service, route, frequency, and reliability. The question of alternative forms of service also arises : bus, minibus, train, private and shared taxis, chartered special-purpose buses, 'community' buses, personal travel vouchers, all may have a part to play in increasing responsiveness to individual needs. The way in which transport authorities explore, consult, and take their decisions is thus of great importance. A single form of operation presents less flexibility and choice to consumers.

User control in transport thus seeks to ensure basic rights of access to services, the maximum choice of transport for individual needs, and good standards of service performance. User control also implies the need to control transport developments and infrastructure (i.e. airports, roads, volume and type of traffic) so that they do not adversely affect other people's transport means or the collective environment.

Transport policy up to 1979

Looked at historically, the provision of transport has always been an important part of the economic and social structure, a subject for statutory regulation and government involvement. Turnpike trusts, canals, and then railways all required Acts of Parliament before they could be built; railway charges were regulated by a public tribunal, road maintenance was the responsibility of local government, and many towns ran their own bus and tram services. Earlier laws allowed for social provision, for example cheap early-morning railway fares for workmen. But the view that mobility and access to services are of such importance as to make the provision of public transport rank as a social service has only recently emerged. Furthermore, the impact on the living environment of roads and traffic is such that their negative effects are now considered to be as detrimental as air and noise pollution, lack of open space, or other forms of environmental deprivation.

The greater consciousness of transport arrangements as a part of the public services has developed as the full consequences of private car ownership have been felt. Increased opportunities for the growing number of people who have access to the use of a private car have been accompanied by relative disadvantage for the 40 per cent of the population who do not. The groups most dependent on public transport – the elderly, women, young people, and households of low income – now suffer from poorer provision and from the loss of shopping, social, and employment facilities which are located increasingly in areas to which they have no ready access. Traffic congestion and heavy lorries in urban areas have the greatest impact on pedestrians, cyclists, and the poorest income groups. Transport policy in the 1960s and 1970s was thus seen as one important way of remedying the social disadvantage of households without cars, and of contributing to the broader social goal of providing a healthy living environment. It does not relate to an established social service with well-defined statutory responsibilities. It is concerned with a much broader spectrum of powers, ranging from highway planning, local plans, lorry weight regulation, and traffic management on the one hand, to the planning and financing of public transport services on the other.

The development of policy is complex because of the varied framework within which decisions are taken. National and local government both take important transport planning decisions. Transport operators may be state or (increasingly) private operators, but are regulated by statutory provisions, and often are dependent on government for important decisions. Thus, decisions on the building and siting of major installations, such as motorways, national airports, or the Channel Tunnel, are taken by central government, as are the vital decisions on maximum lorry weights, fuel tax and vehicle licence duties which affect transport operators. Government effectively determines the investment programme of British Rail, subsidizes rural and commuter train services, and can veto line and station closures. Local authorities plan and maintain all roads except motorways and are responsible for traffic management schemes. In making decisions about land use planning, they effectively determine the need for transport to provide access to schools, hospitals, shopping centres, and workplaces. They also have powers to subsidize public transport, though these have been reduced by recent statutes. Traffic Commissioners license public transport operators at local level, and as Licensing Authority members they also license heavy goods vehicles. Finally, the police have important areas of discretionary authority in traffic regulation.

Developments under the Thatcher governments

The movement of policy up to 1979 was to enlarge the role of local authorities both in financing and controlling public transport and in the overall co-ordination and control of transport planning. Many local authorities used the powers conferred by the 1968 Transport Act to subsidize public transport services. From 1974, they were required by central government to produce annual rolling plans for transport investment and expenditure (Transport Policies and Programmes) which covered investment in both road-building and public transport, and included revenue support for public transport. The general effect was to shift local authority capital expenditure away from roads in the 1970s and to increase revenue expenditure on support for public transport (Wistrich 1986). From 1970 to 1975, British Rail was explicitly subsidized for its 'public service obligation'. The general watchword was integration and co-ordination of transport services.

The Thatcher government has sharply reversed these trends. It has slammed the brakes on subsidy to public transport – even if it has taken some time for the movement to slow down – and it has shattered the move to integration. The new policy has been to fragment transport planning, to privatize transport operations leaving the determination of services to the market, and to reduce government's role to a minimal regulation. The exception is road planning and building, where government powers have been augmented and funding for programmes has been enhanced. The Transport Act, 1985, the most thoroughgoing exercise in privatization and deregulation of any public service, has required the sale of bus fleets owned by local authorities to companies which they may own but may not directly control for day-to-day operations. The National Bus Company is being broken up into smaller units and sold to private operators. The Act has provided for almost total deregulation of bus services, allowing licensing only for the safety of vehicles. Only in London is the new London Regional Transport Authority allowed through its subsidiary to own bus fleets and to determine the routes of services. Elsewhere, the operators run services along routes which they themselves determine, with stops, fares, and frequencies of their own choice. Local authorities, however, retain the power to subsidize unprofitable routes or journeys, and to subsidize concessionary fares, within overall financial limits determined by the Secretary of State (Transport Act, 1983). In transport planning, there has been an important shift in power. The abolition of the GLC and the metropolitan county councils in 1986 left the big conurbations without elected strategic planning authorities. Their powers were dispersed to the London borough and metropolitan district councils, while some were transferred to the Department of Transport. For example, 'guidance' can be given to local councils on traffic management and highway planning. The shire county councils have retained their transport planning powers but bids for government grant for transport expenditure (TPPs) may no longer be used to balance expenditure on road building and subsidy to public transport but only for capital expenditure. Overall, there has been a reduction in the role of local government in relation to transport.

These developments are very recent and the consequences for transport planning and provision are only beginning to emerge. There is a clear gain for the influence of central government in transport planning in the urban areas, for example in the 'corridor' reviews of motorway provision currently being carried out in London. New proposals for £5 billion expenditure in the 1990s were put forward in July 1988 by government-appointed consultants. These included a revived proposal for a south circular road, linking Westway in Kensington with the M4 and then going right through to the Rochester Way Relief Road in Kent. Moreover, increased government power brings with it an increase in the influence of the commercial transport lobby and the motoring organizations which have ready access to the Department of Transport.

In the provision of public transport, the first evidence since the 1985 Act was of comparative caution among operators who have tended to keep to familiar routes. Competition was less than the government had hoped, and new operators fewer, with the large companies still predominant (SEEDS 1987a). Three-quarters of past bus routes continued to be run commercially, but between a third and a half of rural mileage and of uneconomic early, late, and Sunday services had not been registered in 1986 and required subsidy to be continued (*Economist* 1986). In Scotland, it was found that there was little overall change in the extent of the bus networks in 1986/7. There was an increased number of bus operators and greater vehicle mileage operated, but although there were more urban peak-hour services, there were fewer rural ones, and less service in the evenings and on Sundays (Scottish Office 1988). In Great Britain as a whole, fewer bus journeys were made, although the number of route miles operated, especially by minibuses, had risen (TRRL 1988). BusWatch, an independent nationwide bus-monitoring project sponsored by a number of voluntary organizations, analysed responses from passengers' regular experiences submitted by a group typical of users dependent on buses. They found a mixed result. There had been an increased number of initiatives in bus services, especially minibuses, and more service promotions, mostly on urban routes and for day-time services. But the service was more fragmented, and information and comprehensive fare offers had been reduced, so that the traveller had difficulty in working out and comparing convenient routes and prices. Reliability and quality of the travel experience had also suffered to some extent, although minibuses were found to provide a friendlier travelling environment (BusWatch 1988).

The government's clear intention is to put public transport wholly back into the private sector, and to limit its own role to a minimum of regulation and subsidy for social need. In planning, integration is no longer the watchword. In urban areas in particular, greater central government powers are likely to favour more road provision, and land use planning which benefits the car user. Thus the market is to determine provision and the citizen is in the role of consumer or customer, exercising choice and the possibility of change to an alternative operator or mode. With full competition, the government anticipates that the needs of customers, both actual and potential, will be met as operators plan to provide for them. Consultation and participation in decision-making should then be unnecessary, as should action by government bodies to provide and regulate services. 'User control' in the government's view would be satisfied by the effective operation of the market. 'Externalities' – for example the road repair costs of heavy goods traffic – can be taken care of by the tax system when they are only indirectly influenced by market factors. Planning can be minimized, simply to conform to basic health and environmental requirements, but should respond to operators' needs. It is argued that the demand by

41

transport operators for road-building should be seen and accepted as the reflection of consumer demand for more road capacity for car travel and lorry use.

Influencing transport planning

The exercise of voice, and participation by the public in planning decisions, have often been discussed and analysed (e.g. Boaden *et al.* 1982, Cockburn 1977, Skeffington Report 1969). The problems are familiar: the authorities may refuse to consult 'hostile' groups, they may use the process to legitimize decisions already made, professional workers may dominate decisions, the most disadvantaged groups are least able to present their views, and the pressure groups usually include a preponderance of knowledgeable elitist persons with the sharp elbows of the middle class well to the fore. From the viewpoint of business, too, there have been problems, namely the inordinate length of time taken by public authorities and inquiries before decisions are reached (Dobry 1975).

Local authorities retain important powers in planning which affect transport, and it is important to consider how local opinion and needs can be more effectively taken into account if 'user control' is to be extended. A particular problem with transport proposals is that they may cover a wide geographic area and often disadvantage some areas and groups while benefiting others. For example, a one-way system of traffic regulation or a bypass road will benefit car users, lorries, and those relieved of traffic, but disadvantage the immediate neighbourhood of the newly designated route. To gather and assess viewpoints over the spectrum involves a careful weighing of the views of different 'communities'. For this reason, decentralist solutions, often suggested as a method of 'user control', which propose to devolve decisions to local area units, may serve only to articulate one area's views in relation to another's. That does not discount the value of area opinion, but it does not allow the transfer of transport planning decisions into local hands except where they concern only the immediate locality. Many decisions have to be weighed and taken at local authority level in an essentially political balancing exercise. A local interest which wants to win the decision therefore has to lobby and persuade the local council, and if necessary capture its consent at a political level.

However, the bigger problem is how to introduce effective voice into wider decision-taking affecting whole regions or the nation as a whole. Local authority procedures are well defined and established but there are no corresponding regional authorities, while some issues which bear on local areas are taken at national level (e.g. motorway bypasses). Central government engages in extensive consultation exercises with recognized pressure groups. In these the influence of national commercial lobbies is strong. The decisions then taken are poorly scrutinized by parliament. The public inquiry procedure for projects with major national implications is lengthy and expensive because it is largely based on an examination of those whose business and property interests are directly affected and who are inevitably represented by legal counsel. Moreover, ultimate decisions are strongly influenced by major government policy. It is, for example, unlikely that the proposal for Stansted Airport would have been rejected by the Thatcher government whatever the inquiry result. Even so, a public inquiry for another major issue, the Channel Tunnel, was turned down in favour of the faster route of a hybrid bill in Parliament with limited opportunities for consultation once the main decision had been taken.

For such national proposals, the best way of extending public voice would be to expand the role of the Commons Select Committee on Transport to examine the essential policy and political implications of proposals before decisions are made. Some steps have already been taken in this direction by the committee's own initiatives (Ganz 1985). It was able to examine the options for a Channel link well before the government had made its decision and it recommended the rail-only scheme which was finally adopted. It also inquired into transport in London and recommended the setting up of a metropolitan transport authority, again before the government had reached a decision. In 1981, it decided to question the members of the committee which produced the Armitage Report on Lorries, People and the Environment, before decisions were taken on future lorry weights.

It should be possible to extend the Commons Select Committee's work with the aid of more staff and professional advisers and assessors to consider all major transport proposals. The procedures used would aim to expose the issues, whether technical or economic, and to examine their social impact. It would be relatively informal and open ended, and would provide assistance to voluntary groups in presenting their case. The committee would build on its experience of examining reports and witnesses, both from within and outside government. Its past experience suggests that a non-partisan approach by MPs of different parties can be made to work effectively to produce reports which are not divided on straight party lines. In an examination of a major new proposal, the technical aspects could first be examined by professionals and challenged by interest and voluntary groups with professional expertise at an open inquiry assessment. Local residential and other 'lay' pressure groups could simultaneously be given the opportunity to present their viewpoint to an experienced assessor. These inputs would be fed into the Select Committee's considerations and its subsequent report submitted to Parliament. Public procedures would thus be established by which organizations outside government and the people personally affected could express their opinions directly to their political representatives. The report would ensure that information was made public, opinions expressed, and influence exerted at a political level before the government of the day made its decisions.

Where proposals are of regional rather than national significance, it should be possible to adopt a similar procedure with a subcommittee of the Select Committee including local MPs (or members of the Committee on Welsh Affairs or the Scottish Grand Committee) to consider proposals. Another method would be to use a regional group of local authorities. As there is no elected tier of regional government, it would be necessary to create *ad hoc* joint committees of local authorities, and to empower them to require evidence for their inquiries. The abolition of planning authorities at conurbation level for London and the metropolitan areas is in this respect a grievous gap which should be repaired. At present there is a variety of *ad hoc* consultation bodies of uncertain function and little known effectiveness in London, and member-level liaison is split politically between the Association of London (Labour) Authorities and the London Boroughs Association (Conservative). However, in the former metropolitan county areas, some district councils have usefully retained research and information units at county level (Leach 1987).

Public transport decisions

The clear intention of the 1985 Transport Act is that public transport should not be planned or operated under the policy guidance of local authorities. The operators, both at local level and in the case of British Rail and national coach companies, must run on commercial principles. Subsidy for the elderly and for routes not registered for commercial use may be given within overall limits set by the Secretary of State. The questions which must therefore be asked are: first, does the new framework eliminate the possibility of transport being run as a public service with a significant degree of user control? and second, if it does not, is the new arrangement to be preferred or should it be replaced by any other?

To answer the first question, it is necessary to consider whether the services provided can be influenced to meet the full needs of both actual and potential users. That involves determination of those needs, and the ability to plan and operate services to meet them, to influence investment and prices, if necessary with subsidy, and to monitor the effects. The marketing function of an organization seeks to satisfy the market needs of users by designing its service accordingly. It has been described as 'a democratic rather than elitist technology .... Effective marketing is user oriented and not seller oriented' (Kotler 1982). Marketing methods used by operators provide an important check on excessive influence on service provision by its producers – in this case professional engineers, transport trade unions, or long-serving executives using their professional, or the organization's cultural, norms.

But a fuller analysis of need must go beyond the need 'expressed' by market demand or potential demand. Need based on individual want cannot always be met by the market when individual purchasing power is lacking to make it effective or where the need is of a small or scattered group. Need may also arise from the deprivation of specific groups within the community compared with their fellow citizens.

The concept of transport deprivation has been defined as lack of access to activities and services which are required (Banister 1979). Such deprivation varies from one individual to another depending on their age, location, and pattern of activities. For example, an elderly person living in a rural village without a car suffers multiple deprivation in lack of access to shopping, medical services, and social and leisure facilities.

There has been a development of techniques within local authorities and academic institutions to measure such needs. For example, Dyfed County Council in rural Wales has assessed the needs of its population and examined the extent to which they were being met and how they could be better provided (Dodd 1984). At the other end of the rural/urban spectrum, the GLC before its demise used its Popular Planning Unit to examine the transport needs of women (GLC Women's Committee 1985–7). The London Strategic Policy Unit financed by eight London boroughs (aptly named 'the GLC in exile') continued this work by examining the transport needs of black and other ethnic minority groups. The technique used for the women's study was a combination of consultation and survey, involving first exploration and consultation with representative community groups, then the framing of a questionnaire which was sent to a random sample of women for reply. The aim has been to uncover the neglected or unknown needs of hitherto unregarded groups. In the case of the women's study, for example, it revealed the fear which frequently inhibits women from making the journey to desired activities and from using public transport. Other studies had already been carried out in East Anglia and Devon (NCC 1978), in South Oxfordshire (Banister 1979), in Bedfordshire (Blowers 1978), and most recently in Basildon (SEEDS 1987b). Such studies extend the traditional marketing procedures of profit-making organizations to a deeper analysis of need. Qualitative research into the attitudes of particular client groups can also be a useful procedure where it is helpful to analyse complex motivation and relationships (Heiser 1985).

Thus data can be explored and need assessed by a combination of statistical analyses, survey techniques, and group consultation procedures. The results of this analysis can then be applied to service provision.

The next question is whether local authorities currently have the means to see that services can be supplied to meet the needs which have been identified. Local authorities no longer have direct powers to influence the policy decisions of bus operators, direct or guide their investment programmes, influence vehicle design or control fare structures and levels, integrate different services, or invest in new buses. They can still plan the development of new 'metro' systems like Newcastle's and seek to finance them by raising the capital. They retain important, though limited, powers to subsidize particular routes by designating those which have not been registered by commercial operators and then offering them by tender to operators with a subsidy attached. The system can also be used to influence the commercial services indirectly, for example, to influence fares policy since many routes are a mixture of commercial and subsidized journeys. By subsidizing a more frequent service than that proposed by the commercial operator, the local authority can help to bridge the gap between commercially profitable services and unexpressed need. Local authorities may also offer subsidy for the elderly and disabled, who may then receive concessionary fares. They can help to support voluntary organizations running transport services. Dyfed County Council, for example, has financed a 'county cars' scheme operated by the Womens Royal Voluntary Service which provides transport for occasional essential use such as health service visits (Dodd 1984). Subsidies have also been given by local authorities to minibuses operated by community groups and by private operators and to post buses in rural areas (NCC 1978). Local councils can also review their own transport services to see if they can be adapted to include other groups: both education and social services run considerable bus fleets in many areas which could be further used. School buses, for example, might be used to take the elderly to lunch and recreation clubs, and made available for weekend use. These means could be used to supplement commercial services, based on fuller assessment of need.

The possibility of using vouchers for transport purchase can also be considered. One study has proposed the replacement of general transport subsidies by a system of 'access credits' for individuals, to be used on all or any transport or telecommunications facility (CSS 1986). Vouchers are a useful enabling device which can offer the consumer maximum choice between modes of transport, and are particularly valuable where access needs are specific and unusual. For example, disabled people may use them for taxis, or, where available, a dial-a-ride service, or for running a special vehicle of their own. There may well be other disadvantaged groups who could benefit from a voucher system for specific purposes, for example visiting relatives in long-stay institutions.

Under the present legislation, local authorities lack the powers to plan and oversee a fully integrated service, and may not directly operate their own public transport services. If, as has been argued, the assessment of need should be directly related to service provision, there would need to be new powers at the local level. Several important questions need, however, to be resolved. The first is whether the authority which plans and monitors the services should also be directly reponsible for their operation. The second is whether either of these functions should be in the hands of elected local authorities or of statutory authorities not directly democratically accountable. The argument in favour of single-authority planning and operation lays emphasis on unity of purpose, co-ordination, and long-term planning potential, plus the building up of experience and expertise. Against it is the fear that such authorities may become 'closed' organizations, dominated by professional groups and trade union interests, and excluding fresh views, lay assessment, and consumer and user input. It is a criticism often made, for example, of the National Health Service and the Atomic Energy Authority.

A counterweight to 'closed' control is exercised in local authorities where elected councillors are aware of and responsive to local needs and interests, and provide a lay viewpoint. The problem here has always been to persuade councillors to abstain from close detailed control of operations and administration, lately intensified by the stronger ideological views taken on particular management issues. The 'politicization' of local government has often been argued as undesirable, usually in the context of criticisms against the Left. But the Widdicombe Committee found that the level of political organization in local government is similar for all parties, although the degree of political conflict between the parties had sharpened. In its recommendations, it was concerned to reinforce an open process of decision-making in local government which recognized the role of political parties but ensured that neither party, nor sectional, nor pecuniary interests should dominate decisions, and that senior officers should continue to act as permanent and politically 'neutral' officials (Widdicombe Report 1986). In general, the role and record of local authorities in pioneering new services and running existing ones responsive to the needs of their communities make them a good choice for exercising the main planning responsibility in the transport function.

There are stronger arguments in favour of separating the planning and operational functions. First, large-scale public transport is a considerable industrial operation which for efficiency needs to be separated from the more usual procedures of local authority administration. Second, the authority which assesses, plans, and monitors ought to stand back from the operational side, and not to understand its problems too easily. Too great an involvement may prevent an overall view from being taken with the danger that the service becomes producer- rather than consumer-orientated. Third, if flexibility and variety in transport provision to user needs are the aim, then the planning authority needs to be able to choose between alternatives, whether provided by public authorities or by voluntary ones and the private sector.

The solution advocated is therefore to empower local authorities to plan for transport need and to use their resources between capital and revenue expenditure, and between road, public transport, and other means as they think best, but to avoid direct operational responsibility for any large-scale services. On the basis of their plans, they would contract or franchise public transport operators and monitor their operations. They would fund subsidy or grant loans for capital expenditure as they saw appropriate and could lay down rules for minimum conditions of service for employees of the contracting organizations. A model for this type of planning and contracting authority would be based partly on the past experience of the GLC and Metropolitan County Councils as well as the new experience of Passenger Transport Authorities and district councils. This operational-level solution is advocated by a transport expert with experience of London Transport (Quarmby 1985). It allows the local authority to combine and co-ordinate planning and transport powers and to set a 'user' rather than a 'producer' orientation.

In developing this model, the consultative procedures already established by some local authorities could be used to good effect. Neighbourhood groups and decentralized centres for service delivery set up by urban local authorities would have a part to play, as would parish councils, in representing area interests. Particular social groups, for example the disabled, mothers with small children, or the frail elderly, could be contacted through health, social service and voluntary agencies. Their involvement and constant monitoring of operations could be used to ensure that the services remained responsive to user need. 'User control' operated in the way described could be a reality at sensitive and crucial points in the operation of the service.

The role of Transport Consumer Councils

Consumer councils were set up as part of the transport statutory framework when the railways were nationalized in 1947. They were originally intended to consider changes in charges and proposed reductions in services for both rail and nationalized road transport. After 1962, however, their remit was restricted to railways. The councils may not consider charges or fares but they are required to be consulted about station and line closures. Their main task is to consider individual complaints about services and to seek a remedy for them with British Rail. They are also concerned with general issues affecting services, such as train reliability, catering services, and station facilities, on which they make reports and representations. There are eight regional Transport Users' Consultative Committees (TUCCs) and one central one whose members are appointed by the Secretary of State. Their constrained remit and powers ensure a low public profile and limited effectiveness.

In London, arrangements are somewhat different. The London Transport Passengers' Committee (LTPC) was set up in 1969 to represent consumers in relation to both bus and underground services provided by London Transport. It could not consider station or line closures. Its remit also excluded British Rail suburban routes and stations within London, and thus effectively removed its influence from a large (predominant in South London) part of the transport network. The LTPC had a working relationship with both the transport operator (LT) and the GLC which under the 1969 Act was given responsibility for LT as well as for broad transport planning questions. The GLC could set financial targets and directives for LT. The LTPC had therefore a considerable opportunity in its dual relationship to influence passenger transport policy within a well-defined spatial area. LTPC members were appointed by the GLC and, from 1972, selections were made from those nominated in response to public advertisements. (Most of these came from user and pressure groups within London.) It also reported to the GLC. The LTPC listened to and made representations to LT about passenger service complaints and complainants were invited to attend the committee to put their case. But it also set up working parties to consider much broader issues: access to hospitals, women and transport, and access to public transport by people with disabilities were reported on, as well as more specific issues like transport in Docklands and in Croydon. The committee was often able to pick up and develop general issues arising from the incidence of individual complaints. Many of these were the subject of representations to either LT or the GLC; these had a considerable degree of success although not always as a direct and immediate result. In the relationship which evolved, LTPC was a friendly and supportive critic, valued for the contribution it made (Kilvington 1984).

In 1984 the LTPC was replaced by the London Regional Passengers' Committee (LRPC) under the new Act which took control of London's passenger transport services away from the GLC, giving them to the new London Regional Transport under the direct control of the Secretary of State. The new LRPC is appointed by the Secretary of State and, since LRT includes British Rail routes in London within its remit, it may also consider the services of British Rail in the London area. It has a new power: to be consulted by LRT or BR if they propose to close a station or line; it thus corresponds with the TUCCs for the rest of the country. The new committee thus has a wider overall remit for rail, underground, and bus services. It continues to review major policy issues such as the proposed Channel Tunnel terminus in London. It also considers individual service complaints.

Transport Consumer Councils, like their fellow consumer councils for other services, provide an opportunity for monitoring the service from a consumer viewpoint. They are clearly important where there is no possibility of direct democratic input. The existing councils are, however, restricted by their limited remit (outside London) and by their limited powers to inquire into and to affect decisions. They all greatly depend on the goodwill and informal relationships which can be built up and they lack democratic legitimacy. While representing user organizations and pressure groups they often include those interested and active persons who make their contribution without great pretensions to being representative of a broader group.

The need for consumer representation and a voice in decision-making at national level was put forward in the 1970s, where it was seen as an equivalent for the large national transport operators to the arrangements for the major publicly owned utilities for gas, electricity, and the post office. The National Consumer Council in 1977 proposed a National Transport Council to include operators, consumer representatives, and the government in order to ensure a consumer voice at national level. In 1978 the White Paper on the Nationalized Industries proposed a National Transport Consumers' Council to include consideration of both rail and bus services, with regard to fare structure, services, and facilities. The Labour Party's most recent transport policy statement *Fresh Directions* (1987) revives the idea of a National Transport Authority with user representation.

At national level, any such measures to provide consumer input are a welcome counterbalance to both government and producer influence. A National Transport Consumers' Council could ensure a mouthpiece for the consumer voice, but for it to make any impact there would have to be a right to information and a legal obligation on the government and transport operators to consult it. A National Transport Authority with consumer representation would not on its own provide sufficient leverage, as the consumer voice could easily be outvoted.

The question of local consumer councils for transport needs to be considered separately. The framework suggested in the previous section puts local authorities into the position of contracting for local services among operators, rather than running them directly themselves. In such circumstances, the role of the councils would be to survey need, consult and plan the services, and monitor response. Aided by local committees involving user and client groups and with the direct input of councillors, they should be in a strong position to carry out these tasks. They would no longer be in the ambivalent position of seeking to justify the services from the producer viewpoint as well as representing the consumer position. In such circumstances, local transport consumer councils, with weaker popular links and a lower public profile, should not be necessary. However, there must be a reservation based on the limited time of busy councillors and their interest in transport matters. A councillor whose main interest lies in other services will not devote him/herself assiduously to transport affairs. The experience in London of the LTPC suggests that there may be room for a forum where user and pressure groups can make their contribution, and where members do not have to make the larger commitment of time to council work, or the full political commitment. The balance of judgement must therefore lie between the possibility of duplicating consumer work on the one hand and of neglecting the useful work of a more independent committee on the other. Local factors could be of importance here and the best solution might be to leave the setting up of local transport consumer councils as an option to be decided by local authorities with transport responsibilities in consultation with government. Where local consumer councils were set up their areas of competence would need to correspond to transport catchment areas. It would be important to ensure that their remit extended to bus as well as train services, that they had full rights to information from the transport operators, and that they had the right to be consulted and adequate staff to enable them to carry out their role.

Finally, the question of individual redress needs to be considered. Complaints about the levels and reliability of publicly owned public transport services are now dealt with either informally or through the limited representations which can be made by the existing consumer councils. A question to be raised is whether gaps in service, cancellations, and persistently late arrivals in public transport should be the subject of more formal complaints procedures, with possibly a fine for the operators and compensation for the consumer at the conclusion of a quasi-legal process. Such consideration enters the territory of consumer legal rights in service industries and appeal procedures, but it should be noted as an area for some further investigation.

Conclusions

In this account, the basic right of citizens in relation to transport is defined as the right of access to forms of activity and to services which are essential to their daily lives. These should include access to employment, to public and social services, to shops, and to some degree of social contact. To realize this basic right, individuals require mobility, which may be achieved by private means (walking, cycling, and private vehicle) or by public transport. Both access and modes are affected by the decisions of government at different levels. Policies to improve access and to extend citizen influence and user control therefore involve the use of collective action (in relation to planning, road building, traffic management, etc.), as well as policies which seek to extend individual transport choice.

Personal choice is limited by individual resources: the option to use a private car as against a bus service is limited to those who can afford one or, within a car-owning household, have access to it. Of all households 40 per cent do not have regular access to cars. There are important groups – women, the elderly, and the poorest in society – who rely on public transport. To increase choice, policies are needed which improve both the range and quality of public-service provision, and provide or facilitate alternatives.

The Thatcher governments have set out to privatize and deregulate public transport, to reduce the powers of local authorities in transport planning, and to allow the provision of transport facilities (both public and private) to be governed by market forces. Central government finance and activity remain strong in road building, but local authorities retain reduced powers to subsidize public transport. A future policy which intends to increase access for all social groups and to further empower users should include the following measures:

1. The procedures for inquiry and consultation over national decisions which affect transport should be improved, in particular to include more democratic and consumer input. In the case of major policy proposals of national significance, the role of the Commons Select Committee on Transport should be extended to make an assessment and report to Parliament before the government's decision is made. The committee's investigation would take the form of an open inquiry into the technical, economic, and social issues and would use assessors to examine the evidence on technical issues and from local groups.

Regional issues should be examined similarly by a representative subcommittee of the Select Committee, in co-operation as necessary with the Committee on Welsh Affairs or the Scottish Grand Committee. An alternative method would be to constitute special *ad hoc* joint committees of local authorities affected, empowered to conduct the investigations and assessment.

2. Local authorities should use both their planning and transport powers to increase access and to improve the responsiveness of public transport services.

(i) They should develop techniques which assess the access and travel needs of their populations. The examination of basic statistical data, group consultation procedures, surveys, and questionnaires, and intensive attitude research with particular groups all have a part to play. Indicators of transport need should be established. The views of local groups and communities on the way in which transport arrangements and structures affect them should be examined through the processes of consultation. The aim should be actively to involve local people as consumer/citizens in the planning of services.

(ii) Local authorities should use the information gathered and views obtained as a basis for the exercise of their planning powers, i.e.:
   a) future planning of their own services (schools, welfare clinics, etc.) to improve access
   b) development control for factories, shops, offices, and residential areas to improve access
   c) road planning and traffic management.

(iii) Local authorities should similarly use this information:
   a) to designate and subsidize non-commercial public transport routes and to monitor their operation
   b) to offer financial assistance or services to specific groups – whether to women, the elderly, the disabled, or otherwise disadvantaged – to facilitate mobility and access, either by fare subsidy, vouchers, grants to voluntary organizations, or other unconventional forms of public transport
   c) to review the use of their own transport fleets to see whether they can also be extended for further social use
   d) to monitor public transport services.

3. Local authorities should have adequate powers to choose what forms of transport they decide to contract, promote, run, and assist. They should be able to use transport grant at their discretion in accordance with the consumer need they have identified. They should not directly run major public transport undertakings, so that they can identify themselves with the consumer rather than the producer viewpoint in monitoring the service provided. They would use the tendering and contract

procedures as well as subsidy to ensure good service provision as well as adequate conditions of employment.

References

Banister, D. (1979) *Transport Mobility and Deprivation in Inner Urban Areas*, Farnborough, Hants: Saxon House.

Blowers, A. (1978) 'Future rural transport and development policy', in R. Cresswell (ed.) *Rural Transport and Country Planning*, Glasgow: Leonard Hill.

Boaden, N., Goldsmith, M., Hampton, W., and Stringer P., (1982) *Public Participation in Local Services*, London: Longman.

BusWatch (1988) *Deregulation from the Passenger's Viewpoint: a Summary of the BusWatch Survey Findings*, London: BusWatch.

Cockburn, C. (1977) *The Local State*, London: Pluto Press.

Council for Science and Society (CSS) (1986) *Access for All? Report of a Working Party on Technology and Urban Movement*, London: CSS.

Dobry Report (1975) *Report of G. Dobry on Review of the Development Control System*, London: HMSO.

Dodd, A. (1984) 'Rural transport: a view from a county council', in P. Cloke (ed.) *Wheels within Wales*, Lampeter: Centre for Rural Transport.

Economist (1986) 'Private transport', 11 October.

Ganz, G. (1985) 'The Transport Committee', in G. Drewry (ed.) *The New Select Committees*, Oxford: Clarendon Press.

GLC Women's Committee (1985–7) *Women on the Move*, Reports 1–10, London: GLC and London Strategic Policy Unit.

Heiser, B. (1985) 'Qualitative research with users', *Local Government Policy Making*, March 1985.

Hirschman, A. O. (1970) *Exit, Voice and Loyalty*, Cambridge, Mass.: Harvard University Press.

Kilvington, R. (1984) 'The London Transport Passengers Committee', in M. C. Dix, R. P. Kilvington, and A. Layzell, *Participation in Commuting Policy*, Dublin: European Foundation for Human Living and Working Conditions.

Kotler, P. (1982) *Marketing for Nonprofit Organisations*, 2nd edn, London: Prentice-Hall.

Leach, S. (1987) 'The transfer of power from metropolitan counties to districts', *Local Government Studies* 13: 2.

National Consumer Council (NCC) (1978) *Rural Rides,* London: NCC.

Papadakis, E. and Taylor-Gooby, P. (1987) 'Consumer attitudes and participation in state welfare', *Political Studies* xxxv: 3.

Quarmby, D. (1985) Evidence to the House of Commons Transport Committee, vol. II HC 38.

Scottish Office (1988) *Bus Deregulation in Scotland*, Edinburgh: Scottish Office.

Skeffington Report (1969) *Report of the Committee on People and Planning*, London: HMSO.

South East Development Strategy (SEEDS) (1987a) *All Change*, Stevenage, Herts: SEEDS.
——(1987b) *Bus Transport*, Stevenage, Herts: SEEDS.
Transport and Road Research Laboratory (TRRL) (1988) *Bus Deregulation in Great Britain: a Review of the First Year*, London: HMSO.
Widdicombe Report (1986) *Report of the Committee of Inquiry into the Conduct of Local Authority Business*, Cmnd 9797, London: HMSO.
Wistrich, E. (1986) 'Reversing the ratchet?: transport policy change under the Thatcher government 1979–86', paper delivered to the Public Administration Conference of the Joint Universities Council for Public and Social Administration.

4

Housing

David Clapham

The aim of this chapter is to look at the extent of the user control of housing and the ways in which this can be developed. The case for user control in housing is strong. It rests both on the general case for giving people more control over their lives, and on the particular features of housing as a commodity basic to human needs, whose use is, or should be, solely the concern of the occupier. The only exception is the relatively few instances where there are implications for other occupiers, most of which can be dealt with by occupiers acting collectively. Unlike some other public services, the use of housing does not require specialist skills, except of course for the technical skills associated with the structure of the house. Armed with the advice of building surveyors, a household is the best judge of how to make maximum use of a dwelling.

Nevertheless, there are some issues which have implications for society as a whole. The most important one is the distribution of housing where substantial inequality can have a profound impact on some disadvantaged groups, resulting in homelessness for example. Public policy should be concerned with such issues, but the argument throughout this book is that user control is itself an important social objective and should receive more weight than it has in the past.

Because the case for user control is partly built on the specific features of housing which distinguish it from other services considered in this book, the nature of housing as a commodity must be the starting point of the discussion. This is followed by an examination of user control in each of the three major tenures, private renting, public renting, and owner occupation. There is then a discussion of the necessary general policy framework before, finally, proposals for extending user control are drawn together.

The nature of housing

Housing is different in a number of ways from other public services. First, the degree of control exercised over the use of housing depends on the rights and obligations associated with different tenure forms. It may be argued that only one tenure form – public rented housing – can be considered to be a public service. Acceptance of this narrow definition would mean that the housing situation of two-thirds of the population would be ignored, and the majority of public expenditure on housing would be considered to be irrelevant. Although the £3.1 billion direct expenditure on housing in 1984–85 was mainly devoted to the public sector, £3.5 billion was lost to the Exchequer as a result of mortgage interest tax relief. Owner occupation is not only publicly subsidized, it is also influenced by a whole range of public policies. For example, there are controls over the development of new housing and over housing stock considered to be unfit for habitation. In addition, there are a number of specific interventions to support owner occupation such as the provision of improvement and repair grants, and the legal right of council tenants to buy their houses, often at a large discount. Some local authorities have sought to encourage the development of owner occupation by providing land for development at below-market prices or through homesteading or rehabilitation for sale (Booth and Crook 1986).

In the private rented sector the government regulates key features of the relationship between landlord and tenant as well as providing a mechanism for setting rent levels. In the public rented sector there is a move away from the direct public provision of housing through local authorities. In the 1987 White paper, *Housing: the Government's Proposals*, the government laid out plans for reducing the role of local authorities as providers and managers of rented housing. Instead, it is envisaged that the management and sometimes ownership of council housing are to be vested in a variety of bodies such as housing associations, co-operatives, trusts, and private landlords. The Housing Act, 1988, has provided the mechanisms for this transfer through the so-called 'pick a landlord' scheme and the creation of Housing Action Trusts, which are centrally accountable bodies designed to take over and improve areas of council housing with a view to subsequent disposal to alternative landlords.

Therefore, although there is still public provision of housing, it is more accurate to see housing as a publicly regulated service. However, the degree and type of regulation vary considerably from one tenure to another, and so they must be considered separately. The rights and duties associated with the three major tenures lead to differences in the degree of control exercised by users. It is where ownership and occupation coincide that user control is maximized. Before considering these issues, however, it is necessary to look at some of the other special features of housing.

Houses are relatively long lasting and, once built, there are limits to the changes to the fabric which can be made, not least in terms of cost. As a large part of the use value of a house is determined by its physical structure and facilities, control should extend to the process by which the nature of these facilities is determined. In other words the extent of control over the production of housing should be considered.

However, the benefit derived by the occupier of a house is not limited to use of the physical structure itself, because, in choosing a house, the nature of the local area plays an important part. Location determines the nature of the physical and social environment, as well as access to amenities such as shops and recreational facilities. Location can also determine access to public services such as health care and education. These are usually organized on an area basis and there are substantial variations in the quantity and quality of services between different locations.

The durability of housing and its expense compared to household incomes mean that, for home owners, it is the single most important constituent of household wealth. The value of this wealth can change over time either upwards or downwards. The ownership of an appreciating housing asset is an important means of accumulating wealth which can be used to increase current consumption or can be passed on to later generations. The inheritance of a house is becoming a very important mechanism for the intergenerational transmission of wealth (Murie and Forrest 1980).

The importance of housing as a major part of household expenditure, as well as the access it can give to other private or public services and to capital accumulation means that the housing system can be an important influence on the distribution of income and wealth. It is vital that any discussion of user control considers its implications for the achievement of other socialist goals such as movement towards the equalization of the distribution of income and wealth.

The assumption so far has been that the term 'user control' is unproblematic. It is straightforward enough to define the user of a house as its occupier rather than its owner. In this sense almost everyone is a 'user'. But control can be exercised individually or collectively. Whitehead (1984) argues that most of the benefits of housing accrue to the user, not to the community at large. This would seem to be a good argument for increasing individual control at the expense of public or collective control. However, the benefits of housing can depend on decisions made by other users. The most obvious example of this is in a multi-dwelling building where it is in the interests of individual users to combine to make decisions about the fabric of the building and the use of common areas. But even in separate dwelling units, the benefit derived depends on the attributes of the neighbourhood, so there is an incentive for individual users to get together to maximize their collective benefit. User control in housing, therefore, has both individual and collective elements, and the balance between them will vary according to the house type. The rights and obligations associated with different tenures are also important in determining the boundary between individual and collective control. For example, leasehold ownership tends to lead to more developed mechanisms of collective control than freehold ownership.

The exercise of control can bring with it costs. These may take the form of time spent in deciding on the colour of paint, or, more concretely, the money spent on buying it. The costs associated with the control of housing can be large. For example, running a housing co-operative takes up a great deal of the time of some of its members. Owner occupiers can spend large sums of money keeping their houses in good repair. To be effective, control needs to be associated with the resources appropriate to exercising it, whether financial, time, or knowledge resources.

In summary any discussion of the extension of user control in housing needs to consider each of the major tenures separately, as well as looking at the overall situation which can determine control over the choice of tenure. Throughout these discussions the unique features of housing must be taken into account. In particular, consideration must be given to the importance of the production process as well as to consumption; to the balance between individual and collective control; to the impact of the extension of control on objectives of equality; and to the need for control to be effective.

The private rented sector

The decline of the private rented sector from 90 per cent of dwellings in 1914 to less than 10 per cent today is well documented, as is the bad physical condition of much of the stock. Eighteen per cent of privately rented dwellings were unfit and 42 per cent required repairs costing more than £2,500, according to the 1981 *English House Condition Survey*. In addition, 12 per cent of households in the sector lacked a bath or inside wc or both. Nearly 300,000 properties in the sector in England are houses in multiple occupation (HMOs), and it is estimated that 2.6 million people live in accommodation of this type, three-quarters of them in single rooms (Thomas 1986).

New policy initiatives have been introduced such as 'assured tenancies' and 'shorthold tenancies' which are designed to make letting more attractive to private institutions and individuals. However, the decline of the sector is due to deep-seated factors which could only be rectified by fundamental changes to the housing finance system. In 1988 the government made available tax concessions to private investors through the Business Expansion Scheme. This allows individual investors in private renting to claim income tax concessions and to avoid capital gains tax on their investment. However, these measures only last until 1993, and although they may result in some new investment in the short term, unless this is consolidated in the longer term, there is likely to be a continuing stream of households and dwellings leaving the sector. There may well be a continuing role for the private rented sector in catering for young, middle-class single people such as students (Whitehead and Kleinman 1986). However, the sector is likely to continue to offer poor value for money, especially in the furnished sector where rents are high, and where user control is less developed than in any of the other tenures.

The divorce of ownership from the use of a dwelling, which is inherent in any rental form of tenure, leads to a reduction in user control, and can lead to conflict between owners and tenants who may have opposing interests. This is especially true in the current situation in the private rented sector where the interest of landlords is in maximizing rental income, minimizing expenditure on repairs and management, and increasing the asset value of the property. The landlord's concern about the asset value of a house means that there is unlikely to be any user control over matters relating to the physical fabric. Landlords are not likely to want major changes carried out which are not reflected in an increase in the value of the house, and tenants are unlikely to want to carry out changes for which they will receive no recompense. Any proposal to give tenants a right to carry out improvement work and to be compensated for it would be bound to be opposed by landlords on the grounds that it would infringe ownership rights, reduce the incentive to let property, and, therefore, lead to further reductions in supply. There is undoubtedly some truth in this and, in a situation where supply is dependent on the decisions of individuals whose primary interest is on gaining a financial return from ownership, this will act as a major constraint on the extension of user control.

Most state intervention to increase user control has been concerned with altering the perceived imbalance in the contractual relationship between landlord and tenant by legislating to increase the individual rights of tenants. The major areas covered by legislation have been the level of rent, security of tenure, and the physical condition of the property. The two major criticisms of this approach are that the legal rights are not effective or sufficiently wide-ranging.

Legal rights are only effective if they can be easily enforced and this does not always seem to be the case. Knowledge of legal provisions among tenants seems to be low and access to legal advice is limited. The number of advice centres is inadequate, and the delay and costs involved in taking a case to court are prohibitive.

Housing disputes are dealt with by a number of legal bodies, and litigation can take place in a number of arenas. Landlords seem to have greater access to the legal machinery than tenants, and are more likely to have legal representation in court (Satsangi 1987). These criticisms have resulted in demands for a specialist housing court which could proceed in a less formal and more expeditious way. The London Housing Aid Centre (SHAC) have suggested a two-tier model of an upper housing court and a lower arbitration and conciliation service with the objective of avoiding the need for litigation. The major drawback with this proposal is the extra cost which would be involved. It is also likely that without extra resources devoted to the provision of information about legal rights and improvement of access to legal representation and advice, merely altering the legal procedures would have little impact.

The second criticism has concerned the limited scope of the legal provisions. These rarely cover the management issues which may have an important bearing on the use which can be made of a property. Issues such as responsibility for keeping gardens tidy or for internal decoration are rarely made explicit, especially in furnished accommodation and in HMOs.

An approach taken in Denmark to widen the rights of tenants has been to formulate an optional model tenancy agreement. Alternatively the *Report of the Inquiry into British Housing* (NHFA 1985) suggested that some leverage over management issues could be achieved by setting up a register of approved landlords, an idea which builds upon the 'approved landlord' aspect of the Assured Tenancy scheme introduced in 1980. Similarly, the government has introduced a 'social landlords' charter' for housing associations taking over council housing, but this is restricted in scope and does not cover private landlords. It is difficult to see how this kind of approach can have more than minimal impact on tenants' rights. It is not clear what criteria should be used to assess the acceptability of landlords or whether tenants will be able to have any say in decisions not to approve landlords. Although a register may be an effective mechanism for dealing with gross misconduct, it is difficult to see how it could be discriminating enough to put pressure on landlords who do not provide an efficient management and maintenance service.

Attempts to extend user control through the introduction of individual legal rights would seem to offer only a limited potential. The imbalance in the landlord/tenant relationship means that it is difficult to make rights enforceable.

The most effective strategy will be to build on the collective strength of groups of tenants. In Britain, although there have been some examples of collective action by private tenants, most notably in the rent strikes in Glasgow in 1915, these have not developed into a permanent, powerful force. This is in stark contrast to countries such as Sweden where there is a long history of collective tenant organization in both the public and the private sectors. Tenants' associations have won the right to negotiate with landlords over a wide range of issues and make available a number of services to individual tenants including information about legal provisions and legal advice and representation.

In Denmark, tenants in blocks of more than twelve units can elect representatives to deal with the landlord. They have the right to see the balance sheet of the property and discuss the budget, and have to be consulted on the use of funds set aside for the running and maintenance of the building. Also, they have to be informed about the appointment and dismissal of staff, and can work out house rules and make proposals for physical improvements to the block (Harloe 1985).

Improving the collective strength of tenants seems to offer more scope for the extension of user control than concentrating on extending individual legal rights. However, the lack of a strong tenants' movement in Britain is a limiting factor on what can be achieved. Nevertheless, there is room for a legislative framework along Danish lines within which groups of tenants could gain the right to organize and be represented in discussions with their landlord.

Whatever changes are made, they are unlikely to alter the view of many tenants that they would prefer to be in another form of tenure because of the poor service they receive. Any extension of user control should, therefore, include the ability to change tenures and leave the sector. The framework within which this could be achieved will be discussed later (pp. 77–9) as it implies changes to the housing system as a whole. However, there are some measures which could be taken within the existing framework to extend to private tenants the rights which have recently been granted to public-sector tenants. These include the right to buy at a discount calculated according to the length of residence; the right to form a co-operative; and the right to choose one's landlord. The only factors which should prevent these rights being given to private tenants would be if the distributional consequences are inegalitarian and if the rights are impractical. The rights to form a co-operative and to choose a landlord involve the transfer of property at market value, but the right to buy at a discount would result in landlords not realizing the market value of their property. This is particularly important because many landlords are scarcely richer than their tenants. To avoid such losses, poor landlords should receive the market value assessed on the basis that there is a sitting tenant, and the discount should be borne by the state.

However, there are also practical problems which would make the drafting of any legislation difficult. For example, in an HMO where most of the dwelling units are bedsits, a co-operative solution is obviously more practicable than individual tenants taking up a right to buy. It would be difficult to define the precise circumstances in which each solution would be more suitable. Randall (1984) argues that the best course is for the property to be transferred in the first instance to a local authority who could then decide whether to retain ownership or to transfer it to a housing association, co-operative, or other form of tenure such as owner occupation. However, safeguards would have to be built into such a system to ensure that the wishes of tenants were followed wherever practicable. Given likely public expenditure constraints it is also difficult to see how such a programme could be financed unless resale was the usual option.

In summary, a strategy to extend user control of private rented housing would involve improvement and extension to the individual rights of tenants by providing a new legal framework and making these rights easier to enforce. Steps should also be taken to improve the collective strength of tenants through help for tenants' groups. At the same time, it should be recognized that the supply of private rented housing is likely to decline further. Given poor conditions in the sector, and the inherent disadvantages of private landlordism and the concomitant restrictions on the extension of user control, public policy should follow this trend and provide the opportunity for existing tenants to change their tenure.

Public rented housing

As in the private rented sector, in public rented housing ownership is divorced from use, the difference being that ownership is vested in publicly accountable bodies such as local authorities and housing associations.

In practice, public rented housing has allowed a relaxation of the rights associated with ownership and, therefore, increased potential for user control. Nevertheless, public ownership has resulted in two constraints on user control. First, there is the rigidity inherent in the large, bureaucratic institutions created to build and manage public housing. These have tended to generate a dynamic of their own and have been largely resistant to influence from tenants. Second, public ownership has brought with it the belief that management should be responsive to the public interest as well as to the interests of tenants. Often the public interest has been defined in moralistic terms and has been used to control tenants rather than to promote self-expression and responsibility through expanding choice and increasing tenant control.

These two factors have limited the growth of user control in public housing, although some progress has been made at both the individual and collective level. Individual control has been improved through legislation which has stipulated that the terms of tenancy, including the rights and obligations of both landlord and tenant, must be written down and be freely available.

In most cases where tenancy agreements are revised, the new conditions are imposed on tenants without their effective participation, with the result that many tenants are still subject to terms of tenancy which contain unwarranted restrictions on their use of their house which leave them in a weak position to demand services from the public landlord. In such cases it is up to tenants to go to court to prove that any condition is unreasonable, inappropriate, or unduly burdensome (Atherton 1983).

Glasgow District Council took the opportunity provided by the legislation to revise completely its terms of tenancy, embarking on a negotiation process with tenants' representatives which lasted two years. The result was a document which has been held out as a model for others to follow (Atherton 1983).

Tenants also experience problems in enforcing their rights. Most complaints are dealt with by the officers of the public housing authority, who regard them defensively rather than constructively. Local authority tenants have the additional opportunity of channelling complaints through their local councillors, but few know who these are or how to contact them. Also, councillors are largely dependent on information from the officers providing the service. Tenants are then put in a position of trying to enforce their legal rights through the courts. Kay, Legg, and Foot (no date), in a review of the impact of the 1980 tenants' rights legislation, concluded that this remedy was rarely used. They found that many tenants did not know their legal rights and found the prospect of going to court intimidating. Few tenants had easy access to legal advice, and most did not know that they could claim legal aid.

Where no legal duty is involved, tenants can complain to the ombudsman. Complaints about housing constitute a large proportion of ombudsmen's work and, in many cases justice is achieved for the complainant. But their findings are not always implemented and there can be long delays. A few local authorities have set up independent arbitration panels to deal with complaints but they remain a very small minority and little is known about their effectiveness.

Similarly, the collective rights of tenants are undeveloped. Although there are many tenants' associations, these do not seem to be able to form the alliances which would bind them into a powerful campaigning force at the national level and enable them to fight for an extension of control. Only a minority of housing authorities have a policy of supporting tenants' groups and few have any formal mechanisms for tenant participation. The 1980 Housing Act laid a duty on housing authorities in England to consult their tenants on any matter of housing management which substantially affects them, but few do more than invite comments by sending out letters informing tenants individually of proposed changes.

Despite some important exceptions, the general picture seems to be of a poor service provided to tenants who have little control, either individually or collectively, over the type or quality of service received. However, this picture is changing significantly and many innovations are being tried with the aim of making the management of public housing more efficient and responsive, whilst increasing both individual and collective user control.

Individual control

Three approaches are apparent which aim to increase individual control: improvements to the conditions of tenancy; increasing the scope for choice; and improving the effectiveness and responsiveness of service delivery through the decentralization of management. Each of these will now be considered in turn.

The problems of enforcing tenancy agreements are similar for both public and private tenants. Common solutions should be sought by providing information about rights, by improving access to legal advice, and by instituting a quick, easy, and informal method of enforcement. Similarly, a common framework of rights should be sought. The existing framework available to public-sector tenants is insufficient in terms of both coverage and the way in which rights are framed. For example, the obligation of local authorities to carry out repairs is often expressed in such vague terms as to make it meaningless. Some local authorities have sought to tackle the important question of repairs by stipulating times within which they should be carried out. If these are not met, tenants are free to get the work done themselves and be reimbursed. This is a particularly good form in which to cast terms of tenancy because it provides an incentive for the housing authority to perform well, at the same time giving the tenant the freedom to go elsewhere if an adequate service is not received. The right to go elsewhere is an important one to consumers, because it offers a significant element of control through choice. However, it is difficult for producers to give up control by surrendering what is essentially a monopoly position. Ceding such a right should be regarded positively as a challenge to improve service, rather than viewed negatively as a threat to the status quo.

One important area in which many council tenants are restricted is the choice of house. Owner occupiers can compare different houses and choose freely which one they would like to buy, subject of course to their ability to afford the price. Council tenants, however, can be forced to wait years to be allocated a dwelling, and then may only be offered one on a take-it-or-leave-it basis. Many local authorities put a limit on the number of offers applicants can refuse without forfeiting their place in the queue, and none offers more than one property at a time to allow a choice between alternatives. The prevailing attitude seems to be that applicants should think themselves lucky to be offered a tenancy, and if they turn it down there will always be someone else who will accept. This attitude seems to be breaking down because of the growing realization that many properties are difficult to let and this, coupled with the failure to let properties quickly, is resulting in a loss of rental revenue. Practices such as accompanied viewing of properties and the more detailed refinement of an applicant's preferences are essentially designed to let properties more quickly, but they do also increase consumer choice.

Choice for existing tenants can be improved by making mobility easier within an organization's stock. Although local authority tenants have a legal right to exchange, the difficulty of finding a tenant living in an appropriate house who wishes to do so limits the number of such transfers which can take place. Mobility can best be eased by removing the often tight restrictions placed on tenants wishing to move. For example, only certain reasons for wanting to move are considered to be legitimate; moving closer to friends or relatives would not usually qualify. In addition, the number of offers of tenancies which can be refused is often limited.

Movement of tenants between different organizations, and especially local authorities in different parts of the country, is even more difficult. The National Mobility Scheme, which was designed to help alleviate these difficulties, is only voluntary and is constrained by the number of lettings available in the more popular areas. The reluctance of housing authorities to make dwellings available to people outside their area when there are urgent pressures to house local people means that the scheme does not nearly meet the demand for rented accommodation from those wishing to move (Conway and Ramsay 1986). There is a need for the number of lettings under the scheme to be increased and for membership to be mandatory. Achievement should be monitored and sanctions imposed on recalcitrant authorities. However, many of the problems occur because of a mismatch between the demand and supply of houses in particular locations. This can only be solved by increasing the overall level of investment in rented housing and by ensuring that most of this goes to areas of high demand.

Another approach towards increasing the individual influence of tenants has been to decentralize housing management by setting up local offices and offering them some autonomy to respond to the needs of local people. This is envisaged in association with a service-orientated philosophy which aims to improve access to services and relevant information, and to respond to the individual needs of consumers in a friendly and flexible manner. It is difficult to imagine any effective user control without these essential ingredients. But decentralization is not the only way of achieving these objectives, which are only the first step towards any degree of user control. For example, it is desirable that tenants should know where they are on the transfer list and how long they will have to wait, but this is no substitute for being able to move freely. The hope among advocates of decentralization is that the exposure of staff to the needs of consumers will result in policy change. But this is a very slim hope when most major decisions are still taken at the town hall which is usually too far away to be subject to any effective influence except indirectly through the ballot box. In some authorities there have been plans to set up local committees to exercise control over decentralized offices, but the problems of agreeing the appropriate make-up and terms of reference of the committees have proved in most cases to be insurmountable. There has been an understandable reluctance on the part of some councillors to devolve responsibility for a service to a group of people who may pursue the policies of other political parties.

Decentralization has also proved to be very expensive. The Priority Estates Project has shown that the extra costs of staffing, equipment, and office space can sometimes be more than offset by reductions in repair costs and environmental upkeep, as well as increased rental income through a reduction in voids. However, the achievement of these savings is likely to vary between different areas, although it is generally unlikely that they will be large enough to offset the extra costs involved. Therefore, decentralization is likely to cost more but provide a better-quality and more responsive service. Many local authorities have chosen to go ahead with widespread decentralizaiton on this basis without consulting tenants. In so doing they have exposed the superficial nature of their commitment to the extension of tenant control because this is an important issue over which tenants themselves, either individually or collectively, should have control.

A framework can be devised for tenants to control the quality of service by relating it to the level of rent. On an individual basis, it is possible to give tenants an optional set of services, such as internal decoration or the carrying out of some minor items of internal repair, which can be purchased if necessary, or carried out by the tenants themselves, either with their own labour or by hiring their own contractors. Some local authorities allow tenants a degree of choice when their houses are modernized. For example, Glasgow District Council runs a tenants' grants scheme under which tenants can determine priorities in the modernization of their kitchens, bathrooms, and heating systems. They can select the type and colour of fittings and choose a contractor to carry out the work. The council provides a grant to cover basic work, but tenants are free to choose a higher standard and to meet the costs themselves. Although few tenants have opted to provide extra finance themselves, most have appreciated the choice they have been given (Jones, Graham, and Wilkinson 1983). However, the scope for enlarging control in this way is wider on a collective than on an individual basis.

Collective control

The difficulties involved in implementing decentralization in a way which leads to effective tenant representation and accountability show the need for changes in the power relationship between councillors and housing managers on the one hand and tenants on the other. In order to change the imbalance in this relationship there is a need to empower tenants by expanding collective control. The most widely adopted method of extending user control in public housing is through the support of tenants' associations. The most effective support can be in the form of small grants to cover administrative costs of setting up and running an association, which can include items such as stationery and typewriters. Help with finding meeting places through the provision of community flats or tenants' halls is also important. Other forms of help can include the provision of information or specific assistance with financial, technical, or secretarial matters. In a survey in 1982, forty-seven of the authorities provided help to tenants in this way out of a sample of 132. Thirty-nine authorities employed tenants' liaison officers to encourage tenants' associations and help them in their ongoing activities; and a further six authorities provided grants for tenants' associations to employ their own workers (Kay, Legg, and Foot, no date).

However, this kind of help has the disadvantage that it is usually small and piecemeal in nature; moreover, it is under the control of the housing organization with which any tenants' association may find itself in conflict. Attention has, therefore, turned to the idea of a levy on rents paid by all tenants, collected by the housing organization and paid to tenants' associations (TPAS 1985). Although there are examples in other countries such as Sweden, for a long time the only example of a rent levy in Britain was in Sheffield, but a number of councils have now followed this example.

There are three important issues which have to be resolved in any levy scheme: the way the amount of the levy is decided; who receives it; and any arrangements for contracting out. In Sheffield it was decided to fix a set amount (2 pence per week at the outset) rather than make the levy a proportion of rents, as this can lead to accusations of collusion in rent increases. It was decided that all the proceeds of the levy would go to local tenants' associations, although they were asked to pay approximately a third to the tenants' federation as an affiliation fee. The local associations have to be recognized by the city council which imposes conditions on the minimum membership level, their openness to all tenants in the area, and the democratic nature of their constitution. Individual tenants are allowed to contract out of paying the levy, and about 15 per cent have done so.

A rent levy has the advantage of providing a stable source of income for tenants' groups which is relatively independent of the housing organization whose only major role is to collect the money. However, the levy system needs to be designed carefully, particularly as regards its distribution, since this will determine the structure and nature of the tenants' movement in the area. For example, in Sweden the levy is received by tenants' associations organized on a local-authority-wide basis. The result has been a relatively centralized and unresponsive movement which only now, after considerable effort by many tenants, is beginning to channel funds to an estate level.

Once a well-organized tenants' association exists, it is necessary for it to possess some means of exerting influence over the housing situation of its members. However, there is very little information available about the relative merits of different ways of exerting influence. Answers are not available to questions such as whether it is better to take part in formal tenant participation structures, to rely on other more informal methods of communication, or to adopt a conflictual campaigning style. If a formal approach is taken there is little guidance about what kind of mechanisms are more successful in effecting greater influence.

Some organizations have sought to involve groups of tenants in intensive area-based projects, particularly those designed along the lines of the Priority Estates Project to turn-round difficult-to-let housing estates. Others have concentrated on participation structures at the level of a local authority or a housing association. Both will be needed if the intention is to influence the implementation of policy at an estate level and policy-making at the authority-wide level.

It is important for the experience of tenants' groups and housing agencies in operating mechanisms of tenant participation to be shared as widely as possible. Independently funded agencies such as the Tenant Participation Advisory Service are important as a forum for the discussion and dissemination of ideas and experience, as well as being a source of independent help and advice. Such agencies already exist, or are planned to exist, in each of the four home counties, but they should be expanded and their remit widened to include private-sector tenants.

The capacity to influence the decisions of housing managers is one form of collective control over housing, but some local authorities have gone further by handing over control and sometimes the ownership of the housing to the tenants themselves to run as a co-operative. Co-operatives have been formed in many situations, for example to undertake redevelopment, to house particular groups of people, or to manage short-life property. There are many different forms of co-operative with considerable variation in the degree and scope of member control.

The most common form is a management co-operative. An allowance is paid by the local authority or housing association to the co-operative to carry out management and maintenance. This is usually done through employing management staff and by either engaging private contractors to carry out the maintenance work or using the services of a secondary co-operative. A recent survey by the Department of the Environment identified eighty-eight tenant management co-operatives in England and Wales, most of which were in London (Tinker *et al.* 1987). Some of these co-operatives have been in existence for ten years, and a picture is beginning to emerge of what living in a management co-operative means to the members. (For a review of the research evidence see Clapham *et al.* 1987.)

The overriding advantage seems to be the efficiency of the services carried out, particularly the repairs service. This is perceived as a greater advantage by most tenants than the ability to control the services. However, the two aspects cannot be separated because the efficiency of the service is largely due to its control by tenants, and has been achieved through the hard work of co-operative members. Indeed, one of the major constraints on the formation of co-operatives is the amount of work involved, especially at the beginning. There appears to be a commonly held view that the philosophy of co-operatives involves members carrying out work for themselves, whereas the essence of co-operation is co-operative control. The most successful examples of housing co-operatives, such as those in Scandinavia, have evolved a structure which ensures effective control over housing but enables the relevant support to be given to members (Clapham *et al.* 1985). Such a structure has yet to evolve in Britain, although some secondary housing co-operatives are well placed to take on such a role.

Despite the problems, the general experience of tenant management co-operatives in Britain has been very encouraging, although the failure of the idea to catch on in a big way is disappointing. The major reason for this is undoubtedly lack of support from local authorities, but the general situation facing public housing may have been important. The deteriorating physical condition of the public-sector stock and the growing incidence of social problems among tenants mean that any co-operative is taking on a difficult task with few tools at its disposal.

The powers of a tenant management co-operative are in reality quite limited. For example, members have little control over the fabric of the properties apart from those minor matters which can be dealt with through day-to-day repairs. Defects in the structure of the properties, if not dealt with by the local authority or housing association, can create considerable repair problems which would need to be met from money set aside for jobbing repairs. The size of this allowance is determined in negotiation with the local authority, although it is usually based on an average of costs in similar housing still in local authority or housing association ownership. This means that the co-operative members have little control over the resources devoted to management and maintenance and there is no direct link between rent levels and the quality of service received.

An initiative has been undertaken in Glasgow involving the transfer of council-owned stock into the ownership of tenants through the formation of a par-value co-operative. Although tenants as members of the co-operative will collectively own the property, they will not receive a share in the equity when they leave. There are two different models being implemented, the first of which involves funding through the Housing Corporation in England (or the equivalent body in Scotland and Wales) in the same way as housing associations. This means that 'fair' or 'affordable' rents apply, and rehabilitation of the properties and ongoing management and maintenance are monitored by the Housing Corporation and carried out within financial guidelines set by them. The second model has involved putting together a funding package of loans from private financial institutions and improvement grants. Rents will then be set at a level to cover costs and will be under the direct control of the tenants. Both schemes are at a very early stage, and it will be a number of years before the success of the initiatives can be gauged. Nevertheless, considerable interest has been created and there is a demand for similar schemes by other groups of tenants. Co-operatives offer a considerable degree of user control and should be given an added impetus to increase their numbers (see Clapham 1989).

Another important way of expanding collective control is through allowing tenants to choose their landlord. Legislation passed in 1988 has enabled local authority tenants to opt out of the sector by agreeing to a transfer of ownership to another body such as a housing association, trust, or private landlord. However, it is evident that the real purpose of the legislation is to reduce the size of the local authority stock rather than to offer tenants a real choice. For example, the right is only open to local authority tenants and not to tenants of other bodies such as housing associations or private landlords. Further, the decision to opt out is taken on a once-and-for-all basis, with no right to opt back in if the new landlord does not provide an adequate service. To compound these failings the government has imposed unfair conditions on the ballot of tenants needed for the transfer to take place by stipulating that opposition has to be expressed by a majority of all tenants eligible to vote (rather than a majority of those who actually vote) before a proposed transfer can be rejected.

The case for a right to choose a landlord, open to tenants of all agencies on a continuing basis and not subject to unfair ballot procedures, is a strong one. However powerful tenants' groups may be, they are not in a good position to insist that a reluctant landlord provide a high-quality or efficient service. If tenants were given the collective right to opt out and choose another landlord, a big incentive for efficiency would exist, even if the right was rarely used in practice. The effect would be to make landlords compete for tenants.

Nevertheless, the option of changing landlord is bound to entail a difficult and long-drawn-out process which is only used as a last resort. An easier and more desirable system operates in the co-operative sector in Scandinavia where individual co-operatives can choose who carries out management and maintenance functions on their behalf. The incentive for efficiency and responsiveness this creates is one of the major reasons for the co-operatives' success (Clapham *et al.* 1985). It would be possible to create a similar system in Britain providing competition and choice without the transfer of ownership.

So far, the discussion of collective control in public housing has concentrated on consumption issues, but there are many examples of collective control over the production process, whether building new houses or rehabilitating older ones. For example, housing co-operatives in Liverpool and Glasgow have exercised control over the design of their houses. This has been made possible by the trend towards forms of community architecture, and has not been confined to co-operatives: there are examples of tenants' groups being involved in the design of public rented housing. There are many problems inherent in user participation in design, not least the difficulty, in some cases, of identifying at an early stage occupants who will have to wait a number of years before their house is ready for occupation. There has also been criticism of the degree of control allowed by some architects and of inappropriate techniques used. Nevertheless, the scope for extending control over design is wide.

The extension of user control in public rented housing raises questions about the potential impact on the equitable distribution of housing. This applies in two major ways: in the allocation of tenancies and in the potential for some people to buy better housing.

There has been considerable criticism of projects, whether co-operatives, local lettings initiatives, or general tenant participation, where tenants have some control over the allocation of tenancies. The argument is that, put in this position, tenants will discriminate against some prospective tenants, whether homeless people, single-parent families, or particular racial groups. No evidence is ever put forward to justify this view, despite the existence of many examples of tenants influencing lettings. Also, if such discrimination should occur, it would be possible to set up monitoring arrangements so that it could be detected. Action could then be taken, either through anti-discrimination legislation, by corrective action through nomination rights, or through the framework of a local agreement (for example, the right to make further tenancies could be suspended if discrimination were proven). It is, therefore, possible to create a framework within which user control can be extended within limits designed to protect the rights of others.

There is not such an easy solution, however, to problems created by the extension of control to payments for the use of housing. There are very strong arguments for relating payments for housing to the quality of service received, and for offering a choice between different levels to individual or groups of tenants. Tenants can then decide on the relative amount to be spent on housing as opposed to other goods, and can gear the quality and quantity of housing management services to their needs and wishes.

However, there are also strong arguments for pooling major capital costs, and fixing rents in relation to the amenity afforded by the dwelling. The ideal is probably a mixture of pooled capital costs and variable management and maintenance costs which are controlled by tenants. When this was tried in Sweden, most tenants opted for higher rents and a higher quality of service than they had traditionally received (Clapham and Millar 1985). The problem with such an approach is that some tenants can afford more than others. Paradoxically, given the present system of housing benefit, it is the poorest who would be able to afford the highest standard, and those just above the housing benefit level who would be in the greatest difficulty.

A dilemma also arises in decisions about the extension of control to the asset value of housing. In a system where capital appreciation can be achieved by many owner-occupiers, should this be extended to groups of tenants through co-operatives, or to individuals through co-ownership schemes? One argument is that to deny council tenants access to a major form of wealth accumulation is unfair and leads to greater inequality. This is a strong argument, but the unfettered accumulation of individual wealth in this way is bound to lead to great inequalities in the long run. The only way out of this dilemma is to allow wealth accumulation in the public sector while tackling the problem in a consistent way across tenures.

In summary, it is possible to extend user control in public housing in a variety of ways. Individual control can be improved through a legal framework of easily enforceable rights which should apply to both public and private tenants. Control can also be improved through enlarging choice and providing more local services. Collective control can be extended by the support of tenants' groups and the provision of an independent form of funding through a rent levy. Again, these proposals can apply equally to public and to private tenants. The formation of co-operatives is an important way of increasing tenant control, and every help should be given to tenants who wish to pursue this option. In addition, tenants should be able to exercise a choice of landlord, creating an incentive for landlords to perform well. Control can also be exercised over the production process: the growth of community architecture makes this easier. However, control in all these forms should only be extended within a framework which can ensure that some people are not denied access to public housing, and that it is distributed on a reasonably egalitarian basis.

Owner occupation

Owner occupation is evidently the most developed form of user control in housing. Most owner occupiers have control over the use of their dwelling, subject only to minor restrictions which may be imposed by the financing institution, and to general powers of government institutions to intervene in the public interest through, for example, planning and building controls or compulsory purchase powers. In practice, these restrictions are generally unimportant and do not inhibit the control exercised by most owner occupiers.

Control over use of a dwelling is allied with choice over which dwelling to purchase. This is only subject to a household's ability to afford the purchase price; also to the range of housing available and the household's knowledge of the options open to them. Of course, for many people on low incomes this means that they have no effective choice: many are excluded from the sector altogether or end up in poor accommodation. Nevertheless, for the majority of people owner occupation offers the most effective way of exercising control over their housing situation.

The most important limits to this control are that it does not extend to the production of housing and that sometimes households are not in a position to be able to exercise effective control. On the first point, most owner-occupied housing is built speculatively, i.e. it is built by developers who then seek to sell the houses on the open market. In this system there is little room for direct involvement of users in the production process. Any control can only be exercised indirectly through market mechanisms, i.e. if developers build houses which no one wants then they will not be able to sell them. However, this is an optimistic view of how markets function and, in practice, the range of type and location of houses open to purchasers is limited. An increasing number of people are choosing a more direct form of control over production by building their own houses. Self-building has a long history in Britain reaching back to the early terminating building societies. These were formed by groups of people in order to arrange, finance, and organize the building of houses for themselves. Members paid an amount each week to cover costs and, when a house was completed, it was allocated to one of them. When all the members had been allocated houses the society was disbanded. But during the nineteenth century, the link between saving with a society and being allocated a house was broken, and the permanent societies, with which we are familiar today, became predominant.

Since the 1970s the number of self-build houses has grown until it was estimated that over 8,000 such homes were completed in 1982 (the last year for which figures are available). This means that self-builders as a whole were second only to Barratts who completed 11,500 homes (Rhoades-Brown and Fraser 1986). Since 1974, the Housing Corporation has had a statutory duty to promote and assist self-build societies. Local authorities can also provide assistance. Both can provide help with loans, the provision of land and services, and publicity and training. However, there is evidence that, in practice, little help is given. Self-building has many advantages, most notably the made-to-measure house and the sense of achievement on completing the work. However, self-builders are at a disadvantage compared to speculative builders at many stages in the development process. They can experience difficulties in raising finance and are inexperienced in construction techniques and management. Professional assistance at these stages would help many self-builders, and would encourage others to take this route in order to extend control over their housing situation.

On the second point, concerning the limitations on effective control, there are some owner occupiers, most notably those on low incomes, who, although they have formal control over the use of their property, cannot exercise it because of a lack of resources. Some households have problems with heating houses, and therefore have difficulties with condensation. Many have problems in identifying disrepair and in paying for appropriate work to be carried out, or are unable to ensure that they have use of basic amenities such as an inside wc. There are housing programmes designed to deal with these issues, through the provision of repair grants for example, but major problems still exist. Most emphasis has been placed on the plight of the low-income older owner occupiers, and there have been programmes such as 'Staying Put' or 'Care and Repair' specifically aimed at meeting their needs. Most schemes include an agency service which can help older people to identify problems of disrepair and suggest appropriate solutions, as well as providing advice and support during the process of applying for grant aid and in choosing and supervising building contractors. Help is also usually given in paying for the repairs, either by making small sums of money available or by arranging for loans. These schemes have been focused on small geographical areas; therefore their overall impact has been limited. Nevertheless, they do highlight the problems which many older people, and others, have in translating formal control over their housing situation into a reality. Expanding owner occupation will not by itself increase user control if owners do not have access to appropriate resources.

Large regional disparities in house prices mean that many owner occupiers enjoy only a restricted opportunity to move. For example, the media have highlighted numerous cases of unemployed people from the north getting a job in the south but being unable to move house, either because low demand meant they could not sell their existing property or because it was impossible for them to pay southern prices. The most effective way of dealing with this problem would seem to be through an effective regional policy, because attempts to expand significantly the supply of rented or owner-occupied housing in the south are likely to lead to increased social and economic costs through congestion and other problems associated with the over-concentration of population.

There is more that can be done through housing policy to reduce another barrier to movement: the high cost of buying and selling a house. This could be significantly reduced by simplifying the procedures and opening out conveyancing to free competition.

Despite these reservations, owner occupation is a very effective and successful means of user control of housing. However, in the present circumstances, this control is achieved at the expense of other socialist objectives, notably the pursuit of equality. The distribution of housing in the owner-occupied sector is largely dependent on ability to pay. The link between a household's income and the quality of housing achieved is, therefore, very strong (Clapham and Kintrea 1986). Given the impact of housing on access to other services and to the accumulation of wealth, this is a substantial drawback. The only way to alleviate this problem without sacrificing the advantages of user control is to recast fundamentally the system of housing finance and subsidies to redistribute housing purchasing power in favour of lower-income groups, and to prevent housing wealth acting as a major source of the intergenerational transmission of inequalities of wealth. Achievement of these aims would involve changes to the current system of tax relief on mortgage interest payments and of exemption from capital gains tax. These changes should be integrated into a policy framework which would enhance user control whilst regulating the impacts this may have on the distribution of income and wealth.

The policy framework

The current policy framework is important in inhibiting user control in two major ways. First, the imbalance in financial help for different tenures prevents households exercising a free choice. Second, controls exercised over public housing by central government are framed in such a way as to restrict user control.

Because of the different rights and duties associated with different forms of tenure it is important that households should be able to choose an appropriate one for them from a range of options. At present this choice does not exist for most people. The lack of investment in both the public and private rented sectors has meant that, in many areas, they are unable to meet demand. Although there is little hope of reversing the trend of decline in the private rented sector, the size of the public sector has been limited by government restrictions on capital expenditure (McCulloch 1987). Mechanisms have been created through the right-to-buy legislation for public-sector tenants to become owner occupiers, but no mechanism has been created for private-sector tenants to become owner occupiers or for those in other tenures to become public rented tenants or members of co-operatives.

The emphasis on owner occupation means that user control is being extended to those who are able to take advantage of the incentives to enter the sector, but is effectively denied to those who cannot enter. As has already been argued, owner occupation in its present form also leads to problems of inequality in the distribution of wealth.

Effective user control demands a policy framework where a free choice is made possible through a neutral financial regime which does not discriminate in favour of particular tenures. This is easier to state than to achieve in practice, for both technical and political reasons. The technical reasons relate to difficulties in defining neutrality in any meaningful way when different tenures confer different rights and obligations. Does 'neutral' mean that costs in each tenure should be equal, or should they be equivalent to the rights held, or does it just mean that the subsidy should be equal? The political difficulties relate to the fact that, however the technical difficulties are resolved, a tenure-neutral policy is bound to mean curbing expenditure on tax reliefs for owner occupiers.

The second major condition of extending user control is that the restrictions on public rented housing exerted by central government on local authorities must be lifted. The rationale behind the restrictions is the restraint of public expenditure, but they go much further than would be needed to achieve this aim. For example, it is now possible for central government directly or indirectly to influence local authority rent levels, thus preventing user control over the level of rent and preventing a direct relationship between the quality and quantity of management and maintenance services and rental payments. Controls operated through the Housing Corporation have been even more onerous with rents being fixed through the fair rent system and specific allowances made for management and maintenance costs. For both local authorities and housing associations, controls over building programmes restrain the amount of building, but also limit the detailed choices of house design and quality of finish which can be made.

The centralized nature of the overall policy framework places important constraints on user control, particularly in the public rented sector. Although it is necessary to have a system of accountability for public expenditure, the system should be designed with the extension of user control as one of its major objectives. This means in practice, that central government and the Housing Corporation should be concerned solely with the amount of total public expenditure and its distribution between competing agencies. Detailed decisions on how the money is spent and the achievement of value for money, should be left to the agencies and the users to determine, because they are the ones who suffer most from bad decisions or poor value for money. A system needs to be designed to create the incentives for the control of expenditure and the achievement of value for money whilst ensuring that the users of housing can make effective choices about the type and standard of housing to be achieved.

This would mean central government and the Housing Corporation taking a back seat on detailed issues whilst concentrating on the more strategic questions. Such an attitude is taken by governments in other countries like Sweden, where financial help to the co-operative sector takes the form of low-interest loans. The incentives for the restraint of expenditure and the pursuit of value for money ensure that no detailed assessment of plans for specific developments is needed (Clapham *et al.* 1985).

However, even if a system is devised to give control to users at an individual or very local collective level (say at the level of an individual co-operative) certain strategic issues – such as the distribution of subsidy between different agencies in the public sector, or the legal framework of rights in all rental sectors – should still rest with elected representatives at central or local government level who have the job of reconciling conflicts between different groups of users and potential users. Nevertheless, it is important that the voice of all users should be heard before such decisions are made and that all users should be able to combine in such a way as to ensure that their voice is heard. This is particularly important for private- and public- sector tenants who, because their numbers are smaller and their political position is generally less powerful than owner occupiers', may have difficulty in making their voice heard. This gives added importance to the need to build a stable and powerful tenants' movement in Britain.

Conclusions

Wide-ranging changes are needed in the housing system if user control is to become a reality for most households. As outlined in the previous section, the overall policy framework needs to be altered by the delegation of decision-making to as local a level as possible, and by allowing control over the choice of tenure to create the climate within which user control can take place. Without these two basic changes user control is bound to be partial and unsatisfactory because of its limitation to minor issues, with major decision-making power on issues such as the level of rent retained at the central government level.

This raises the major question of whether specific measures to extend user control should be pursued if the overall climate remains unfavourable. I would argue that in most cases it is worth while, because only through households experiencing the limits to user control will the political impetus be generated to overcome them. However, care must be taken to judge the impact of each individual measure, and ingenuity must be exercised in order to maximize the extent of control within the overall national framework.

Individual control can be improved through an extension of the individual rights of tenants in both public and private rented housing and through the provision of an effective form of redress. It makes a lot of sense to create a similar legal framework for the two groups of tenants as there is no logical reason why their rights should be different. An effective method of enforcing these rights should be created by simplifying existing procedures and making the process more accessible to tenants. At the same time, the provision of legal advice to tenants should be improved by increasing the number of advice centres.

More emphasis needs to be given in the public sector to extending the choices open to tenants, whether this applies to the colour of their bathroom suite or the choice of house to rent. Local authorities and housing associations, given the right policy framework, could be encouraged to offer a number of optional management services such as internal decoration, which tenants could opt to pay for.

The extension of individual control is necessary to create appropriate forms of redress for users of housing, and to ensure individual choice and access to information about the service and the rights and duties of all the parties involved. Measures to extend individual user control could easily be enacted by politicians at a national or local level. The fact that this has not been done shows the threat to their position which many professionals and politicians see in extending user control. The only way of meeting this situation is by empowering users collectively, so that they can challenge the power of those who resist change. Only in this way will services become accountable to users who will then be able to participate in discussions and decisions about service provision and delivery.

The collective power of rental tenants can be improved through the support of tenants' associations. They should be given help to organize themselves through the provision of premises and the payment of starter grants. Once organized they should be given an independent source of funding through a levy on rents, and a framework should be created so that they can influence policy. As yet it is not known which framework is the most effective, or even whether a uniform framework is possible or desirable. Advisory bodies such as the Tenant Participation Advisory Service should be expanded and their coverage increased in order to monitor participation arrangements and to facilitate the exchange of information and experience. Many tenants will be happy to extend their control through participation in housing management and maintenance, but collective control can be taken further through the creation of co-operatives. There are many forms of co-operative which are applicable in different situations, and no one model is superior to any other. However, models which involve collective ownership as well as control over day-to-day issues offer more scope for the exercise of effective control.

There are limits to the extension of user control in housing, some of which can and should be overcome, notably the overemphasis given to ownership rights in both public and private sectors and the definition of the public interest as acting in a regulatory rather than an emancipatory way. But there are others which impose effective restraints on how far user control should be taken, notably its impact on the achievement of objectives of equality. Although there is room for a compromise between objectives of equality and emancipation through user control, the emphasis between them should be amended with the latter being given more prominence.

An example of an effective compromise is the granting of control over the allocation of tenancies in the public rented sector to tenants themselves acting collectively, whilst monitoring the outcome and reserving the right to nominate households for a tenancy in order to ensure that no groups are excluded and that the rights of potential users are protected.

In the owner-occupied sector, objectives of equality dictate that action should be taken to control the accumulation of wealth through capital gains. Action should also be taken to redistribute purchasing power by changing the system of tax relief on mortgage interest payments. At the moment, the subsidy is concentrated on the better-off and, although owner occupation potentially offers a large degree of control over the use of housing, many of those on low incomes receiving little or no subsidy do not possess the necessary resources to make this control a reality.

Housing is, then, a field of public policy in which user control over provision and consumption can be extended to a substantial degree without impinging on the proper preserve of representative democracy or creating undue problems of inequality. The nature of housing as a commodity has meant that it has been at the forefront of the Right's attempts to promote individualism and market provision and consumption. But housing could also be at the forefront of the alternative approach outlined here which can achieve a form of user control designed to empower all users, not just those who have the resources to use market power effectively.

Note

I would like to acknowledge the help of Peter Kemp and Robina Goodlad who both made useful comments on earlier drafts of this chapter.

References

Atherton, G. (1983) *Terms of Tenancy*, Glasgow: Scottish Consumer Council.

Booth, P. and Crook, A. (eds) (1986) *Low Cost Home Ownership*, Aldershot: Gower.

Clapham, D. (1987) 'The new face of public housing', in D. Clapham and J. English (eds) *Public Housing: Current Trends and Future Developments*, London: Croom Helm.

——(1989) *Goodbye Council Housing?*, London: Unwin Hyman.

Clapham, D. and Kintrea, K. (1986) 'Rationing choice and constraint: the allocation of public housing in Glasgow', *Journal of Social Policy* 15: 51–7.

Clapham, D. and Millar, M. (1985) 'Restructuring public housing: the Swedish experience', *Housing Review* 34: 120–2.

Clapham, D., Kemp, P., and Kintrea, K. (1987) 'Co-operative ownership of former council housing', *Policy and Politics*, October.

Clapham, D., Kintrea, K., Millar, M., and Munro, M. (1985) *Co-operative Housing in Norway and Sweden*, Discussion Paper No. 4, Glasgow: Centre for Housing Research, University of Glasgow.

Conway, J. and Ramsay, E. (1986) *A Job to Move*, SHAC Research Report No. 8, London: SHAC.

Department of Environment (1982) *English House Condition Survey 1981*, Report of Physical Condition Survey, London: HMSO.

Gauldie, E. (1974) *Cruel Habitations*, London: George Allen & Unwin.

Harloe, M. (1985) *Private Rented Housing in the United States and Europe*, London: Croom Helm.

Jones, H., Graham, P., and Wilkinson, D. (1983) *Glasgow Tenants' Grants Scheme: an Assessment*, Central Research Unit Paper, Edinburgh: Scottish Office.

National Federation of Housing Associations (1985) *Report of the Inquiry into British Housing*, London: NFHA.

Kay, A., Legg, C., and Foot, J. (no date) *The 1980 Tenants' Rights in Practice*, London: City University.

McCulloch, D. (1987) 'The financial aspects of change', in D. Clapham and J. English (eds) *Public Housing: Current Trends and Future Developments*, London: Croom Helm.

Murie, A. and Forrest, R. (1980) 'Wealth, inheritance and housing policy', *Policy and Politics* 8: 1–19.

Randall, G. (1984) 'The demise of the private landlord', in Labour Housing Group, *Right to a Home*, Nottingham: Spokesman.

Rhoades-Brown, G. and Fraser, C. (1986) *Self-Build Housing. The Neglected Alternative*, Occasional Paper 2/86, London: Department of Town Planning, Polytechnic of the South Bank.

Satsangi, M. (1987) 'Housing costs: a review of the evidence', Discussion Paper No. 19, Glasgow: Centre for Housing Research, University of Glasgow.

Tenant Participation Advisory Service (TPAS) (1985) *What Price Tenants' Groups?*, Glasgow: TPAS.

Thomas, A. (1986) *The 1985 Physical and Social Survey of Houses in Multiple Occupation in England and Wales*, London: HMSO.

Tinker, A., Dodd, P., McCafferty, P., and Dougall, S. (1987) 'Co-operative housing – interim results of a DOE national study', *Housing Review* 36 (1): 13–16.

Whitehead, C. (1984) 'Privatisation and housing', in J. Le Grand and R. Robinson (eds) *Privatisation and the Welfare State*, London: George Allen & Unwin.

Whitehead, C. and Kleinman, M. (1986) *Private Rented Housing in the 1980s and 1990s*, Occasional Paper 17, Cambridge: Department of Land Economy, University of Cambridge.

White Paper (1987) *Housing: the Government's Proposals*, London: HMSO.

5

Police

Rod Morgan

Using the police and being policed: making a reality of policing by consent

In Britain police officers and most politicians are apt to say that we have 'policing by consent'. They seldom specify what the phrase means or how the consent is demonstrated. But whether it refers to aspiration or achievement, 'policing by consent' is an intriguing notion. In what sense can it exist and is user control, the phrase employed elsewhere in this study, consistent with policing by consent? To tackle these issues we have to begin by asking what policing is.

The nature of policing and the police

The word 'police' derives from the Greek *polis*. Originally it referred to organized government and civil administration generally. Nowadays we use the word more specifically. Policing concerns the enforcement of rules framed to order relationships and procedures. To police means to monitor, regulate, enforce, and discipline. In any society or organization there is policing; it may be diffuse or specific, everyone's duty or the function of specialists variously called auditors, inspectors, examiners, or security officers. All these functionaries police but, since the nineteenth century, *the police* has been a title reserved for that arm of the state entrusted generally with the duty of maintaining public order, administering certain regulations, and enforcing those rules embodied in criminal law.

It is often alleged that the order maintenance and law enforcement role of the police lends them a unique character among public services. All political philosophies which recognize the need for a state apparatus maintain that the security of the citizen's person and legitimate possessions is not merely the proper concern but the first duty of the state. Thus though there is argument between the political Left and Right about whether the state needs to provide other goods and services

– health, housing, education, etc. – there is no such dispute about policing. The provision of armed forces for external defence, and police for internal defence, is the primary justification of the state. The legitimacy of having police forces is not in question. Ideally, policing is a public good. Criminal offences are committed not just against individuals; they offend the Queen's, that is to say the state's, peace. Vendetta and vigilante are pejorative terms. There are good collectivist reasons for removing from individuals the capacity to determine the allocation of punishment. Were victims and complainants able to control the policing outcome of their complaints, then the police would be no more than the agents of private retribution.

Two things follow from these opening remarks. First, if all citizens benefit from policing, then, indirectly all are users. Second, the concept of the Queen's peace implies that user control should first and foremost mean the political accountability of the police, not control of police decisions by direct individual users at the point of service delivery.

Accepting policing as a public service does not mean there is no room for argument about the breadth of the police mandate. Neither does it mean that policing is for the police alone. It is possible that some of the tasks currently allocated to the police – for example, looking after lost property, regulating licensed premises, checking on aliens, or providing crime prevention advice – would be better undertaken by other agencies. Moreover, the massive growth of the private security industry (more than twice as many persons are employed in private security as in the police), and the current emphasis on community involvement in crime prevention, indicate the extent to which there is scope for the privatization and voluntarization of aspects of policing. As the Labour Party Manifesto for the 1987 General Election recognized, for example, there is a case for offering grant aid to the most vulnerable and deprived sections of the community to enable them better to protect themselves against crime. It is generally agreed, however, that the core policing functions – maintaining public order, enforcing the law, and detecting crime – belong irreducibly to the state.

It is often said that the police as law enforcers have a monopoly of the legitimate use of force. Much that the police do is non-conflictual but in the last resort they may properly resort to coercion: a proportion of the people who come into contact with the police resist rather than welcome their attentions. In fact these adversarial characteristics are not unique to the police. The Inland Revenue and environmental health departments also act against (indeed prosecute) offenders, and Social Services, armed with court orders, intervene in domestic situations where their presence is bitterly resented. Moreover, the common law power of citizens' arrest – resorted to regularly by bailiffs, store detectives, and other policing agents to detain persons they reasonably suspect of having committed an offence – means that some force is used by others. What distinguishes the police is the extent of their adversarial contact and the fact that it is backed, in the last resort, by the use of their own considerable force. When other agencies cannot peaceably resolve their adversarial relations, it is to the police that they turn for coercive assistance.

It follows that offenders and suspects, many of whom may prove to be innocent, are less users of the police than persons used by the police. Clearly there cannot be policing by consent in the sense that offenders must first agree to proceedings against them. Like complainants, they cannot be allowed to determine police actions. However, because many police actions involve the use of legal powers which have implications for individual rights and liberties there is especial need to ensure police procedural propriety and impartiality. There is need to state and safeguard the rights of citizens in the face of police actions and the police must be the politically and commercially disinterested agents of the law. This concern has increased as the police have become more specialized and powerful. As recently as 1929 a Royal Commission described the police as citizens in uniform (Cmnd 3297, paras 15–16). That concept, always a romantic fiction, has now been laid firmly to rest. Police officers are armed with a battery of statutory powers, many of them recently extended and codified by the Police and Criminal Evidence Act, 1984 (PACE). The corollary has been for the police to assert that they are primarily accountable to the law itself: this relationship, they argue, must stand proud of all arrangements for their governance.

It is this notion of accountability to the law that lies at the heart of what police officers usually mean by 'policing by consent'. We may call it the legal version of consent. Constables exercise original, not delegated, powers. They enjoy a freedom from control by elected representatives which is unique in English public law. Parliament democratically determines the criminal law and the powers of the police which the police maintain they use impartially to enforce the law. Thus, so the argument goes, we have policing to which the people democratically have consented. It is this legal doctrine which is used to justify constabulary independence. Before considering whether the unique legal position of the police is justified by the character of policing as a service, we need first to understand the current constitutional arrangements for the governance of the police.

Constabulary independence

Constitutionally there is no such body as the British police. In England and Wales there are forty-three separate police forces tied to local government. Scotland and Northern Ireland have their own local police forces. Each of the local provincial forces in England and Wales is governed by an arrangement set out in the Police Act, 1964. There are three parties to the arrangement: the chief constables; the police authorities; and the Home Secretary. Chief constables are responsible for the 'direction and control' of their forces (s.5(1)), police authorities are responsible for the 'adequacy and efficiency' of forces (s.4(1)), and the Home Secretary has a formidable array of powers over all forces which he must exercise so as 'to promote the efficiency of the police' (s.28).

Within this 'tripartite' arrangement chief constables occupy a position quite distinct from chief officers of other local services. Whereas directors of social services or education exercise control over their services and subordinates only in so far as it is delegated to them by the county councils to whom they are answerable, chief constables exercise control in their own right. 'Constabulary independence' has been upheld since 1964 in several celebrated court judgements. In the words of Lord Denning, a chief constable is 'independent of the executive'. It is his duty 'to enforce the law of the land'. To this end he 'must take steps to post his men so that crimes may be detected; and that honest citizens may go about their affairs in peace ... but in all these things he is not the servant of anyone, save for the law itself' (*R. v. M.P.C., ex.p. Blackburn*, [1628] 2Q.B.118). It is this authority which has led chief constables jealously to guard what they claim to be their sole responsibility for 'operational' matters and to resist attempts at what they claim to be political interference by police authorities (Oliver 1987).

There are four major deficiencies with the related concepts of constabulary independence and accountability to the law. First, the law is of little value in determining or monitoring most policing decisions. It is true that police officers may be held accountable in law if they misuse or exceed their legal powers. But that is not usually the issue in contention. Most arguments about policing concern the wisdom and appropriateness, not the legality, of police actions. In most of the situations that confront officers in the course of their duties there is available to them a range of equally lawful options: the choice they make between options is largely a function of individual judgement, training, and force policy. On these issues the law is silent.

Second, given that police resources are always limited, it is not possible for officers to enforce all the laws all the time. Priorities have to be set. Priorities determine how officers exercise their unavoidable individual discretion, and priorities are implicitly embedded in the decisions made by police managers regarding the disposition of personnel. On these questions the law is also silent.

Third, the police are concerned with more than mere law enforcement. The most recent Royal Commission on the Police maintained it to be the duty of the police to maintain both law and order (Cmnd 1728, 1962) and listed no fewer than eight police functions. This suggests a possible conflict of objectives within the police mandate. As Lord Scarman observed in his Report on the 1981 Brixton disorders, 'if law enforcement puts at risk public tranquillity, he [the police officer] will have to make a difficult decision' (para. 4.57). In Lord Scarman's judgement tranquillity comes first, but whether he is right or wrong the dilemma for the police remains, and it is a judgement on which the law, again, offers no guidance.

Fourth, none of the key terms used in the Police Act, 1964, or since to delineate the increasingly controversial boundary between the proper domains of politicians and professional police officers – adequacy, efficiency, police policy, operational policy, etc. – is anywhere defined. The Police Act, 1964, is full of contradictions and ambiguities (Marshall 1965). How, for example, is the police authority to be responsible for securing that there is an 'adequate and efficient' police force if many important aspects of policy – such as the distribution of resources or the setting of priorities – are held to be not their business?

In a sense the tripartite arrangement was always a fudge which relied on an amicable partnership between politicians and professionals, central and local government. The 1962 Royal Commission based its recommendations on an existing division of labour which though ill-defined 'rarely gave rise to practical difficulty' (para. 79). The Commission was content to allocate to police authorities a role that did not 'extend beyond the giving of advice' as far as policy was concerned (para. 166). The assumption was that chief officers would exercise their independent 'direction and control' in a manner sensitive to the advice of politicians. It was an approach which emphasized openness to public opinion as part of an ethos of professional accountability. As Kogan (1986) has argued, the concept of professional accountability is fine as long as consensus prevails and there is congruence between the objectives and methods supported by professionals and politicians: the problem arises when they are incongruent. The question then is whether there is policing by consent in the general normative sense of congruence between the values and actions of the police and the public they allegedly serve (Bayley 1983).

The tripartite arrangement since 1964

Local government has always occupied the weakest corner of the tripartite arrangement. But since 1964 the influence of local government has further diminished. Indeed it is arguable that whereas *de jure* we have local police forces politically accountable locally, *de facto* we have a national police force locally administered.

Consider the Police Act, 1964. Given that 49 per cent of police spending is provided locally, and that police authorities determine the establishment of their forces, equip them, and fix their budgets, it might be thought that in spite of constabulary independence the power of the local purse is considerable. It is not. In fact local authorities provide less than a quarter of police spending because half their contribution is eligible for Rate Support Grant. Central government largely pays the piper. Further, 85 per cent of police spending is taken up by staffing costs, and it is the Home Secretary who makes regulations 'as to the government, administration and conditions of service of police forces' (s.33) including their: rank structure; duties to be performed; hours of duty, leave, pay, and allowances. Moreover, to earn the 51 per cent specific police grant-in-aid Home Office approval is required for changes in force manpower establishments. The room for local authority manoeuvre is minimal (Lustgarten 1986). Most of the powers available to police authorities – for example to appoint and dismiss their chief constables (s.4(2) and s.5.(4)) or to ask for special reports from them (s.12(2)) – are hedged about by the arbitrating powers of the Home Secretary. Finally, by far the largest and strategically most important police force, the Metropolitan Police, has no locally elected police authority at all. The Home Secretary is the police authority for London and the London boroughs are bound to pay whatever precept is levied on them.

Since 1964 various centralizing measures have increased the effective control exercised corporately by chief constables and the Home Office.

First, the number of police forces in England and Wales has been reduced by amalgamation from 125 in 1962 to the present forty-three. Second, the creation of larger police forces has meant that a diminishing number coincide with single local authorities. Police authorities outside London comprise two-thirds councillors and one-third magistrates. Ten of these forty-one provincial authorities are 'combined' (multi-county) authorities: these bodies are wholly independent of their constituent county councils which must pay whatever precept is levied on them. Third, the police authorities which in recent years have done most to take their duties seriously, the six provincial metropolitan authorities, were abolished in 1986. They have been replaced by 'joint boards', the elected members of which are drawn from their constituent district councils. Joint boards: have more parochial affiliations than their predecessors; have no function other than for policing and their members therefore meet infrequently; and for the first three years of their life, must seek approval from the Home Secretary for their budgets, precepts, and manpower levels (Local Government Act, 1985, s.85). Compared to the old metropolitan authorities the new joint boards are weak *vis-à-vis* the police (Loveday 1987).

Fourth, the majority of police authorities are hung politically and, because not wholly elected, are less able to present a strong front against the police or Home Office. Combined and joint board authorities are most likely to be hung. Even when there is a political majority among elected members, the statutory co-option of magistrates makes it rare for there to be a majority overall. Magistrates tend to be impatient of challenges to the police or Home Office and increasingly use their casting votes to place in power political groups whose views they favour even when those groups constitute a minority of political members (Widdicombe Report 1986). Thus, contrary to the non-political leavening influence envisaged for them by the 1962 Royal Commission, magistrate members are aggravating rather than cooling the increasingly partisan political conflict over policing (Morgan and Swift 1988).

Fifth, the Association of Chief Police Officers (ACPO) has gradually built up its national organization and influence and the Home Office has increased its use of circulars – the draft texts of which are discussed closely with ACPO – to influence the shape of policy development. Policy-making is more and more determined corporately at the centre. Sixth, the consequence of the present government's commitment to curtailing public expenditure, particularly that of local authorities, has made it even less likely that local councils will wish to invoke Home Office opposition. If they do so they risk not just the loss of police grant-in-aid but rate-capping.

The irony is that at a time when their potential to influence policy is diminishing, police authorities' desire to shape policy is increasing. Until the late 1970s authorities were largely non-controversial non-decision-making bodies (Brogden 1977) and sparingly used their powers to call the police to account (Harris 1977). Today police authorities are among the most party political and controversial of local government committees with members flexing their vestigial muscles as never before (Morgan and Swift 1987). We need to understand why, quite apart from the constitutional considerations already cited, this is so.

The politicization of policing policy

Britain is passing through a stressful period of change. Unprecedented levels of unemployment, industrial decay, and heightened socio-economic divisions have stimulated conflicts into which the police, as enforcers of law and agents of order, have necessarily been drawn. When liberal 'rule of law' doctrines are widely questioned, then policing logically bears the strain. Few readers will need to be reminded of the most spectacular manifestations of these strains. The 1970s and 1980s are likely to be remembered as a litany of places that were the scene of violence, fire, and tumult. As never before our television screens have been filled with pictures of angry citizens locked in conflict with the police – Saltley, Grunwick, Orgreave, and Wapping, St Paul's, Brixton, Handsworth, and Broadwater Farm. For many people these places, and others like Stonehenge that previously had a more idyllic ring, will summon up battleground images. The picture of Dixon of Dock Green with his rarely used whistle is a far cry from the phalanxes of officers clad in flame-proof suits and NATO helmets, clutching riot shields, wielding long batons, and spilling from transit vans armoured with steel-mesh grids. In so far as 'policing by consent' is *procedurally* manifest by the police being unarmed and employing the minimum force – something the British have in the past taken pride in – times have dramatically changed.

There is doubtless a symbiotic relationship between the methods employed by the police and those resorted to by criminals and groups engaged in civil disobedience. The police justify their public order training, formation of specialist control squads, and increased purchase and deployment of riot control equipment, with reference to the growth of terrorism, the increase in recorded crime (particularly crimes of violence), and the greater mobility and organization of protest groups and workers involved in industrial disputes. Conversely many of those in conflict with the police justify their actions with references to police brutality, discrimination, and generally oppressive methods.

As conflicting accounts of events leading up to particular confrontations illustrate (for example, on the events at Broadwater Farm, see Metropolitan Police (1986) and Gifford (1986)), it is not easy to trace the causes of the escalating resort to force. But force is now more readily employed and policing policy, which used to enjoy almost bi-partisan political support, has become a controversial area (Reiner 1985). The question we must examine is the extent to which these explosions of acrimony reflect more general problems and the decline of everyday consent.

From the available survey evidence it would appear that the police continue to enjoy the support and confidence of the overwhelming majority of citizens (Hough and Mayhew 1983; PSI 1983). Most people, however, have little contact with or knowledge of the police (Southgate and Ekblom 1984). Their contacts are self-initiated, non-adversarial, and fleeting: people really do ask police officers for the time or the way, and these contacts are invariably positive. A minority of people, however, are approached by the police, a few of them often: these contacts are generally adversarial and, not surprisingly, much more likely to be negative. This negative side should not be overstated: the majority of persons stopped by the police in their cars or on foot say that the police behave in a polite manner and have good reason to stop them (PSI 1983). Nevertheless, the evidence is that young people and some socially and economically disadvantaged groups – the unemployed and black people in particular – are most likely to have adversarial contacts (being treated as suspects or offenders) and to have certain police powers used against them disproportionately; and are much the most likely to report that the police behave in an impolite, oppressive, or corrupt manner (Willis 1983; PSI 1983; Jones *et al.* 1986).

These pockets of mistrust and hostility are disturbing because they invariably occur in disadvantaged neighbourhoods where the incidence of crime is a major problem (Kinsey 1985; Jones *et al.* 1986). Further, those social groups with the most adversarial contacts are also the most likely to be the victims of crime. Moreover, there is some evidence that this discontent is associated with unwillingness to assist the police with inquiries or witness evidence (PSI 1983), a matter of vital concern given the reliance of the police on members of the public to clear up crime.

Mistrust often precipitates mutually reinforcing patterns of avoidance behaviour. The system for making complaints against the police, recently changed and long considered inadequate, clearly does not enjoy the confidence of many groups who consider themselves ill-handled by the police. Further, the evidence suggests that the police also tend individually to avoid contacts with groups they know or assume to mistrust them (Southgate and Ekblom 1986). Finally, a good deal of more general concern has been expressed that whatever level of background confidence prevails – and in most areas it appears to be relatively high – the police have become physically more distant from the public; that they are generally less accessible.

The degree to which this is true is difficult to assess. It is certainly the case that the police are now more mobile and thus more likely to patrol in cars, are equipped with better communications and intelligence technology (radios, computers, etc.), and that many now operate in specialist squads. It is also true that few constables now live in local beat police houses and that many small police stations have in recent years been closed. Moreover, the creation of larger police forces, and the substantial pay rises awarded the police since 1979, mean that officers are more likely to move during their careers and more commonly commute to their duty stations. This pattern of specialization and professionalization is said to have distanced the police physically and culturally from the communities in which they operate, a pattern observed in other service occupations.

There are counter-arguments. There are now many more police officers per head of population than at any time in the past, and the public demand for foot patrols has led most chief officers to claim that they are deploying a greater proportion of available manpower on community beats. Moreover, many forces are experimenting with local surgeries or drop-in centres, practically all have specialist community liaison officers, and, in response to PACE s.106 and Home Office advice, most have set up subdivisional community consultative committees in co-operation with their police authorities (Morgan 1985). Most forces are also introducing panels of lay visitors to police stations (Kemp and Morgan 1989). Further, with the encouragement of Her Majesty's Inspectorate of Constabulary, the application to policing of the government's Financial Management Initiative (Prime Minister 1984) has resulted in a vogue for 'policing by objectives' (Butler 1984): many chief constables are now promulgating policy objectives annually and a few are actively encouraging the participation of their police authorities and local consultative committees in force planning cycles. The use of public opinion surveys and the formulation of police performance indicators, some of which involve user satisfaction data, are additional ingredients in current police management thinking (Horton and Smith 1988; Morgan and Smith 1989).

The police argue that the public have rose-tinted memories. Officers, they say, never were as available on the streets as is claimed. And the public make incompatible demands. They want visible local beat constables. But they also want the sort of rapid response to incidents that can only be provided by mobile patrols. There is a trade-off between these demands that users do not understand.

Data on the disposition of police officers are not sufficiently available to determine whether the number of officers actually on foot patrol has declined or increased. What seems likely is that there is now less continuity of personal contact between particular officers and residents of local neighbourhoods than used to be the case. This is probably due to the increased mobility of the public at large as well as the police, but for the police, this greater mobility, combined with increased professionalization, is said to result in officers defining their role (including the manner in which they exercise their unavoidable discretion) more in terms of the police culture (the views of their peers) than with reference to the standards and priorities of the communities in which they operate (Cain 1973). It was to this process that Lord Scarman drew attention when he wrote that the police 'run the risk of becoming... a "corps d'elite" set apart from the rest of the community' (1981: para. 5.3).

The problem with all such references to professional groups and the community is the implication of cultural homogeneity on both sides. The police are not a monolithic body. Apart from the differences between forces, sociologists of the police refer to 'canteen' and 'management' cultures and to the divides between the uniform and CID branches, the specialist squads, and so on (Holdaway 1983). The same is true of neighbourhoods. Whether we think of 'community' in terms of locality, identity, or shared interests or values (Plant 1974; Willmott 1984), most neighbourhoods are not consensual wholes but comprise cross-cutting groups of individuals who, as we have seen, have different experience of the police and very different views about what they should do (Shapland and Vagg 1988). Further, the spate of local surveys conducted recently demonstrates how large are the differences between neighbourhoods both in terms of their experience of crime and their expectations of the police (Kinsey 1985; Jones *et al.* 1986). It follows that in the case of most 'police–community' conflicts there are invariably divergent accounts as to which groups of officers behaved badly or well, and whether the police had a mandate to do what they did not merely in law but in terms of requests from citizens for police intervention against another group within the community (see Morgan 1987).

Conclusions

From this review we can glean three broad lessons. First, it is plain that whatever approach one takes to the concept of policing by consent – legal, political, normative, or procedural – no one institution or mechanism is likely to satisfy the different groups using the police and being policed. If policing by consent is to have any meaning for all citizens, there has to be a chain of interlocking mechanisms which make the police accountable politically, which sensitize the police to different user interests and needs, and which safeguard the rights of those who have adversarial contact with the police. Enhanced political accountability, through police authorities empowered to determine general policing policy (as the Labour Party (1987) propose), would on one level be a radical step but one unlikely to impress those economically and politically marginal groups who complain of police harassment. More incisive monitoring of police decisions and a complaints system which inspires greater confidence are likely to be more relevant. Moreover, it is doubtful whether county councillors have currently sufficient information adequately to judge the quality of police service delivery at the grassroots (Day and Klein 1987). Decentralization of police management dovetailed to greater public participation in framing local police services may be a more important determinant of the quality of services and public satisfaction with them. It is not a question of favouring political as opposed to legal or managerial initiatives (Hambleton 1988). These are not alternatives: all these mechanisms mutually reinforce any notion of policing by consent worthy of the name.

Second, though the police service does have distinctive characteristics, it is not as different from other public services as it is often claimed to be. The differences are less fundamental and more of degree. Thus, though the police are accountable in law for much of what they do, many policing policy decisions are as much political and moral as legal, and unavoidably so. There is no case for avoiding political accountability for these decisions. Indeed, quite the reverse. The more controversial questions of policing policy become, the greater the need for well-informed public debate and responsible decision-making.

Third, it is evident that the existing framework for the governance of the police no longer accords with the contemporary distribution of power between central and local government and between politicians and professionals. As a consequence, there has been a singular absence of political accountability for the dramatic changes in the nature of policing in Britain during the last decade. Neither Parliament nor the local police authorities have adequately debated or determined these changes because neither body is technically responsible for them. The consequence has been the encouragement of dangerously irresponsible posturing by politicians on the Left and Right, posturing which has drawn an important public service into partisan disrepute and done nothing to promote the positive resolution of the very difficult dilemmas which confront the police. The following proposals comprise an attempt at operationalizing the doctrine of policing by consent in the light of these tensions and deficiencies.

Proposals

The number of police forces and their functions

The operation of neither national nor local police forces is free from problems. The competing arguments for equity and national standards as opposed to local diversity, sensitivity, and identity are equally powerful. The *de facto* development of national policing might formally be recognized through the creation of a national force accountable to Parliament via the Home Secretary. That way Parliament would have the clear responsibility for policy developments which, aside from the Metropolitan Police, it currently lacks. However, the creation of a national force would be unlikely to enhance the user sensitivity of the police, even were local advisory and administrative mechanisms instituted: police geographical career mobility would almost certainly further increase; there would be a tendency to adopt nationally uniform policies for the distribution of resources and the setting of priorities irrespective of local needs; and the voice of local minorities would be less likely to be heard. We are committed to public services on a human scale. There is a strong case for retaining, with minor amendments, the same pattern of local police forces as at present. Certainly there is no case for further force amalgamations.

There are already distinct problems of scale in some of the metropolitan areas, however, The abolition of the provincial metropolitan counties makes it timely to consider the case for restructuring such large forces as the West Midlands and Greater Manchester Police. In an area like West Midlands, for example, there is a good case for hiving off distinct areas such as Wolverhampton and Coventry to neighbouring forces, leaving Birmingham and its adjacent district councils with a police force more closely attuned to local needs and conditions.

London presents the most difficult problem of scale and police public relations. Because of the capital's unique constitutional arrangement it deserves urgent and radical attention. Almost one in four of all police officers in England and Wales serves in the Metropolitan Police. The Met provides specialist national services for all other forces and caters also for problems which, though not peculiar to the capital, are disproportionately centred on it – the protection of the royal family, Parliament and politicians, embassies and diplomats, etc. Finally, the Met has no locally elected police authority and contains in the very heart of its geographical area the smallest local police force in the land – the City of London Police – which is accountable not to a local authority but to the Common Council of the City. This complicated and anomalous package, the subject of increasingly bitter controversy, needs to be redesigned.

It would make sense to abolish the City of London Police and amalgamate it with the Met. It would also be sensible to provide London with a police authority the membership and powers of which are the same as the provincial authorities. The historical reason why it is not so, and the stumbling block against doing so now, are the national strategic functions of the Met. The remedy lies in handing over these national strategic functions of the Met to a small national police force fully accountable to Parliament via the Home Secretary. This would leave the Met a slightly smaller (though still by far the largest in the land) but genuinely local force.

Constitutional issues

Whatever the number of police forces, the most pressing need is to ensure their political accountability. The tripartite arrangements in operation since 1964 have been overtaken by events and no longer command the confidence of politicians or professionals. What is required is a framework within which elected politicians take those policy decisions which are unavoidably political so that police officers can sensibly make the day-to-day operational decisions which are properly theirs.

A new Police Act, which might be preceded by a Royal Commission or some other official inquiry, is required to amend the 1964 provisions for the governance of the police. The new provisions should include, *inter alia*: making politicians, not chief constables, responsible for determining the broad aspects of policy; clarification as to which aspects of policy are the responsibility of the Home Secretary (and thus subject to the approval of Parliament) and which that of local police authorities; removing magistrates (unelected and non-accountable members) from police authorities; and permitting police authorities to co-opt members of local consultative committees, lay visitors to police stations, and other user-group representatives.

It cannot be pretended that these questions will easily be resolved which is why they should preferably be considered first by a searching inquiry. There is, for example, no clear dividing line between general and day-to-day policy decisions. Yet it is also clear that members of other professions, social workers and teachers for example, are the servants of their departments directed by elected committees without those professional workers' capacity to make impartial decisions in individual cases being undermined. There is no reason why the same should not be true for the police. There should be no more question of politicians being able to interfere in the application of the law to individual offenders than there is interference in the way social workers assess the degree of disturbance in children or teachers judge the quality of pupils' essays. Revising the doctrine of constabulary independence should not rob police officers of their vital independence of judgement in particular cases.

Space allows me to do no more than suggest how power to determine policy might be divided between Parliament and the police authorities. There are some obvious spheres of appropriate responsibility. For example, there seems no good reason to devolve important decisions about police equipment and procedures. Whether the police should have access to plastic bullets and the circumstances for their issue, the general criteria for cautioning rather than prosecuting offenders, codes of practice for video-recording the interrogation of suspects in police stations, etc., are all policies the safe and equitable application of which transcends local circumstances and to which Parliament should pay close attention. By contrast, the distribution of police personnel by subdivision, their allocation by specialism (and thus policing priority), the siting of police stations and their hours of opening, etc., are all examples of policies which need properly to be tailored to the needs of different neighbourhoods. These are properly matters for police authorities.

If police authorities are made responsible for aspects of general policing policy this will not diminish the need for partnership between politicians and professionals. On the contrary, like local authority committees responsible for other statutory services, police authorities will be heavily reliant on the recommendations of their chief constables. Moreover, police authority responsibility for policy will not of itself guarantee that policies are in accord with those the public approves. It will be necessary, therefore, to open up the policy-making process. There should be introduced a statutory requirement for police authorities, after consulting with their chief constables, to make and publish annually a detailed plan for the policing of their areas. Plans should include statements of objectives and priorities, data on the disposition of police officers, points of access for the public, arrangements for police–community consultation, etc. At present police authorities have no such powers and most are effectively excluded by their chief constables from this policy-making process.

The publication of plans is vital for political, managerial, and general public accountability. Plans will better enable local councillors and their constituents to monitor the day-to-day delivery of policing on the ground. In any service an annually published plan will always be an approximate statement of intent which never perfectly accords with services delivered. Indeed because so many aspects of policing are contingent, reactive, and therefore unplannable, the gap between intent and outcome is likely to be greater in policing than in most services. But plans will enable everyone concerned to know when departures – the abstraction of community beat officers or the temporary closure of a police station, for example – need explaining and to test how valid are the reasons offered by senior officers for those departures. It goes without saying that chief constables should be under a clear obligation, as they are not at present, to report on major departures from plans agreed with their police authorities.

Sensitizing the police to users' needs and interests

Making public services formally accountable politically does not guarantee their sensitivity to users. Policing is no exception to this rule: those social groups most in need of policing services are often those in conflict with the police; they tend also to be those groups marginal to the political process. There is need therefore to ensure that policing on the ground is attuned to local concerns and that managers and politicians responsible for policy have the means of knowing that relationships at neighbourhood level are sound. The government has introduced mechanisms which lay the foundation for this process, though arguably they will prove ineffective in the absence of arrangements for ensuring political accountability on the lines set out on pp. 96–7. The recommendations which follow build on the current government initiatives. The aim is to maximize the congruence between police objectives and methods on the one hand and community priorities and values on the other.

To have an impact on the quality of life within neighbourhoods policing needs to be closely related to the delivery of contiguous public services. Neglected neighbourhoods where lighting is poor, rubbish is not collected, homes are physically insecure, and social facilities are lacking, tend also to be areas where social incivilities abound, and the reality and fear of crime flourish. Effective policing involves inter-agency co-operation. It is desirable, therefore, for police administrative areas – divisions and subdivisions – to coincide to the greatest possible extent with local government (district and borough council) boundaries so that police middle managers can establish effective liaison with their counterparts in other agencies and with local councillors.

At present such liaison is discretionary. In some forces it is encouraged and good, in others it is frowned on and poor or non-existent. It would be beneficial were police authorities (currently police forces) obliged to inform lower-tier local authorities of proposals to redistribute police personnel permanently by area or specialism (e.g. changing beat arrangements) or to change public access to police services (e.g. closure of a police station or the opening of a police surgery). There should be a similar obligation to inform the police community consultative committees which in most areas have been set up by police subdivision under s. 106 of PACE. Such an obligation would serve to educate local communities about the policing of their areas and ensure that police authorities considered the views of local communities.

Granting rights of information and advance warning of policy proposals to consultative committees needs to be balanced by obligations and resources to permit those obligations to be fulfilled. At present consultative committees have no clear role and seldom any resources. In most parts of the country committees are almost wholly dependent on the goodwill of subdivisional commanders, though there are exceptions (some London boroughs and a few provincial police authorities maintain independent police 'support' or monitoring units or employ one or two full-time staff to service consultative committees). To ensure that consultative committees either represent, or make it their business to investigate, a wider constituency, police authorities should make it the duty of committees to investigate, monitor, and report on the adequacy of grassroots consultation between the police and the public normally represented by community beat officers and community groups such as parish councils, residents' and tenants' groups etc. To facilitate this process consultative committees should be given a modest budget to hire halls, advertise meetings, etc., and should be aided by a small staff employed by the police authority.

Organizational issues

If the political reforms proposed on pp. 96–7 are to have impact they need to be dovetailed to a police organization shaped to receive and implement the product of greater public participation. 'Community policing' is a much-used weasel phrase which needs to be given operational substance.

The police know about most crime only because members of the public choose to tell them. By the same token most crimes are solved only because the police are told who the culprits are. They can do very little about crime without public trust and co-operation. Only by working with the grain of public opinion is police work effective. Further, the vast majority of crime is parochial, committed by people in their own neighbourhoods according to peculiarly local social, economic, and physical characteristics. If police organization is not geared to these parochial patterns they will neither understand people's concerns nor benefit from the product of that policing by the public – watching, noticing, intervening, etc. – which goes on in all neighbourhoods (Shapland and Vagg 1988). Not only do most members of the public want to see more police in their locality but it follows that the bedrock of effective policing by consent is the beat patrol officer.

It would not be sensible for beat policing always to be done on foot – many rural areas would never see an officer on that basis. Nor is it plausible to suggest that beat officers should live in police houses situated in the neighbourhoods they patrol – most officers no longer accept 'tied cottage' working conditions and in any case many urban areas have never contained police houses. But there is a pressing need to structure police careers, their functional division of labour, and their duty rosters, to maximize continuity in the allocation of personnel to neighbourhood beats. Local team policing, involving uniformed and detective officers, offers the best prospect of ensuring that: the public get to know their officers; the police become familiar with local concerns and values; and there is a reciprocal flow of information between the police and those local community groups which lie at the heart of neighbourhood identity, organization, and social control. Some centralized specialist police squads and para-military public order training are obviously necessary but the vast bulk of police work, in all parts of the country, comprises incidents – crimes and incivilities – of a relatively minor nature brought to police attention by disturbed residents. A more decentralized, functionally integrated and community-orientated police organization is more likely to generate police managerial measures of effectiveness congruent with public expectations of police performance. Further, given the improved mutual confidence which agreed measures of effectiveness should bring about, police efficiency should also be increased.

Safeguarding the rights of suspects

Because persons coming into adversarial contact with the police cannot be allowed to determine police actions, it is vital that suspects and offenders have procedural rights. Further, it is vital that there be means for investigating complaints against the police which command the confidence of all concerned.

Police powers have recently been comprehensively revised by PACE following the Report of a Royal Commission (Cmnd 8092, 1981). The Act is controversial. Some critics maintain it has greatly increased police powers and that the alleged safeguards for suspects are inadequate (GLC 1985; Baxter and Koffman 1985). Others, particularly the police, argue the Act has hamstrung them, sunk them in a sea of paper, and undermined their ability to detect crime and bring offenders to book (Oxford 1986; Curtis 1986). The truth lies somewhere between these extremes: certainly the early evidence suggests that the worst misgivings on both sides are unlikely to be borne out (Irving and McKenzie 1989). Yet whatever the merits and demerits of the legislation it seems sensible to reserve judgement until more data are available. For the same reason it is premature to propose further legislative changes in the sensitive realms of police powers regarding: stop; search and seizure; arrest; and the treatment of suspects in police custody.

Yet precisely because PACE has stimulated such fierce argument and suspicion, it is important that the public understand how the new police powers are being used. The police need to make more transparent their operational decisions. In one or two instances the Act obliges the police to publish information on the use of powers (s.5 on road checks, for example), but this is not generally the case. It is desirable, therefore, that the police make available in annual reports to their police authorities, and locally to consultative groups, regular data on the use of their more important powers under PACE (e.g. numbers of persons stopped and searched, numbers of persons detained in police stations by periods of detention, numbers of detainees requesting and receiving access to lawyers, etc.).

Further, it is desirable that what happens in police stations be above suspicion and the public confident about the proper treatment of suspects. Lord Scarman recommended in his report on the 1981 Brixton disturbances that there be appointed for this purposes lay visitors to police stations, persons who would regularly visit stations to inspect conditions, make themselves available to suspects, and report on what they found. His recommendation was given no place in PACE, but in 1986, by means of a Circular (12/1986), the Home Office commended the introduction of panels of visitors. The commendation is sensible. Panels should everywhere be instituted, should include members of subdivisional consultative committees, and should regularly make available public reports on their findings.

Finally, there is the question of complaints against the police. This issue also is controversial and has recently been the subject of legislative change: PACE s.87 created a new Police Complaints Authority (PCA). But it is clear that however assiduous and penetrating the oversight of members of the independent PCA, they will continue to be subject to the criticism that it is not they but police officers who are responsible for investigating the facts of the cases that come before them. There is a fundamental dilemma here. It is a question of whether insiders pull punches or outsiders do not know how to throw them. It is claimed by some observers that investigations conducted by lay persons will elicit less information than is currently gained by serving officers familiar with police work and culture. Whatever the truth of this insight it is the case that the present system contravenes the principle – more honoured in the breach in British public life – that no group should investigate itself, a contravention which has undermined, and will undoubtedly continue to undermine, the credibility of the PCA in the eyes of many. This is of as much symbolic as practical importance. Accordingly, it would be sensible were the PCA provided with a body of independent investigators, some of whom might be ex-police officers, to investigate the facts of serious complaints (defined by PACE s.116) or to re-examine less serious complaints about which the PCA is not satisfied.

The future

There never was a golden age when all citizens looked favourably on the police and their actions. Were it so there would be no need of them. There have always been groups hostile to the police and the laws it is their duty to enforce. Nevertheless, repeated opinion polls suggest that the police remain among our most trusted institutions: the 1962 Royal Commission claimed that 80 per cent of the public judged their police to be the best in the world. Both assessments, the critical and the satisfied (and possibly complacent), have some validity. There can be little doubt that unlike the police in many countries, the British police command a high degree of general confidence. There are danger signs, however. In the 1980s the police have been sucked into conflicts which would scarcely have been imaginable twenty years ago. The use of force against and by the police is now more commonplace than within living memory. Further, policing has been politicized to a disturbing degree. Some politicians and senior police officers have gone on record to suggest that effective and impartial policing and respect for the rule of law are the interest of only one political party, and that the police might find it difficult to work with a future Labour administration (see, for example, *Guardian* 4 October 1984, p. 5 and 6 October 1984, p. 14).

The events that have led to this state of affairs are varied. Arguably the law and, by implication, the police, have been used in a partial and socially divisive manner by the government. Certainly the elected representatives of the people, at Westminster and in local government, have witnessed profound changes in the direction of policing policy without being able to shape it. Moreover, by virtue of their growing specialization, centralization, and increased reliance on technology, the police, like other professions, have lost some of the contact with the community which formerly they had. There is need to re-establish political accountability for policing policy and develop new mechanisms for transmitting the consent on which ultimately all effective and efficient policing is reliant. The proposals in this paper are designed to that end.

References

Baxter, J. and Koffman, L. (eds) (1985) *The Police: the Constitution and the Community*, London: Professional Books.

Bayley, D. H. (1983) 'Accountability and control of the police: some lessons for Britain', in T. Bennett (ed.) *The Future of Policing*, Cambridge: Cropwood Conference Series No. 15.

Brogden, M. (1977) 'A police authority – the denial of conflict', *Sociological Review* 25 (2).

Butler, A. J. P. (1984) *Police Management*, Farnborough: Gower.

Cain, M. (1973) *Society and the Policeman's Role*, London: Routledge & Kegan Paul.

Cmnd 3297 (1929) *Report of the Royal Commission on the Police*, London: HMSO.

Cmnd 1728 (1962) *Report of the Royal Commission on the Police*, London: HMSO.

Cmnd 8092 (1981) *Report of the Royal Commission on Criminal Procedure*, London: HMSO.

Curtis, L. (1986) 'Policing the streets', in J. Benyon and C. Bourn, *The Police: Powers, Procedures and Proprieties*, Oxford: Pergamon.

Day, P. and Klein, R. (1987) *Accountabilities*, London: Tavistock.

Gifford Report (1986) *Report of the Broadwater Farm Inquiry*, London: Karia Press.

Greater London Council (GLC) (1985) *The Police Act 1984: a Critical Guide*, Police Committee Discussion Paper No. 3, London: GLC.

Hambleton, R. (1988) 'Consumerism, decentralisation and local democracy', *Public Administration* 66 (2), Summer.

Harris, J. C. (1977) *Survey of Police Authorities' Current Practice*, London: AMA/ACC.

Holdaway, S. (1983) *Inside the British Police*, Oxford: Basil Blackwell.

Horton, C. and Smith, D. (1988) *Evaluating Police Work*, London: Policy Studies Institute.

Hough, M. and Mayhew, P. (1983) *The British Crime Survey: First Report*, Home Office Research and Planning Unit, London: HMSO.

Irving, B. and McKenzie, I. (1989) 'Interrogating in a legal framework', in R. Morgan and D. Smith (eds) *Coming to Terms with Policing*, London: Routledge.

Jones, T., MacLean, B., and Young, J. (1986) *The Islington Crime Survey: Crime Victimization and Policing in Inner-city London*, Farnborough: Gower.

Kemp, C. and Morgan R. (1989) *Behind the Front Counter: Lay Visitors to Police Stations*, Bath: Bath Centre for Criminal Justice, University of Bath.

Kinsey, R. (1985) *Crime and Policing on Merseyside*, Liverpool: Merseyside Metropolitan Council.

Kogan, M. (1986) *Education and Accountability: an Analytic Overview*, London: Hutchinson.

Labour Party (1987) *Labour Manifesto: Britain will Win*, London: Labour Party.

Loveday, B. (1987) 'Joint boards for police in the metropolitan areas: a preliminary assessment', *Local Government Studies*, May-June.

Lustgarten, L. (1986) *The Governance of the Police*, London: Sweet & Maxwell.

Marshall, G. (1965) *Police and Government*, London: Methuen.

Metropolitan Police (1986) *Public Order Review: Disturbances 1981-1985*, London: Metropolitan Police.

Morgan, R. (1985) *Setting the PACE: Police Community Consultative Arrangements in England and Wales*, Bath: University of Bath.

——(1987) 'The local determinants of policing policy', in P. Willmott (ed.) *Policing and the Community*, London: Policy Studies Institute.

Morgan, R. and Smith, D. (eds) (1989) *Coming to Terms with Policing*, London: Routledge.

Morgan, R. and Swift, P. (1987) 'The future of police authorities: members' views', *Public Administration*, Autumn.

——(1988) 'Magistrates and police authorities', *Justice of the Peace*, July.

Oliver, I. (1987) *Police, Government and Accountability*, London: Macmillan.

Oxford, K. (1986) 'The power to police effectively', in J. Benyon and C. Bourn (eds) *The Police: Powers Procedures and Proprieties*, Oxford: Pergamon.

Plant, R. (1974) *Community and Ideology*, London: Routledge & Kegan Paul.

Policy Studies Institute (PSI) (1983) *Police and People in London*, 4 vols, London: PSI.

Prime Minister (1984) *Progress in Financial Management in Government Departments*, Cmnd 9297, London: HMSO.

Reiner, R. (1985) *The Politics of the Police*, London: Wheatsheaf.

Scarman Report (1981) *The Brixton Disorders 10–12 April 1981*, London: HMSO.

Shapland, J. and Vagg, J. (1988) *Policing and the Public*, London: Routledge.

Southgate, P. and Ekblom, P. (1984) *Contacts between Police and Public: Findings from the British Crime Survey*, Home Office Research and Planning Unit, London: HMSO.

——(1986) *Police–Public Encounters*, Home Office Research and Planning Unit, London: HMSO.

Widdicombe Report (1986) *The Conduct of Local Authority Business*, Cmnd 9797, London: HMSO.

Willis, C. (1983) *The Use, Effectiveness and Impact of Police Stop and Search Powers*, Home Office Research and Planning Paper No. 15, London: HMSO.

Willmott, P. (1984) *Community in Social Policy*, London: Police Studies Institute.

6

Social Services

Marian Barnes, David Prior, and Neil Thomas

For social workers have an intrinsically difficult, if not impossible task. They are very different from doctors. People consult doctors because they want to, or manifestly need to. They do not in the same way consult their social worker. They are referred to a social worker, whether they like it or not: the social worker is 'put onto' them. The social worker is therefore extremely likely to seem intrusive and interventionist, imposing his own values on the reluctant or uncomprehending client.

(Warnock 1987)

Introduction

Before we can start to consider what 'user control' can mean in the context of the personal social services, we need to explore briefly the purpose and nature of those services and the varying circumstances in which people come to be users of them. It is our contention that such circumstances are less easily defined and more variable in nature than is the case in relation to many of the other services considered in this volume.

We will discuss the confused statutory definition of personal social services in the following section. Here we want to make a more general point about the lack of an agreed definition of what social care means, and thus the lack of a coherent statement of the purpose of social services in general, as opposed to the purpose of any specific service provided by those statutory agencies established to deliver them.

Social care in practice is provided when people experience problems to which their existing caring networks (if any) are unable to respond. A major characteristic is thus its 'alternative' or 'substitute' nature, replacing that which more advantaged citizens have access to from resources in their more direct control. In practical terms that alternative care may be provided by means of accommodation, day-time activity, practical and personal care assistance, or supportive and enabling relationships of varying types. In practice, the relationships between service providers and users may not always be experienced in those terms. The social distance between the disadvantaged service user and the professional service provider is one factor which can cause the user to feel devalued and powerless:

> because we are trained to think in terms of cases, we have an inherent tendency to separate those we work with from those who do not call on our help. We begin almost to think of clients as a separate homogeneous group, about whom myths are constructed which often prevent us from seeing them as real people.... We forget that 'client' is descriptive not of a person, but of a relationship.
>
> (Simpkin 1979)

In general, use of personal social services is concentrated in those groups within the population who have least power and least opportunity to choose between different problem-solving strategies. Referral is made at a time in people's lives when they are experiencing severe difficulties in material circumstances, interpersonal relationships, and ability to care for themselves or those dependent on them. The history of such problems may be lengthy, and turning to social services may be a last resort, prompted in part by a wish to find someone else to share the burden. Involving social services staff often means the involvement of strangers in the most intimate aspects of life.

Referral to social services in some instances is not only a substitute for preferred but unavailable options, but runs explicitly counter to the users' wishes. This applies when employees of social services exercise their statutory duties in relation to receiving children into care, and making application for people experiencing mental disorder to be compulsorily detained in hospital. These examples illustrate another major dimension of the purpose of social services, which is concerned with the exercise of social control in circumstances in which certain types of behaviour are regarded as unacceptable or dangerous.

In such circumstances the concept of 'service use' is itself questionable, and that of 'user control' poses major dilemmas. Certain groups of people with mental health problems regard themselves as 'survivors' of services, emphasizing their experience of a complete lack of control over what has been done to them. We will consider some of these dilemmas in subsequent sections.

In general, we consider the term 'consumer' of services, which makes a frequent appearance in the increasing number of discussions about the need for 'consumer-sensitive services', to be an inappropriate one. The term 'consumer' has connotations of exercising choice in the market-place and this is not the model of use of the personal social services. Neither do we feel that the term 'consumption' accurately describes the way in which services are used, whether those services are experienced as helpful or intrusive. For the purposes of this discussion the term 'user' is probably the most appropriate one available, although in using it we acknowledge that not all those who come in contact with social services departments would be happy to describe themselves as such.

This latter point raises another key issue relating to the nature of the use of the personal social services. It is not only the definition of who becomes a user of social services and in what circumstances which may be outside the power of the users themselves; the definition of the problem they are experiencing and thus what might be an appropriate response can be taken from them and redefined to suit bureaucratic, professional, or ideological purposes:

> much of the work which has already been done on definitions has been carried out by people who do not themselves experience the daily problems of disability. This has drastically affected the solutions, and has in turn often served to perpetuate discrimination against us, as well as wasting resources of an enormous scale. The struggle for control over definitions which, ultimately, decide the kind of services which are provided and who gets them is gradually coming to a head.
>
> (Davis 1986)

Radical social work has for some time (see, for example, Bailey and Brake 1975) objected to the 'individual pathology' model which locates problems in inadequate people, rather than seeing them as a consequence of the interaction between individuals and their social environment. Since personal social services are often residual substitutes for more highly valued goods, the temptation is to provide services to 'victims' of the existing social order on terms which blame those victims. The current focus on child abuse is a case in point. Public pressure on SSDs focuses on detection and policing of abuse rather than on its prevention. The advent of the Social Fund is reinforcing this direction as it forces people to become and remain defined as 'mentally ill', 'alcoholic', or in other ways 'sick' in order to obtain basic material support.

The question of who defines the problem to which social services are asked to respond is crucial in discussing user control of such services. The necessity to ration resources, inflexibility in service organization, and externally defined criteria for service provision all affect this. The latter is increasingly a feature of the world in which local government as a whole operates. The changing nature of the relationship between central and local government is resulting in the latter being forced to manage demand in ways which conform to narrow definitions of technical rationality and which minimize protest or place the protesters beyond the pale. This is a far cry from the satisfaction of demand and it reduces the autonomy and self-worth of vulnerable groups in particular.

Of course this is a major reason why the Left has begun to question its belief in state centralist solutions, but it also highlights the constraints on current local responses. As Hoggett and Hambleton (1986) warn: 'By taking upon itself responsibility for the management of urban problems and tensions, local government runs the risk of reproducing the problems that it sets out to solve'.

We shall return to this and other issues raised here in our more detailed discussion below.

Our approach

It is clear that the personal social services include a wide range of services provided to people at different stages in their lives. In this chapter we cannot hope to cover either all the examples of attempts to introduce user control in different service contexts, or all the problems and implications of such attempts. What we aim to do is to select a few services, directed at different target groups, in order to discuss the problems and possibilities which arise when attempting to introduce different degrees of empowerment.

Since we are concerned with large, complex organizations, it is necessary to locate the points at which control can be exercised. We have identified the following points at different levels within the decision-making and service structure:

- in contacts between individual workers and users
- in contacts between discrete groups of workers and users (e.g. in a children's home)
- at the level of the management and planning of a particular service (e.g. children's residential care)
- departmental service/resource management and planning
- committee management and policy development
- local authority-wide and inter-agency management and policy development
- national policy development (e.g. legislation, resource allocation).

In their introductory chapter, the editors make clear that we are advocating more, not absolute, user control and that its nature and forms – as well as its degree – will vary. This is also true *within* social services.

Our intention here is to suggest a number of possible models, both individual and collective, which have potential in different circumstances. To impose a single model would, after all, contradict the principle of choice which is inherent in this process.

None the less, we start with two prerequisites: information and accessibility. People need to know what services are available, when, where, and how to gain access, what conditions of eligibility there are, and what are the rights of users. That information needs to be available in various forms, so that it is accessible to people of different backgrounds and with varieties of intellectual, physical, and sensory impairment. The services themselves also need to be accessible and easy to use.

In addition, service users need to know what information about them is held, while both users and citizens should be told who is accountable for the services and something about their performance.

Beyond these two requisites, our editors have already identified characteristics which give users power. Some of these form a continuum in the degree of participation they provide to – and demand of – users. At the lower end are various forms of *consultation*, through opinion surveys and the like. Then *representation and advocacy* on behalf of individuals and groups is possible. This may be extended to allow for active *participation and partnership* in running particular services. At the top end, users may be given *delegated power* to operate services on the department's behalf.

Other characteristics do not fit neatly into such a continuum. Indeed, the provision of *choice* for users can be seen as an alternative to higher levels of participation. This may also be true of procedures for *appeal*, *complaint*, and *redress*, although these should be present regardless of the level of participation.

We will return to a general discussion of these characteristics at the end of this paper, having outlined various attempts at increased user control in particular services.

Two further preliminary points need to be stressed. First, we must reiterate that, for the most part, these services are aimed at people who may have been excluded from valued, mainstream activities, who are absolutely or relatively powerless within the social structure, and who may have been conditioned to accept that status. Thus, to extend effective control to them is both more difficult and more important – not least as a means of helping them to claim more control over the rest of their lives. The 'new consumerism', with its assumptions of active, confident, unstigmatized users, is an insufficient response to this challenge.

Second, we must stress that this paper is an attack neither on the proper use of bureaucracy, nor on professionalism, nor yet on representative democracy. We seek rather to enrich and strengthen these important features of present services.

User control: the statutory framework

Since many of the activities of the personal social services are defined by statute, it is necessary to set out the main features of this legislation and consider both the rights it gives to users and how it might affect users' abilities to exercise control.

The legislative context

The first point to note is that it is not possible to define the statutory framework governing social services provision by local authorities in terms of either a single all-embracing piece of legislation or a series of statutes which together comprise a systematic and complete framework. This contrasts with, for instance, the education and local planning services. Instead there exists a very large body of legislation of varying relevance to the provision of social services, whose component parts deal with a vast range of issues in a fragmentary and uncoordinated manner and which were enacted at different times, in response to different social, political, and economic pressures, and in the absence of any socially agreed concept of 'social services' as a necessary and desirable feature of contemporary society.

This lack of coherence in the nature of the legislation governing local authority social services, when compared with other public welfare services, can to a considerable extent be explained by the historical relationship between the state and what are now known as the 'personal social services'. There are two key issues here. First, there has been a continuing uncertainty on the part of the state, traceable at least back to the nineteenth century, as to whether the social services are provided primarily to regulate certain sections of society for the safety and well-being of others, or to provide direct help and support to those sections. The history of this uncertainty can be charted from the Victorian distinction between the deserving and the undeserving poor and the debates over the appropriate forms of response to these groupings, through to present-day dilemmas of 'care versus control' in social work. The resulting ambiguities have been fully translated into statutory form.

Second, the development of social services legislation over the last hundred years has been shaped by the gradual and grudging nature of the state's acceptance of the need to assume responsibility for the provision of such services, a reluctance to cross the boundary into the private realm of 'family life' echoed in conservative ideology to this day. The development took the form of a selective and irregularly paced transfer of welfare functions from various philanthropic and charitable organizations into central and local agencies of the state, prompted by political contingencies and social pressures, but rarely, if ever, by a clearly articulated philosophy of service provision. Thus the incorporation of social work (or 'welfare work') into the sphere of public services on any significant scale was only definitively accomplished in the late 1940s, partly as an adjunct to the Labour government's 'welfare state' legislation (in the case of elderly and disabled people) and partly in response to mounting public and professional concerns about standards of service (in the case of child care). Whilst the organizational unification of service provision was achieved substantially (though not totally) with the creation of local authority social services departments in 1970, legislation determining and regulating the nature of the services to be provided has continued to appear spasmodically, and to display a distinct lack of consistency and varying degrees of enthusiasm for the acknowledgement of state responsibility.

Characteristics of social services legislation

One major outcome of the state's historical uncertainty and reluctance *vis-à-vis* the personal social services is the enormous variation in legislative 'weight' which bears upon the different strands of service provision. Thus in relation to the welfare of children, increasing social demands for legislative action have, over recent decades, combined with uncertainty as to what action is required and unwillingness to leave the decision to professional judgement. The result is a vast and complex network of child care law which leaves both the provider and the user of the child welfare services treading through a legal minefield:

> The legal framework governing the state's role in the child care system is an extraordinary patchwork of Acts and regulations .... Numerous inconsistencies, gaps and contradictory provisions exist which not only profoundly frustrate everyone involved in child care but also diminish the principles of natural justice. The dozen or more different 'compulsory' routes into care present a multiplicity of different legal considerations and procedures.
>
> (Colvin 1984)

The provision of welfare services to elderly people, by contrast, is still largely governed by legislation passed in 1948 (later refined and updated to extend the powers of local authorities); this is concerned principally with specifying the kinds of services which should or may be provided. The themes of state uncertainty and reluctance are here manifested in uncertainty as to how many resources should be allocated to services for elderly people and reluctance to intervene in the realm of 'family care' (see Means 1986).

Legislation governing social services for people with mental illnesses, mental handicaps, and physical handicaps falls somewhere between these two extremes. The mental health legislation is complex in its concerns with individual rights and the definition of service providers and users as legal entities, but makes only vague reference to the service provision responsibilities of social services departments. The legislation on people with disabilities is more straightforwardly service-orientated, though in its latest manifestation (the Disabled Persons (Services, Consultation, and Representation) Act, 1986) introduces concerns with service users' individual rights and with issues of users' representation.

Differences in orientation are a second major characteristic of social services legislation. Thus, some parts of the law are orientated towards the provision of care and support for service users; other parts are orientated firmly towards the exercise of official control over users, through provisions permitting the monitoring of individual behaviour, the restriction of activities, removal from the user's own or family home, and the imposition of medical treatment or penal sanctions. Within these categories further differences in orientation occur according to whether the principal beneficiary of the legal provisions is intended to be the apparent subject of the legislation or not (e.g. the child or its parents; the elderly/handicapped person or his/her family). In only the rarest instances is the legislation clearly orientated towards the entitlement of users to exercise any influence over the services they receive.

A third characteristic, which is perhaps obvious but is relevant to any consideration of the possibilities for user control, is the determination within the legislation of who is responsible for the provision of the personal social services. Thus the legislation goes beyond allocating the bulk of responsibilities for service provision to local authorities, by requiring the establishment of a specific committee of the local authority to be responsible and accountable for personal social services provision and requiring the committee to appoint a senior officer to manage those services (Local Authority Social Services Act, 1970). The vesting of statutory powers and obligations in a committee of elected councillors and in a senior officer acting on their behalf has major consequences for the way decision-making in respect of the provision of services is organized, and therefore for the potential for influencing or controlling aspects of decision-making by users.

The rights of users

What rights are users of the personal social services actually given by legislation? The answer, in terms of rights to exercise direct control over service provision, is very few. In the sphere of children's services, the law has generally not concerned itself with such matters: 'Traditionally under the law children have been seen as passive objects in need of protective laws and not as individuals with enforceable rights' (Colvin 1984). Section 18 of the Child Care Act, 1980, does require that local authorities, 'In reaching any decision relating to a child in their care ... shall so far as practicable ascertain the wishes and feelings of the child regarding the decision and give due consideration to them, having regard to his age and understanding.' This is obviously a rather weak acknowledgement of a 'child's right' to be involved in decisions affecting his or her life (children can remain in local authority care up to the age of 18); moreover, it only relates to children who are actually in care. In passing we may note that the situation is no better for the parents of children in care; Colvin refers to parents' legal position as 'reprehensibly vague ... there are no clear answers to questions about parental powers over children's property, medical treatment, nationality, or their rights over education, change of name, or consent to marriage' (Colvin 1984). Foster parents are in a somewhat stronger position than the biological parents of children in care, possessing most of the 'rights' in respect of the child's upbringing that parents ordinarily have. Again, however, there is a lack of legal precision and the powers of foster parents are certainly outweighed by the powers of the care agency which places children with them (see Holden 1980).

For the parents of children who are not in care but are of concern to social services agencies, some improvement in their rights seems likely under new legislation currently being considered. This promises the replacement of the twenty-eight day Place of Safety Order, which allows children to be removed from their parents, with an eight-day Emergency Protection Order to which parents would have the right of challenge. The new law is also likely to remove the power of the local authority to take children into care by means of the administrative order known as a 'parental rights resolution'. In future the local authority will be required to argue its case in court.

For disabled people, which includes those disabled by physical or mental handicaps or mental illness, the Disabled Persons (Services, Consultation and Representation) Act, 1986, introduces some important new rights. In summary, these are: the right of a disabled person to be represented in dealings with a local authority by a person authorized to speak on his or her behalf; the right of a disabled person to demand full assessment of his or her need for services provided by a local authority; the right to receive a written statement, following an assessment of what services the local authority intends to provide or why it proposes not to provide services; the right of disabled persons' carers to have their needs taken into account; and the right of disabled people's organizations to be consulted before any person is co-opted to a formal committee to represent disabled people's interests.

Whilst this Act certainly increases the power of disabled people to influence decisions concerning services provided to them, and opens up the possibility of local authorities being sued for failure to provide appropriate services, it is too early to judge how much improvement in the ability of users to exert control over services will actually result. At the time of writing, key sections of the Act have not yet been implemented, so its effectiveness has not been tested. There are, moreover, serious questions about the priority which local authorities will give to meeting the demands likely to be unlocked by the Act in the face of a continuing squeeze on local government finance. However, it is worth noting that the fact that the Act is on the statute book at all owes much to the pressure exerted by user groups.

Specifically in relation to people with mental illnesses, the Mental Health Act, 1983, contains two important provisions which enhance users' rights. First, the establishment of the Mental Health Act Commission created an independent body to monitor and protect the rights of detained patients. Second, the Act strengthened the role of Mental Health Review Tribunals, to which people formally admitted to hospital for treatment under the Act can appeal against their continued detention. The Tribunals have the power to order the discharge of the detained person.

However, these rights only follow compulsory detention in hospital, which many people experience as a complete loss of control over what is happening to them. This will be discussed in more detail in a later section (p. 123). The general point to emphasize here is that legislation exists which defines those circumstances in which people can be forced into a relationship with welfare services against their will, but remains silent about the rights of those experiencing mental health problems or their carers to receive help which could prevent crises from arising. In this context, any good intentions embodied in the Mental Health Act designed to limit the use of compulsion are compromised by levels of locally available resources which are inadequate to meet the needs of those who want help.

User control in practice

We now turn to selected areas of service provision to consider what evidence of user control there is in current practice, and how user-control principles could be introduced and extended.

Services for children at risk

Two preliminary but vital questions need to be raised before we discuss in detail the possibilities for user control in the sphere of services for children at risk. First, what is the nature of the risk that is being referred to? Second, who actually is the user – the child or his/her parents?

'Risk' tends to be defined by service providers in three different ways:

- the risk that a child may suffer physical or emotional abuse or neglect, which may lead to death, injury, psychological damage, or failure to grow and develop normally
- the risk that a child may become involved in criminal activities, which may result in his/her entry into the juvenile justice system with the further risks of penal sentences which are disruptive of family life, schooling, and career prospects
- the risk, often consequent upon the previous two 'risks', that it will be necessary for the child's welfare to remove him/her from his/her family either permanently or temporarily, thus depriving him/her of the experience of being raised in his/her 'natural' family and causing at least temporarily the breakdown of family life.

The question whether it is the child or the parents who are the users of child care services is dependent on which definition of risk underlies the way in which services are provided. Where risk is defined in terms of family breakdown, services are likely to focus on the needs of the family as a whole. The child will, as far as possible, be seen as a part of the family unit and as the 'normal' responsibility of the parents. Services will have a strong orientation towards helping the parents fulfil this responsibility adequately; thus the parents can be regarded as the primary users of the services.

Where risk is defined in terms of child abuse or neglect, services focus more specifically on the needs and rights of the child. Protection of the child and prevention of further abuse will be the main service orientation, including the removal of the child from his/her family and the provision of a substitute home. The interests of the child will take precedence over the interests of the family unit; thus it is the child who can be regarded as the primary service user.

Other important questions suggest themselves but cannot be discussed in detail here. For instance, what is the definition of the family? For most children who come into contact with social services, the stable nuclear family is not the norm; this means that 'preventing family breakdown' is not as clear-cut as it sounds. Another issue is the extent to which 'society' is the real user of the child care services, in the sense of being the beneficiary of the services' regulatory and control functions. Certainly such considerations have been a major influence in determining the legislation governing child care.

For the remainder of this section it will be assumed that 'risk' refers to risk of neglect or abuse of the child, and that the 'user' of the services aimed at alleviating or preventing these dangers is the child. This probably reflects the dominant orientation of most local social services authorities at the present time. Such an assumption is, however, clearly simplistic, as recent child care history shows. Judgements about these definitions made by practitioners and their managers in the context of highly complex and pressurized situations are central to social work practice. Invariably, the judgement entails a balance between concern with the risk of damage to the child and of damage to the family, and thus between concern with the rights of the child and the rights of the parents. The consequences of getting the balance wrong are detailed in the reports on the death of Tyra Henry and on the Cleveland sexual abuse cases; one revealing a balance towards parent/family concerns, the other towards child concerns. Whilst these and other recent child abuse inquiry reports (e.g. on the deaths of Jasmine Beckford and Kimberly Carlile) seem certain to generate yet more legislation and thus a shift in official definitions of 'risk' and 'user', it is not at present clear what overall effect this legislation will have. Certainly the events in Cleveland have brought to centre-stage the need for greater clarity on the rights of parents when faced with health and social services personnel acting on behalf of their children. At the same time, the Butler Sloss Report on Cleveland recommends a greater recognition of the right of children to be consulted and to be listened to in the course of investigations into suspected abuse.

Given our assumption about the identity of risk and user, it is appropriate to consider services to children, and the possibilities of extending user control, within two main categories: the process of making the decision whether a child at risk requires a substitute home; and the actual provision of the substitute home.

The service at the heart of the decision-making process concerning a child at risk is the assessment of the child's needs. Assessment may be carried out in a variety of settings, although the current trend is away from placing children in specialist 'observation and assessment' centres and towards keeping them in their familiar everyday surroundings. It is likely to involve a range of professionals in addition to the social worker, including teachers, psychologists, psychiatrists, paediatricians, GPs, health visitors, and police. The outcome of this multi-disciplinary assessment is usually determined in the formal context of a case conference, with all the participants present. The process may continue in the courtroom if the decision is to seek a Care Order on the child, in which case magistrates also become part of the business of 'assessment'.

In all this, the opportunities for the child to exercise any meaningful control over proceedings are minimal, even where s/he may be deemed old enough to have a responsible view on his/her own needs. The extent to which the child's own views, feelings, and reports of events are taken into serious consideration depends on the approach of the individual professional concerned, as does the involvement of the child in actual decision-making. The participation of children (and/or their parents) in case conferences is still very rare, and the bureaucratic style of most case conferences is anyway unlikely to enable children to participate effectively. There is, however, some evidence to show that where, as in Greenwich, a clear policy on the involvement of parents in case conferences is laid down and the co-operation of the professionals gained, the results can be highly positive (McGloin and Turnbull 1986). There seems to be no reason why older children should not be similarly involved.

In court hearings, children who are the subjects of care proceedings can be full participants, but in the context of an adversarial legal system which again is not designed to empower children in any real way. The use of guardians *ad litem* – independent social workers who are appointed to represent the interests of children in legal proceedings – is an important recent step in improving the rights of children to have their views heard and taken into account. Overall, however, it has had a minor impact on the child care system, partly because of legislative tinkering which prohibits the guardian from advocating on the child's behalf in court (Colvin 1984). One important right that children and young people do possess is the power to choose and appoint their own solicitor, and this applies even where a guardian *ad litem* is acting for them. The role of guardian *ad litem* is likely to be strengthened in new child care legislation.

Once children are 'in care' and placed in a substitute home setting, and are therefore users of a local authority's residential or fostering services, the potential for establishing means by which they can exercise real control over services is considerable – although once again this potential has been little realized to date. First, for children in residential homes there is the issue of the way the home itself is run. There is clearly scope for children to be involved in the management of their home, from the maintenance of an open and participative management style in which children are consulted and encouraged to make their views known, to the establishment of a residents' committee as the main decision-making body in the home. Second, in both residential and foster homes the existence of a clear and effective complaints procedure is a vital if basic means of giving children in care some capacity for influencing the service which they receive. Hounslow, for example, provides all children in care with a booklet which gives basic information on what being in care means, what sources of help and advice are available, and how to make formal complaints. Third, all children in care must be the subjects of regular statutory reviews which check on the child's well-being and on the long-term intentions for the child, whether the current placement is suitable, whether they should return to the natural family, be fostered/adopted, etc. Such reviews in theory provide an opportunity for children to make a major formal input into the planning and decision-making process which determines their future. However, the extent to which children are actually involved in their own reviews varies considerably and there is clearly scope for a significant increase in the influence which children in care could have over the child care service through the statutory review process. Fourth, children in care can be regarded as the most knowledgeable sources of information on the quality of substitute home placements. Thus their experiences could be drawn on in an agency's evaluation of its services and in planning future service developments. Involving children in service planning in this way would be a fundamental, if more long-term, approach to enhancing user control of services.

A different perspective on user control, and one which reveals a much greater degree of positive work by local authorities, is provided by the preparation of young people for the experience of leaving care. Careful and sensitive preparation for independent or semi-independent living, perhaps after many years of institutional upbringing, is significant not only in effecting a successful transition from one form of life to another but in equipping the young person with the basic means to exercise control in adult life.

This section has necessarily only scratched the surface of its subject matter. It has also not addressed some of the profound difficulties and dilemmas which make the provision of statutory child care an ideological minefield. One such dilemma which should be mentioned, however, is that between individual and collective issues. It is important to recognize both that children and young people in care experience problems as individuals, and require responses that enhance their personal capacity to influence and change the situations that give rise to problems, and also that they experience problems collectively, thus requiring responses which empower on a group level. Examples of both kinds of possible response have been suggested in this section, where the response comes from the local authority and its professional representatives. We wish to highlight another kind of response, which is that of children and young people themselves taking collective action to address both individual and collective problems. This 'trade union' model has, we believe, considerable potential and is exemplified in the activities of NAYPIC (National Association of Young People in Care). In spite of a high turnover of leadership resulting from age limits on membership, NAYPIC's activities have achieved positive impacts on issues ranging from those to do with control over the individual young person's own image and self-expression through campaigns to abolish 'clothing books', to the provision of socially and culturally appropriate care environments for children and young people from ethnic minorities. In a number of local authorities NAYPIC has been invited to contribute to the development of child care policy and practice, and this kind of openness on the part of statutory service providers to listen to the voice of their users and allow them a role in defining the nature of the provision can only be applauded. Perhaps the most important message to carry forward is that if ways are to be found of making user control in the child care services any sort of reality, then social services departments and their committees must recognize that the users themselves are likely to have practical proposals as to what those ways might be.

Services for people with a mental handicap

In our introductory section we highlighted the 'alternative' nature of many of the services provided by SSDs. Over recent years there has been a recognition that this can stigmatize and devalue service users, and so policies have been designed to 'normalize' services and thus reduce their stigmatizing effect. Such policy developments have been most pervasive in respect of services for people with a mental handicap and have made an impact at a number of levels.

They have prompted the discharge of people with a mental handicap from long-stay hospitals, often miles from their place of birth, into smaller accommodation run by social services rather than the health authority. Within social services there has been a move towards the development of group homes and the use of ordinary housing rather than the expansion of purpose-built hostel accommodation. Where purpose-built accommodation is provided, attempts are being made to furnish and decorate in non-institutional fashion.

Whilst normalization is not explicitly concerned with user control, it does try to address one of the major factors inhibiting mentally handicapped users from taking control over their own lives. As such it can be seen as a precondition for the development of services based on user-control principles. The following discussion highlights some of the dilemmas affecting its implementation.

People's day-time activity is usually determined by their relationship to the productive and reproductive institutions of society. For those outside such mainstream activity, not through choice but as a result of having characteristics which mean that capitalist society has little use for them, the question of how to spend their days is not so easy.

Young adults with a mental handicap have little chance of obtaining employment on leaving school. The importance of employment as a

119

source of status, identity, and economic independence has been well documented. The young mentally handicapped adult is likely to be denied this source of recognition of his/her new adult status and to remain in a position more akin to that of a child attending school than an adult going out to work. Even the best Adult Training Centre is a substitute for what is regarded as 'normal' day-time activity. Rather than being centres of further education which provide the extra education and training their students require before they are ready for work, they are more often the only source of structured day-time activity accessible to adults with a mental handicap for long periods of their adult lives.

Within such centres it is particularly important for users to have the opportunity both to control the activities with which they fill their days, and to ensure that the relationships between themselves and the staff who work in them recognize their adult status. A significant problem in achieving this lies in the low expectations which may have characterized the upbringing of the mentally handicapped young person. Peter Leonard writes of the effect this has on personality:

> For people with disabilities the experience of subordinacy is likely to be even more profound, expressing itself though a range of relationships including those within the family. The child with disabilities, for example, especially if she is mentally handicapped, is less likely to be spoken to as less is expected of her (Shakespeare, 1975, p. 19). Thus in their social production as subjects, the two senses of *subject* to which we have referred may be profoundly unbalanced in the case of people with a disability. Ideological inculcation subjects them to the social order, but it frequently does not qualify or prepare them as actors in that order: they may be expected not to act, but only to be acted upon.
>
> (Leonard 1984)

Communication difficulties may make this worse. Physical impairment as well as limited intellectual abilities may hamper verbal expression. Some people with a mental handicap have virtually no verbal abilities at all. A combination of low expectations and the difficulties experienced by professional staff in communicating with people with a mental handicap often results in very limited conversation. They may not be asked what they want to do with their time, or how they want to live their lives, or about their hopes, fears, likes, and dislikes. Research by Diana Kuh and her colleagues, which involved talking with a large number of young adults with mental and /or physical handicaps, was greeted with surprise by many of the young people concerned as this was the first time that they had been asked directly how they wanted to live (Kuh *et al.* 1986).

One positive outcome of the policy of normalization is that the concept of 'the day centre' is being challenged. Since the purpose of such centres is to provide education or employment, opportunities for people with a mental handicap to follow relevant courses in colleges of further education are being explored in co-operation with education departments, and in some instances sheltered employment schemes have been developed which enable people to become employees rather than clients of the local authority. The opportunity to develop confidence in an environment not exclusively designed for the handicapped can enable young people to play a more active and independent part in their own lives generally.

Assuming day centres of some description will remain necessary for people whose level of handicap means that they would be unlikely to be able to undertake a job or participate in college courses, a number of characteristics would be necessary to enable service users to share in the control of such centres. Users may have to be encouraged to express preferences when this is a new experience for them. And the expression of preferences may have to be made by non-verbal communication: by pointing at visual images, or using facial expression of body language. An example of this is provided by a research project designed to establish the preferences of a group of people being discharged from a hospital in the West Midlands, as to the type of accommodation in which they would like to live (Richards 1985). Of the twenty people interviewed, four were non-verbal, and verbal communication was extremely limited with three others. To overcome this the researcher used photographs of both internal and external features of different types of accommodation to encourage people to express their preferences.

The encouragement of such expression is time consuming, and involves workers learning both to read different signs and to send messages in different ways. It involves intensive work on a one-to-one basis and, where group discussions are involved, the ability to interpret between a number of different methods of communication. Workers in Adult Training Centres (ATCs) have often recognized that one of the best ways of facilitating communication with those who have verbal communication difficulties is by getting other more verbally able trainees to act as interpreters. Perhaps their own experiences make them more sensitive to what their peers are trying to say. Such an approach can assist in reducing the social distance between staff and trainees, and in so doing can potentially reduce the power differential.

Another way of doing this which has been tried in north London is to involve trainees as trainers either alongside or instead of the centre staff:

For our dance therapy work we include Alan as one of the instructors.

Alan is a Down's syndrome man of 30 with a background of difficult behaviour. However, he has worked hard at his dance and three years ago he was included as part of our experimental dance workshops with able-bodied people. He was able to lead an hour's workshop by himself. It is impossible to overestimate the value to both mentally handicapped pupils and their parents and teachers when they see that an instructor is 'one of them'.

(Davis 1987)

In order to establish relationships of this type day centres need to be smaller than they often are now. A number of smaller units, focusing on different types of activity, would also provide a further element of choice.

The tendency to view people with a mental handicap as childlike rather than as adults responsible for making their own choices is sometimes encouraged by parents concerned at the possibility of exploitation. A particularly sensitive area in which this dilemma is experienced is that of sexuality. There have been circumstances in which parents have withdrawn their daughters from an ATC because they were being given sex education and the opportunity to express their sexuality. Most staff of ATCs would be fairly clear that the service user, from their point of view, is the person with a mental handicap. But direct opposition to parents is neither helpful nor desirable, and this is a particular instance in which it is important to recognize that there may be more than one service user with potentially different interests. Giving more control to the young person is likely to involve helping parents come to terms with the lessening of their control over their son or daughter.

Kuh's research identified a dissonance between the young people and their parents in terms of their wishes about the type of home they would prefer. This was usually because the young people wanted a higher degree of independence than their parents wanted for them. An example of this dilemma and suggestions for the way in which the social worker involved needed to proceed to ensure that both the young person and her parents were involved in decision-making was quoted in the report:

Consumer: Jane Smith

Area of concern: Help to live away from parental home.

Viewpoint: General consensus that this is an area of concern but conflict over what may be the most appropriate solution.

Preferred options: Jane wants to live with friends, with some domiciliary help. Mr and Mrs Smith would prefer a place in a care community eventually. Social worker has access to a one-bedroomed adapted flat in a warden scheme for elderly people.

What is preventing the need from being met?: Social worker has not discussed this issue alone with Jane and does not know of her wish to live with able-bodied friends. Parents consider their daughter is too young to leave home.

Next steps?: Social worker to discuss issues with Jane and Mr and Mrs Smith both individually and together and encourage them to talk about the variety of future living options. Meanwhile opportunities need to be found which will give Jane a chance to experience short breaks away from home with friends.

(Kuh *et al.* 1986)

As far as the choice of a home is concerned, the implementation of user-control principles is likely to mean that the social services department is less often the direct provider of accommodation. Where possible, the aim should be to provide the counselling, advice, and support that would enable people to live in their own (probably rented) home. More profoundly handicapped people will probably continue to need purpose-built accommodation, but it should be clear that such accommodation is their home and that they, both individually and collectively, should be able to participate in its organization and have a say in who has access to it.

In general, increasing user control in relation to services for people with a mental handicap means defining the relationship between service provider and service user as an enabling and empowering one. It is probably more appropriate to think in terms of greater control being exercised at the interpersonal, rather than the strategic, level, at least in the first instance. Participation in service planning can be assisted by the expression of preferences which can influence decision-making about, for example, the location of group homes or the type of activities undertaken within day centres. But the long-term aim should be to enable people with a mental handicap to exercise a greater degree of control over their lives outside the arena of social services as well as within it.

Mental health services

Mental health services generally receive low priority within the personal social services. The Audit Commission quote expenditure for 1985–6 of £56 million on mental health services compared with £322 million on mental handicap, £136 million on younger physically handicapped people, and £1,378 million on services for elderly people (Audit Commission 1986). The passage of the Mental Health Act, 1983, introduced new duties for social services departments and this has meant that at least some aspects of work with people with mental health problems have been given more attention over the last few years. But it is those aspects of mental health work concerned with the fulfilment of statutory responsibilities which have been the focus of most attention.

Mental health legislation enables people to be detained in hospital against their wishes, following the application of a social worker approved under the terms of the Act. Section 13 sets out the approved social worker's (ASW's) duties before making such an application. Not only should the social worker be convinced that the person is suffering from mental disorder, and that detention is required, in the interests of her health or safety, or in order to protect other people, but

> Before making an application for the admission to hospital an approved social worker shall interview the patient in a suitable manner and satisfy himself that detention in a hospital is in all the circumstances of the case the most appropriate way of providing the care and medical treatment of which the patient stands in need.
>
> (Section 13(2))

This phraseology is a somewhat watered-down version of the original expression of the embodiment of the 'least restrictive alternative' concept which aimed to promote the civil rights of those suffering from mental disorder. If the conditions outlined above do not apply, the 'care and treatment' required by people with mental health problems should be provided without recourse to compulsory detention, using the least restrictive form of alternative care. Attendance at day centres with a social or therapeutic aim might be one source of alternative care which would enable people to retain a much greater degree of independence and control over their lives than would be possible if they were to enter hospital. Alternatively, if current living arrangements are either exacerbating, or threatened by, the mental health problems of the person concerned, a temporary or permanent new home might be needed before those problems can be addressed directly. However, legislation provides no rights to such services if hospital is not seen as the appropriate location in which to meet the needs of the person concerned.

Evidence from a study of the way in which the Mental Health Act, 1983, is being implemented by social service departments suggests that alternative options are used comparatively rarely (Fisher *et al.* 1987). The single most frequently used alternative to compulsory hospital detention is informal hospital admission. Just how 'voluntary' such informal admissions are when the recipient is aware that, if she doesn't go quietly, a compulsory detention is likely to be ordered, is open to question.

Many of those assessed by ASWs may well be in need of temporary treatment to stabilize their condition. However, ASWs also consider that many enter hospital because an alternative is not available, not because hospital is the most appropriate place for them. In too many circumstances, lack of appropriate resources means that those at the receiving end of services lose immediate control over most aspects of their lives and may also suffer in the long term from the stigma of having been detained under a section of the Mental Health Act. Whilst legislation requires SSDs to provide sufficient approved social workers to carry out the necessary assessments under the Act, no extra resources have been made available for the provision of services which might prevent the crises which often result in assessment followed by hospital detention.

There have also been reports that guardianship (which includes the power to require the person concerned to live in a particular place) is sometimes used not because the social worker feels control is required, but as a means to command resources which would not otherwise be available.

A mental health – as opposed to mental illness – service would include provisions which enabled those with mental health problems to take responsibility and control of their own lives, rather than intervening at times when this becomes most difficult. It would involve social work practice which recognized and addressed the mental health element in a range of problems with which people come for help to social services. For example, currently in many cases which are labelled 'child care' problems, the mental health problems of a depressed and isolated mother may be invisible and thus not a focus for action. This in turn may result in an inappropriate response to the child care problem which may exacerbate the woman's depression by suggesting that she has failed as a mother. Both her feelings of control and the amount of control that she is able to exert over her life would be severely reduced. If social work assistance were addressed to the mother in her own right, she could be empowered and enabled both to define and solve any problems herself.

Such a service would also offer a genuine alternative to the predominantly medical mental illness services now available. Many of those suffering from mental health problems do not regard themselves as 'ill'. The origin or cause of mental disorder is extremely difficult to determine, but there is convincing evidence that social factors play their part. In this circumstance the contribution of a social rather than medical response is vital. From a user-control perspective the possibility to exercise choice in the type of treatment, therapy, or care received is as important to someone suffering from mental health problems as it is to anyone else. Currently, the question posed by many parents of people suffering from schizophrenia – 'What on earth are we going to do when they close all the hospitals?' – is very difficult to answer, but the sufferers themselves are clear that enforced hospitalization is not what they want. The dilemma is that avoiding the use of hospital admission very often means that family and friends continue to provide support in what can be very difficult circumstances, with very little or no assistance from social services (see Barnes *et al.* forthcoming). The right of the person experiencing mental health problems to remain as independent as possible can be at the expense of carers' abilities to choose their own lifestyles. And this is a potential and actual conflict in relation to most groups of social services users.

Community mental health centres are being developed in some areas: in some successful examples users play an active part in determining both the nature of activities and the organization of the centre itself. Tontine Road in Chesterfield is one of the best known. Here the staff have delegated their own powers to a joint group of staff and members called 'Contact'. It has a constitution which sets out the role of staff as advisers and a clearly accountable executive committee with control over the budget. That budget includes payment to some members who take on helping tasks. Members have also been consulted informally about new staff appointments. Both problems and benefits have been identified in relation to this initiative: some members felt that too few of them were capable of asserting their rights in opposition to staff. The disabling effects of past 'treatment' had left their mark. But members had been enabled to regain abilities that they thought they had lost and one member commented 'When I came here I was given back control of my life' (Banks 1986).

Another model of user control in relation to mental health services is provided by the Camden Consortium (see Camden Mental Health Consortium 1986). This provides a forum in which users of mental health services, carers, local people, and professionals can meet to debate mental health issues (although some senior professionals have now opted out). It was successful in getting plans regarding the closure of Friern Barnet Hospital changed, after objections that users had not been consulted about the future of the hospital. The consortium is not purely a users' group and there is the potential for some of the same problems that were identified in Tontine Road. Mixed groups run the risk of being overbalanced by more assertive professionals who are also more used to operating in such contexts. The difference is that the consortium is outside the service provision structure and can be seen as operating more along the lines of a trade union, exerting pressure from outside, rather than being incorporated into the structure.

'Survivors Speak Out' is yet another model and one which is more akin to NAYPIC in the area of child care. Although not exclusively an organization of users (one-third of members are 'allies'), it is clearly aimed at raising consciousness and promoting self-advocacy on the part of users. Professional allies are involved only to the extent that they will support these aims, and the difficulties for both professionals and users involved in breaking free of firmly established roles are well recognized (see Bell 1987). In spite of the difficulties a major achievement of 'Survivors' has been to provide a users' voice and presence on conference platforms where often only professional voices are heard. Thus as well as helping individual users to overcome loss of confidence, they are contributing at a more strategic level to the way in which thinking about mental health services should be developing.

Services for frail elderly people

Frail elderly people are the largest single group receiving help from social services. The continuing sharp rise in their numbers will accentuate this aspect over the next decade. If we add those in need but not receiving help and those who are the primary carers of all these groups, we gain some impression of the numbers affected by the amount and character of the help available. Growing recognition of this 'problem' has coincided with concern about the implementation of 'community care' policies for all dependent adults. Together, they have spawned a minor industry of description, prediction, analysis, and experiment, culminating in the Audit Commission's damning indictment (1986) and the proposals for change enshrined in the Griffiths Report (1988).

Later, we touch on present shortcomings and briefly discuss the Griffiths Report. First, however, we wish to sketch out what services might look like if they were built from scratch on the principle of user control. Whilst it is distilled from recent analyses and experiments, the design sketch is unashamedly Utopian. We recognize that other priorities and other values will limit its achievement, the most powerful of which include:

- the pressure to invest in and reward present and future workers, rather than past workers, of which problem constructions such as 'the pensions time bomb' and 'the burden of old age', and solutions such as 'early retirement' are a by-product.
- the pressure to reward the powerful and successful, emphasized by the present expansion of private rather than collective rights to property and pensions; in this way the inequalities of working age are transferred into old age.
- the pressure to maintain traditional gender divisions which reinforce

women in their 'natural' caring role, whilst denying them rights, both as carers and as recipients of care (e.g. Peace 1986).
• the pressure to allow providers almost unfettered discretion in the way public resources are spent; the paradoxical result has been that, whilst public services for frail elderly people saw real growth in the 1960s and 1970s, many of those services reinforced their dependency, rather than combating it (Phillipson and Walker 1986).

All are agreed about the deleterious effects of this last pressure, but they are being used as a justification for eliminating collective provision – except, of course, for those with no choice, over whom professional discretion and control are increased. The powerfully effective Utopian vision of which this strategy is a part has to be countered by one in which the concepts of need and social justice are brought back to the centre of the political stage (Webb and Wistow 1987: 229).

Since user control of services would not operate in a vacuum, we would need to start with other factors affecting the lives of elderly people. The foundations of such a service would include a decent basic pension, which was much closer to average earnings than at present (currently 20 per cent for a single pensioner) and which kept pace with them (it will be 9 per cent in 2034 if present trends continue). They would also include decent primary and acute health care, in which the focus was on enabling people to be aware of and influence their own health status and on preventing ill health. It would also require much closer attention to the characteristics and needs of older people in the design of everyday products. But perhaps the most important foundation would be political and ideological. Older people would no longer be subject to ageist stereotypes which structure their social dependency. They would understand what normal ageing is, be able to explore the possible components of what is, for them, a good old age, and assert greater control over both physical and social ageing. Part of this would involve their own decision about when to leave the labour market. These ideological foundations would themselves be supported by a thriving polity, centred on old people themselves, but including trade unions and welfare professionals.

Built on these foundations, the major features of the services would comprise the following:

1) Elderly people would have clear rights to services. These rights might be graded according to people's frailty (notwithstanding the problems in measuring this) and perhaps their social resources such as family support, but the grading would be explicit and open to political challenge.

2) People would be able to choose how they exercised that entitlement, not only in terms of the balance between, say, household care and recreation, but also between different types of household care and different suppliers.

3) The range of services would be expanded. For example, intensive domiciliary care would be available, as would residential flatlets, so that heavily dependent people could choose non-communal, semi-communal, or fully communal care.

4) The services would be constructed as coherent packages. Additional income, accommodation, personal and household care, transport, occupation, recreation, and education would be considered together, so that a coherent set of choices could be exercised by individuals.

5) In exercising this choice, elderly people would have access to a broker whose role would include the following: to map out and explore (critically) the available options; to help old people and their immediate informal carers to reach some accommodation about their mutual caring relationship, bearing in mind their potentially conflicting interests; to arrange access to services once a choice has been made; to act as monitor and troubleshooter.

6) Services would be local and flexible. More services would come to the user, rather than vice versa, and those requiring an institutional base would contain a mix, rather than a concentration of one service (such as residential care) designed to achieve dubious economies of scale.

7) Those providing the service would be trained to understand normal ageing and to value it, to help elderly people retain or regain self-esteem, to emphasize growth as well as adjustment to deterioration, to pass on skills and knowledge, to encourage social and political awareness, to be sensitive to ethnic and cultural differences in ageing. They would not, as at present, be largely untrained or mistrained into a pathological view of old age. Consequent on this the existing occupational divisions would not survive in their present form – either between health, social care, education, and housing, for example, or between high- and low-status workers within those services.

8) Mechanisms of user control would include, at the individual level, information, choice, and brokerage which would be augmented by well-publicized complaints procedures and by market research. Collectively, there would be user groups with clear rights to be consulted about day-to-day provision and any proposal for change. These would both negotiate and often join

with groups of paid and informal carers. The mix and co-ordination of services would be proper topics of discussion as well as day-to-day matters of organization and activity. These forums would also provide the ammunition, the training, and the head of steam for the interests of old people to be explicitly considered across the gamut of local authority and other services and so on to national level.

9)   Services would be located alongside valued services for other groups of people. The foundations of good, accessible design and security would mean that frail old people would have access to such services. Transport systems and home-based shopping, information, and education would be especially significant in gaining access.

10)   The complexity in the range of providers would be explicitly recognized. These would include both people who are paid and people who are volunteers in all types of institutions currently in existence – family, self-help groups, co-operatives, formal voluntary agencies, philanthropic and non-profit-making enterprises, commercial enterprises, and public agencies. Self-help and co-operative groups would be likely to increase in a user-controlled service. The prime roles of the public service would shift: its concern would be for the whole of the system, not just for parts of it; it would determine eligibility and probably provide brokerage services; it would develop and implement a trade and industry policy, promoting new services and regulating existing ones; it would also remain a direct supplier, although probably not within the same organizational boundaries as at present.

11)   People would receive the same services, from the same providers, regardless of whether these were paid for from public funds or in some other way.

Such a picture contrasts starkly with the present pattern of services and many recent policy developments work in precisely the opposite direction, despite the rhetoric of community care. Services are often incoherent, most are small parts of separate fiefdoms, managed from afar. Even those within a single organization are often managed in separate sections so that the service received is often a function of which part of the organization initial contact was made with. The system is hopelessly imbalanced towards the provision of residential care and the government has encouraged a major list in the same direction by opening the floodgates of commercial provision. Perverse incentives to shift the burden on to others exist at every level. Families receive relatively little help when they care for frail elders, yet the state – via the NHS, the social services department, or supplementary benefit – often takes over completely when such unpaid and unrecognized support is no longer possible. A social services department short of resources can fail to keep pace with demand, knowing that the private residential sector, funded by the state, will act as a safety net. Hospital consultants are tempted to bypass social services and refer directly to the private sector. Hospital managers are given bonuses for closing long-stay units, even though community services have not been built up to replace them.

Furthermore, our discussion of social services legislation has shown that old people and their families are rarely afforded rights – except the right to join a queue for under-resourced and idiosyncratically rationed services (e.g. Mitchell 1987). Information about services and procedures for appeal and redress are woefully inadequate (e.g. National Consumer Council/National Institute for Social Work 1988) and social workers are forced to act as resource rationers rather than brokers. Authorities are nowadays making more use of consumer and need surveys (e.g. Barnes 1987), but, generally, both individual and collective means of user influence are poor. Statements from government ministers provide strong evidence that this situation is symptomatic of a policy to push responsibility on to individuals and their families, since a collective shouldering of this 'burden' is officially considered so onerous as to threaten our economic well-being (see discussion in Phillipson and Walker 1986: 9). Once more the definition is crucial – the 'rising tide' of old people about to swamp the economically active.

There are, of course, proposals for change, notably those in the Firth Report (1987) on public support for residential care, the Wagner review (1988) of residential care, and the Griffiths proposals (Griffiths Report 1988) on the organization of community care. We discuss these on pp. 134–50. In general terms they are likely to result in more coherent policies, financing, and organizational structures at the price of a considerable centralization of power. However, the effects of any such changes will be crucially determined by the level of resources allocated to them and to basic income support. Here, the auguries are not good. Basic pensions seem destined to slip further behind earnings; there is no sign of proper disability or carers' benefits; the restrictions on Housing Benefit and Attendance Allowance, and the Social Fund with its derisory budget, are all indicators of regress.

At the local level signs are more hopeful. Many authorities have broadened the range of schemes to assist frail elderly people and their carers. Intensive domiciliary support schemes, street wardens, short-term foster and other relief care, night sitters, alarm systems, and so on abound. As yet these are uneven in amount and quality and few have been properly integrated with traditional services or with each other (Social Services Inspectorate 1987). Integration with health, housing, transport, and voluntary services is even less likely.

Four brief examples must suffice to indicate possible ways forward. First, there is Birmingham's Community Care Special Action Project, in which a policy review is taking place across all departments of the local authority and closely linked with the NHS. Central to this exercise is a commitment to learning of users' and informal carers' views about existing and desirable services, and then building such views into the policy and planning process (Jowell and Prior 1989).

Second, there is Sheffield, where the local authority has taken a decision to build no more residential homes for elderly people, but instead to develop local Elderly Persons Support Units (later renamed Community Support Units). These aim to integrate domiciliary, day, health, and recreational services in one location close to elderly people's own homes. A community support worker acts as a focal point of this service which can provide care in people's own homes up to the level of residential care (Macdonald *et al.* 1984).

The focus of the Kent Community Care Scheme (Challis and Davies 1986), our third example, is rather different. People at risk of entering residential care were offered the chance of help from an experimental service in which specialist social workers were entitled to spend up to two-thirds of the cost of residential care in providing community-based services. Their progress was compared with a matched group of people receiving traditional services. Whilst the social workers had access to traditional services such as home helps, much of their development activities went into creating informal networks of paid helpers for each old person and working out a clear division of labour between family, other informal, and formal carers. The social workers therefore acted as assessors, resource people, and case co-ordinators, as well as providing direct help. The opportunities this scheme offers for user control operate at the individual, rather than collective, level.

The last example is the Dinnington Neighbourhood Services Project (Bayley *et al.* 1987). This covered a wider remit than services for elderly people. Two social workers, a housing assistant and the wardens she supported, and the domiciliary health workers were brought together to cover the same patch. They had a common office base and tried to work as a team, using a regular fieldwork meeting to integrate their own work and link with other local professionals. They worked much more closely with informal caring networks and developed new ones.

The outcomes of the Birmingham project are yet to be evaluated. All three of the other examples can claim some success, but also raise issues which still need to be fully resolved in the context of developing user-controlled services. The service in Dinnington coped with a sixfold increase in demand with increased speed, efficiency, and effectiveness.

Overall, too, the Kent scheme was more cost effective than traditional alternatives. It was also preferred by both the old people and their relatives. The old people lived longer, stayed out of residential care longer, and said they felt better.

A users' committee has always been a part of the first support unit opened in Sheffield. The intention was for this to be a management committee, but it has never really been more than a steering committee which has taken decisions about fund-raising activities, letting of premises, and social activities. There is evidence of a certain reluctance on the part of users, who come from a very traditional village community, to take on what are considered to be the proper functions of professionals. It is felt that the move towards a management committee was attempted too quickly with a group of predominantly elderly users, to whom the concept of managing their own service was foreign. The process of determining a constitution for such a committee within a group with more limited responsibilities might have assisted people unused to being in this situation to take on more control.

The Dinnington project also had problems in securing an effective lay participation in managing and running the project. Both this and the Sheffield scheme again serve as reminders that, by definition, user control cannot be imposed. It implies a significant shift in people's expectations of welfare services, particularly in the case of elderly people whose perceptions of such services are rooted in the workhouse. The process of empowerment is as important as the objective. In addition, the Dinnington scheme failed to carry all service providers along and the home help service chose not to be integrated, neither did interdisciplinary management develop to run an interdisciplinary service. This latter serves as a reminder that the process of user empowerment must also take on board the effect that this will have on staff. The experience of many workers in SSDs is that they have little control over the nature and quantity of service that they are able to provide. Consultation with workers about service developments may be both limited and tokenistic. The process of empowering users must involve workers and not exploit them.

The issues raised by the Kent scheme provide another perspective on this matter. Here the concern is with the possible exploitation of low-paid workers in order to devise services more acceptable to the user. The rate per visit (an average of one to two hours) for paid helpers varied between £1 and £3 at 1977 prices. The paid helpers refused to bargain about their fee and were reluctant to talk about the extra work they had done, leaving the social workers to protect the helpers from their own discomfort. There is a danger that schemes such as this add to the development of low-paid casual labour which is seen primarily as women's work.

Controlling and organizing the services

Having looked at some of the problems and possibilities of user control in four specific service areas, in this final section we examine various proposals about the general organization of services, including those contained in the Griffiths and Wagner reports.[1] Inevitably, various ways of disaggregating large-scale services – including both decentralization and the creation of competitive markets – require discussion as they relate to the personal social services, notwithstanding the general discussion elsewhere in this volume. We will do so against some of the generally accepted criteria relating to user control – access, choice, information, representation, and redress. To these we add three others to reflect the general public interest – accountability, cost-effectiveness, and participation.

Access to which services?

There is no doubt that the present strategic and operational fragmentation of services creates major barriers to obtaining packages of services most appropriate to people's needs. The Griffiths Report proposes that there should be a single source of publicly financed assistance for community and social care – the local authority social services department. Those other services with fingers in the pie should have their remit restricted – social security to basic income support, housing to bricks and mortar, and the NHS largely to health promotion and acute care. In so far as these authorities stay in the social care business, it will be as agents of social services. This will bring greater strategic coherence at the price of a considerable concentration of power: if the one door is closed there will be no others on which to knock. We consider whether the proposed counterbalances are sufficient on pp. 144–5.

First, however, we must note that the attempt to clarify organizational boundaries has not been entirely successful. There are uncertainties over the care of people whose chronic conditions have both medical and social elements. There is an attempt to ensure the exchange of information between GPs and social services, but the relationship with community nursing and medical consultants is inadequately explored. For example, to limit the role of psycho-geriatricians to diagnosis and active treatment, when most elderly, mentally infirm people will be in residential care or in the community, would be crass. Similarly, the balance between cash and kind – over disability and carers' benefits, for example – is not properly examined.

In general, the Griffiths Report attempts to clarify the bases on which services co-operate by reducing them to one – simple market exchange. The social services department will specify the help it wants from others and will pay for it. Given that coherent packages of care attuned to users' needs must cross organizational boundaries, it remains to be seen whether this is an adequate basis on which to work. Recently there has been a marked, but fragile, expansion of multi-disciplinary teams. Would they survive and prosper under the Griffiths' system?

Furthermore it is unclear what impact the accompanying changes in the method of central finance will have upon the huge variations in the amount and mix of services which are acknowledged to exist (e.g. Audit Commission 1986). Griffiths rightly claims that the present formulas for distributing central funds to health, social security, and local authority services take no account of community care needs, and his report proposes an earmarked grant to do so. How that grant system will affect the existing variations is unclear. Will there be a levelling up or down? Already there are grounds for concern over the proposals to integrate publicly funded by privately run residential care. It is assumed that the housing elements will be covered by Housing Benefit, leaving social services to pay the rest for care. This considerably understates housing costs and forces a cross-subsidy from social services. In the long run this forms a major incentive to develop community-based alternatives. In the short run community services may be cut to cope with the resultant cash crisis! In short, the theory suggests easier access to a wider range of services and incentives to develop others in accord with users' wishes. The reality may be very different, depending crucially on the level of funding.

The Griffiths Report insists that it is for others to set out a clear philosophy of community care, and clear statements of policies and priorities which are in line with it. Without these, we have no way of knowing, for example, at what point family care ceases to be the best solution, what level of stress carers must suffer before they can expect help, and what sort of respite care and preventive help they should have, as opposed to substitute services when they can no longer cope.

Equally, the crucial issue of service quality will remain obscure. In the Griffiths model the care manager will become a managing agent, letting out contracts which specify the nature, amount, frequency, and quality of services in return for a price. This will be technically difficult, controversial, and hard to enforce. Already the proposals in the Wagner Report over the qualifications of people running residential services and users' rights to single bedrooms have aroused controversy, despite their comparative simplicity – we consider whether care can be treated as a commodity in this way on p. 145. One temptation will be for care managers to rely upon a limited number of agents providing specialist services. This may discourage attempts to gain access to ordinary, normal services for stigmatized groups of people. Here, the Local Government Act, 1988, with its emphasis on tightly defined competitive tenders and its restrictions on the insertion of wider social responsibility clauses into contracts, could act as a further pressure towards residential specialist services.

Access – to whom?

In effect, the Griffiths Report proposes three tests to determine who obtains publicly organized services and at what price. Do they have an officially recognized need? Is it of sufficient priority given cash-limited funds and the competing needs of others? Can they afford to pay? The general criteria for priority would be set by central and local politicians, and interpreted by named care managers who would identify those in need, assess needs, decide what packages of care were appropriate, taking into account users' and carers' wishes, and ration services.

In determining priorities, however, Griffiths echoes current Conservative orthodoxy: the family is the major source of support and public services should be seen as back-ups or substitutes of last resort: even then, means-testing should be consistently applied. The costs of disability and social distress are only to be borne collectively if individuals and families cannot bear them (paras 3.2, 3.3). Some of his predictions for the future go further in that direction: tax incentives, insurance schemes, and occupational cover for these eventualities feature prominently, with no acknowledgement of the resulting inequalities (para. 39). There are, of course, more extreme positions than this. Minford (1987), for example, would impose new legal obligations on people to care for members of their extended family, with a private market growing up to help them meet those duties. The complexities of family form are cheerfully ignored.

In response, the Left seem to be caught between, on the one hand, aspirations to a service for all – especially giving greater rights to women carers – and, on the other, accepting the present reality of a residual service for disadvantaged minorities. One suggested way out of this dilemma is the social maintenance organization, in which social services departments act as care managers and brokers, irrespective of whether services are paid for from public, occupational, or private funds (Davies 1987). This would at least ensure that all social groups received the same sort of services, preserve a form of collectivism, and recruit some of the sharp elbows of the middle class to campaign for good services.

Accessible and responsive services

How services are organized has a profound effect upon accessibility. There are three ways of organizing them: by function (e.g. home helps), by user group (e.g. adults with handicaps), and by locality. All departments permutate all three, but at different levels and in different mixes.

We do not believe that large-scale public services organized along functional lines can deliver accessible, responsive care. The resulting long hierarchies, the divisions between services, the rigid functional specialisms, and the distances between resource controllers and the human consequences of their actions are all inimical to the interests of users. Relevant, coherent, flexible packages of care are almost impossible to construct in such a system. Functional specialsms are needed, but at lower levels of organization and, probably, not those that exist at present.

The Griffiths proposals would remove those functional specialisms from the front line. Locally based care managers, with their own budgets, would act as gatekeepers and orchestrators of care, purchasing the mix of services they judge to be most appropriate to a user's needs, either from within the department or outside it. The care manager thus becomes the primary user, to whom those services must be responsive. This assumes the existence not only of financially skilled local managers, but also of financial information and management systems specifying the true costs of a wide variety of services. Whilst areas such as Surrey have moved some way along this road, many will be starting almost from scratch.

The need for devolved management is acknowledged by commentators from all shades of the political spectrum, provided it is balanced by clearer policy directives within which managers must work. Only in this way can informed dialogue and effective negotiations with users and with various providers be developed. The basis of this devolution is, however, more contentious. The common building block is the neighbourhood: the Dinnington project and the various 'patch' experiments are examples. The protagonists of this approach suggest that multi-purpose general practitioners, with access to specialist help, can provide a high-quality service, enhanced by their new specialist knowledge of neighbourhood networks (e.g. Bayley *et al.* 1987). They argue, further, that the general growth of services and the shift away from large-scale institutional provision make possible the localized supply of a good range of services, without sacrificing too much specialist care.

An alternative is to base services around a user group, as in the Kent Community Care Project. Protagonists of this approach stress the specialist skills developed and the knowledge of special needs, the ability to link with other specialist services (e.g. health specialists), to be based upon a specialist, capital-intensive facility, and to mesh formal care and informal communities of interest, which may be geographically dispersed. Research into the needs of particular groups (e.g. people with visual handicaps) has reinforced this view, stressing the relative ignorance of such special needs among 'general practitioners'. Against it, there is always the danger of specialist ghettos developing.

Neither approach is mutually exclusive and the best compromise will vary according to the social make-up of the locality, the needs of the particular group, and the special skills currently available to them (see Bulmer 1987). The balance of formal and informal resources is crucial: inequalities due to class, race, age, and gender mean that informal resources are likely to be in inverse proportion to needs – in individuals, families, and communities. Whilst all services should demonstrate care in and with the community, in some localities and for some groups the emphasis will need to be upon care for, rather than care by, the community. Resource distribution must reflect this.

However, decentralization *per se* has no necessary association with user control and there is widespread evidence that proximity does not necessarily lead to integration. Bayley *et al.* (1987) identify three stages:

a)   Work 'outside the community' in large hierarchies, with demand filtered through a formal system and fieldworkers working reactively with individualized 'cases', mostly using their own department's resources and contacting other agencies sporadically. There is little or no community dimension and little focus on prevention.

b)   Work 'alongside the community' in local units with direct public access to fieldworkers who work in closer contact with other public services. Faced with higher demand and at earlier points in the development of problems, the fieldworkers focus on the clients' networks and call on more formal resources, but preventive community-based work is an adjunct to mainstream work with clients.

c)   Work 'within the community': local workers from several agencies operate as a team; links with the community are far less formal and they respond to high demands using formal and informal networks, and work with groups or streets as well as individuals and their networks. Thus the roles of 'treatment agent' or 'counsellor' remain, but the other traditional roles of 'advocate', 'broker', and 'co-ordinator' are emphasized. To these are added new roles of 'network consultant' and 'entrepreneur'. Similar roles have been stressed in the Kent Community Care Project.

There remains a further question about the relationship between formal and informal care. Who sets the terms of it? Bulmer (1987) notes the very different motivations and operational philosophies on which these two types of care are based. He predicts that one likely outcome of the attempt to 'harness' informal care is that it will become colonized and invaded by the values of the formal system. Beresford and Croft's critical evaluation of the East Sussex patch reorganization makes a similar point:

> The dominant tradition in personal social services as in British social policy generally has been prescriptive. This is as true of fabian and marxist analyses as of utilitarian and thatcherite ones. In spite of their participatory aspirations, patch and community social work have so far failed to break this mould. Instead of enabling a developmental process that involves people and makes it possible for them to ask their own questions, patch offers *its* answers.
>
> (Beresford and Croft 1986: 286)

In the Griffiths scheme it is clear whose answers count. The care managers will adjudicate in any conflicts of interest between users, carers, service providers, and the public interest. And cost will be a major feature in how the latter is defined.

Choice

As Potter (1988) notes, the principle of consumer choice cannot be treated as an absolute in any public service, given the potential conflicts of interest between users and taxpayers. It is even more difficult to apply to some personal social services, when the choices of family members may collide and society denies people the freedom to behave in certain ways. Nevertheless, we have stressed the importance of maximizing choice within these boundaries and have explored various ways of doing so. These include:

- developing 'partnership practice' in which information is shared, the goals of any task-centred work are mutually agreed, and alternative packages of services are offered (e.g. Fisher *et al.* 1986: 139)
- using interpreters and facilitators to help people with communication difficulties express preferences and adopting means of communication which they find easiest to use
- undertaking consumer research. We particularly applaud approaches such as that of Kuh and her colleagues (Kuh *et al.* 1986). Their survey of young people with handicaps was wide ranging and the questions open ended. Conflicts of view between users, carers, and professionals were allowed for, yet aggregate measures of overall need were developed. The results were incorporated into

individual casework, and user and carer groups were created to discuss common needs. From these, self-advocacy groups, including one for young people with mental handicaps, have grown

- using trial periods before decisions are made about long-term care packages. This is particularly important when users' past experience is limited. Some consumer surveys (e.g. Wilcocks *et al.* 1982) confirm Morrison's conclusion: 'people want what they know rather than know what they want' (1988: 207)

- developing user-orientated performance indicators. The Audit Commission currently represents the interests of ratepayers in its concern with 'value for money', but it is not enjoined to take a service user's view and has been rightly criticized for its neglect of such concerns in favour of least cost solutions (e.g. Miller 1986; Kline and Mallaber 1986). To do so would entail collecting users' views alongside those of professionals in the regular information series used to generate indicators, and considering the implications of those indicators in dialogues between service providers and users

- attempting to reverse the traditional power relations in long-term residential care, so that the residents determine such critical day-to-day matters as when to get up, what to wear, what and when to eat, and when to use the WC – for all of which people with severe disabilities are dependent on others (e.g. Dartington *et al.* 1981). Various proposals in the Wagner Report develop this principle (paras 4.5 – 4.14)

- providing intensive packages of domiciliary, day, and relief care which act as a realistic alternative to long-term residential care (Griffiths and Wagner reports).

These and other specific developments need to be pursued with vigour, but what of more general aspects of service organization?

Griffiths makes two main suggestions. First, public sector managers must internalize the interests and values of the 'consumer' and make them central, just as managers in the private sector are doing (Griffiths 1988). Second, the number of providers should be enlarged and they should compete with each other (Griffiths Report 1988). These suggestions fail to address a number of problems. The question of conflicting opinions and interests is not tackled: here, attempts to develop new philosophies of public-service management which recognize the centrality of political choice may bear greater fruits (Clarke and Stewart 1987).

Nor is the power imbalance between users and providers effectively tackled. Griffiths (1988) argues for a strengthening of the users' position, but his report on community care gives limited attention to this and some of the recommendations may well exacerbate the problem. The monopoly power of the care manager is not countered by any appeal mechanisms or suggestions that independent advocates are necessary. The role of voluntary bodies in providing such a voice is noted, but the potential stifling of it if those same bodies become providing agents of the social services department is ignored and there are no proposals to strengthen that voice. In effect, as well, the provider of long-term care is often in a monopoly position once someone is admitted, since there are few chances of leaving and many means of discouraging the expression of dissatisfaction.

A prerequisite for the exercise of real choice, of course, is for people with a specific recognized need to be granted substantive rights to services. A cash-limited public service faced with long-suppressed and growing demand is unlikely to sign such blank cheques. Perhaps this is the reason why Griffiths gives such little encouragement to voucher schemes, such as that proposed by Bosanquet (1987). Similarly, the Wagner Committee only called for further study of the idea (para. 3.23). The complex specification of needs and rights – necessarily far more elaborate than those recently abandoned as too complicated in the Supplementary Benefit system – is another drawback to voucher schemes. Equally, experience of the nearest thing to a voucher – residential care financed by Supplementary Benefit – demonstrates the vulnerability of some social service users in a dispersed, competitive, and poorly policed system. Finally, choice implies the existence of a surplus: this is not usual in tightly rationed, publicly financed services, where surplus is seen as waste.

Information

Information takes on an even greater importance in the public sector, because the services at stake are likely to be crucial to consumers' welfare, and because the imbalance in the amount of information possessed by providers and consumers is so wide.... [People] need information about goals and objectives, about the standards of services authorities aim to provide and the standards achieved; about their rights to a service and their responsibilities in using them; about the way authorities are structured and the decision-making process; about why decisions are taken and about what those decisions actually are.

(Potter 1988: 153)

A few SSDs take seriously the need to inform the public about their services. For example, they fulfil their duty under the Chronically Sick and Disabled Persons Act to publicize the services available. Some also provide written information about particular services to potential users, such as children about to enter care. Most do not. The closely related brokerage function – including putting people in touch with services outside the department's remit – is often left to the discretion of individual employees and is dependent on their knowledge. This brokerage function becomes more critical if social workers as case managers become gatekeepers to a much wider range of services. In such circumstances the provision of alternative sources of information becomes even more critical. Wagner calls on the public library service to undertake this task (para. 3.2). The same committee rightly recommends that authorities actively seek out informal carers, to discover their needs and inform them of the services available (para. 5.9).

Users' access to the information held in their personal files is also an important safeguard. When the 1987 Access to Personal Files Act is brought into force this will give service users limited access to their social service records, and the chance to obtain copies and have inaccuracies corrected. This will not apply to information collected in the past, or to information given by others on a confidential basis. Equally there are restrictions on access in the case of adoption records and those on people with mental disorder. The potential conflict between the interests of parents and children is again reflected in that parents do not have an absolute right to see records on their children. The new Act consolidates the pioneering work of authorities such as Barnet and Oldham, who acted in advance of the legislation and have developed new recording systems which allow such access, whilst protecting confidentiality. The DHSS has also supported the initiative (e.g. Circular LAC (83) 14). Events in Cleveland have also highlighted the importance of giving children and parents access to – and a voice in – what goes on in case conferences.

However, the quotation from Potter correctly implies that there is a more general level of information necessary – about policies and priorities. Only then can people respond to the political choices being made on their behalf and politicians be held accountable. The Griffiths Report makes a strong plea for such political visibility. It calls for a responsible Minister, a separate money vote and debate, a clear philosophy, and policies in line with resources. Similarly, local politicians are enjoined to set clear local priorities (paras 5.7 and 6.19–6.22). Politicians are notoriously reluctant to accept this classic statement of their responsibilities. Informal indications are that these elements – including the existence of a local social service authority with its own political legitimacy – are the ones which are causing most concern in government circles. The government's reluctance to enact proper freedom of information legislation is another symptom of the same malaise.

These are crucial issues for personal social services. They are, after all, dealing with complex and variable needs arising from problems which the rest of society would rather have hidden from view: Webb and Wistow see social workers as modern nightsoil workers (1987: 212). In these circumstances concealed administrative discretion and supply-side economics are a dangerous cocktail. Death by a thousand tiny cuts can be transferred from income maintenance to social care.

Redress

The need for proper procedures of complaint and redress has been brought into sharp focus by events at Nye Bevan Lodge in Southwark, and in Cleveland. More recently there have been calls for Birmingham Council to pay for independent legal advice and legal action for children in its care who may have been abused (*Birmingham Evening Mail*, 7 September 1988). Such cumbersome mechanisms will be necessary until there is a decent system of no fault compensation. In their survey of local authority complaints procedures, Lewis *et al.* (1987) found those in social services to be the best of a very poor or non-existent bunch. Generally, there existed 'a submerged body of complaints which administrative cultures helped to suppress'.

Not before time, there seems to be a general consensus that something must be done. The Wagner Committee recommends that each residential provider must have a clear and well-publicized system including someone accessible to complain to, someone to ascertain the full facts, a means of adjudicating, and a source of independent advocacy for those unable to present their case unaided (para. 3.19). Similarly, the National Consumer Council/National Institute for Social Work report (1988) calls for a single, coherent, simple, speedy, and comprehensible system. It should contain an independent element and, perhaps, the appointment of a clients' rights officer. The report condemned most existing procedures as 'woefully inadequate'.

In a dispersed, competitive system of provision, such as that envisaged by Griffiths, the importance of systems which are seen to be fair is even greater and they must be closely linked to other mechanisms of quality control. They are, however, a second line of defence. Effective means of quality assurance comes first.

Representation and participation

We have already cited many ways in which one form of representation – enabling the users' views to be heard – could be strengthened. User surveys, user unions, and self-advocacy, independent advocates, pressure groups, implementing the Disabled Persons Act, 1986, and changing child care law to ensure basic procedural justice are some of these. There are, however, major impediments to their enthusiastic adoption. The first is the belief that it is the professional who is the expert and the best arbiter of conflicting views and interests. This view of social workers has many critics, from Barbara Wootton (1959) to Lord Justice Butler-Sloss (1988). It is none the less pervasive and likely to be reinforced by some aspects of the Griffiths and Wagner reports, both of which assume that care managers/nominated social workers can combine the roles of advocate and resource rationer.

One effect of this view is the professionals' insistence that problems and solutions must fit their boundaries, categories, and definitions. This is a major source of frustration for users and their advocates – not least elected councillors. At all levels of the process, opposing views of the world are likely to be excluded from the crucial decision-making forum, be it a case conference or a caucus meeting (e.g. the 'non-competing contradiction' discovered by Saunders (1979)). This goes a long way towards explaining professionals' ambivalence to carers: the 'co-operative' ones are seen as co-workers; the 'stroppy' ones are seen as second-order clients.

Long hierarchies make matters worse since they insulate the resource controllers from the users. A major impact of the Birmingham Special Action Project has been to expose senior managers to the expression of 'raw pain' from both users and carers (Jowell and Prior 1989). Griffiths (1988) both applauds and practises various ways of getting close to the customer as a means of eliminating this problem and he is sanguine about the presence of advocates and pressure groups. But it is left to the managers to direct this process and his report does nothing to build in countervailing forces if they do not. There is, for example, no call to build in rights of representation as a condition of concluding contracts with commercial or voluntary agencies. Of course the Local Government Act, 1988, excludes such clauses.

There is a bigger, but related danger. The social services department would be the single point of access to publicly funded care and central government would control a large portion of its financing via specific grants. We have already noted the rumours that government will seek to make this process less visible. We must also note that many Ministers do not share Griffiths' view of pressure groups: along with others in the New Right, they see them as threats to the proper conduct of government which should be ignored or, better still, suppressed (e.g. Hurd 1986). The likely scarcity of central resources and the high political cost of raising extra money via the poll tax is almost bound to force local politicians and professionals to keep the lid on the expression of user wishes.

In contrast, we see a need to encourage such expression. Many users of social services are demoralized and beset by other pressures, and their past experience has taught them not to expect to exert much control over their own lives. They are hard to unionize and many of the community care initiatives – laudable in themselves – will further disperse them into smaller units. There need to be forums in which they can articulate their own accounts of their needs and explore ways of meeting them. Here, social services need to learn from the 'bottom-up' approaches of community groups and the women's movement.

Such forums should be accessible in terms of the time at which meetings are held, their location, the language in which they are conducted, the availability of advocates and interpreters, the information made available in advance, and the encouragement of participation from all. The model of a council committee is not appropriate. It will often be more appropriate for service users to have the opportunity to meet with each other and develop their ideas together, without the intervention of professionals or council members, before entering into a dialogue. Progress may well be slow, but a commitment to participation must allow time and space for growth. Given such space users may well reject solutions which are constrained within existing organizational boundaries, so the forums themselves should relate to a range of services.

One of the weaknesses of the Griffiths Report is that it tends to treat care as a commodity, to be packaged, priced, and competed over. In at least some parts of the Wagner Report (1988: 73) it is seen rather as a process, whose prime purpose is to enhance the independence of users, or later on to allow them to relinquish it as slowly and with as much dignity as possible. To achieve this, it is often important to go beyond representation and encourage participation. Management control can be devolved to local committees. Any attempts to do this must take staff along with them. The decentralization of services inevitably involves changes in line management structure: workers experiencing such changes may feel doubly vulnerable if users' committees are introduced into this structure. Sheffield MDC has been experimenting with various models of neighbourhood offices and management committees. One of the intended committees was disbanded when the trade union representing home helps objected to the committee being involved in the management of staff. There had been discussion with social workers about this, but not with home helps.

Equally, direct participation can conflict with the traditional roles of elected members. There are also very real questions about the legal position of such committees and conflicting legal opinions have been given in relation to proposed initiatives in Sheffield. One opinion held that it was not possible for the Social Services Committee to delegate its powers to an elected local committee. Another suggested that this would be possible if such a committee were designated as a council subcommittee. However, that would preclude staff from membership, since they could not be both council employees and members of a council committee.

Sheffield has probably gone further than most SSDs in thinking through the implications of power-sharing with users and local citizens, but much is still to be resolved. A group within the department has been considering what might be the elements of the constitution of management committees. Working on the two principles that such committees will in fact manage people, money, equipment, etc., and that such management will be within the context of overall council policy, such a constitution would include details of powers, responsibilities, and accountability relating to the selection of staff, provision of services, and relationships with the local community.

One model currently in operation in the same authority has taken the discussion a stage further to the point at which a group of council tenants employ their own social worker and community worker. Members of the management committee are elected at an AGM from representatives of various community groups on the estate. 'The committee is supported by the two employed workers who are technically members of an advisory sub-committee composed of professional workers with responsibilities for the area' (Derricourt 1987). The highly personalized and sensitive tasks of the social worker have posed their own dilemmas: 'Members have no sense of exerting managerial control over the work of the social worker; rather, the committee asserts that she has to be trusted since the nature of the work is what it is' (Derricourt 1987).

Such moves must not take place in isolation from other democratic processes. There is a grave danger that the involvement of direct users only in the control of each service may be seen as a replacement for general political control – that the multi-purpose local authority may be seen as redundant. Rhodes (1987) warns us that the proponents of such demarchic systems (e.g. Burnheim 1985) ignore the importance of values such as care and citizenship. The threat to disadvantaged groups is more immediate. Having just begun to emerge from the ghettos will they be forced back into them? That those ghettos have become more democratic is small consolation if what their people most want is a life outside. Meanwhile the barriers to their access to normal, valued services may well be raised. Will schools which opt out be anxious to take in pupils with social, mental, or physical handicaps? One of the tests of a service proposed by the Labour Party review group on consumers and the community is: 'Does it safeguard the larger interest of the community as a whole? How far does it reinforce the mutuality, co-operation and inter-dependence of a healthy and civilised society?' The development of specialist, atomized services, however democratic, is unlikely to pass that test: the system as a whole is likely to become less responsive – except to the pressures of the skilful and powerful.

Thus, as users gain experience and confidence from participation within social services, they should be helped to take a more active part in wider forums. Positive action is needed to ensure that such minority interests are represented. In Islington and elsewhere, attempts are being made to guarantee the participation in neighbourhood committees of old people, of women caring for children and dependent adults, of people with disabilities, and of ethnic minority groups, as well as the direct election of general community representatives. Participation must not, however, be seen as an alternative to other forms of representing users' views. When many of them are demoralized, distressed, and beset by other pressures, such as ill-health and debt, most of the initial progress will come from forms of involvement which are less demanding.

Cost-effectiveness

Value for money is a vital criterion in any public service and there is no doubt that the present system is hugely wasteful of resources, inequitable, and with built-in incentives to remain so (Audit Commission 1986). Equally, the Griffiths proposals would go a long way towards reversing that position, given their stress on greater strategic coherence and the power for local managers to devise flexible ways of meeting needs. Beyond this, however, there are some important dilemmas which make the test of cost-effectiveness notoriously difficult to apply. We can measure inputs, but to monitor processes requires the enthusiastic participation of service providers, whilst outputs and, especially, outcomes are much more difficult to assess.

The resultant problems of defining, specifying, and ensuring quality will be brought into sharp relief in a system of dispersed, competitive provision, such as Griffiths proposes. Does an authority attempt to develop detailed, tightly drawn specifications and to police their implementation? Does it try to choose agents it can trust, and to develop a loosely specified partnership with them, through seats on executive committees or boards of directors? What mix of these two approaches is possible? What mix will the regulations allow?

These problems add to the temptation we have already noted to focus on least-cost, rather than cost-effective, services. To counter such temptations those forces pressing for quality services need to be strengthened. Some people have proposed a quality commission, or

wider terms of reference for such bodies as the Health Advisory Service.
Others have suggested the introduction of family impact statements to
assess the costs and benefits of policies. Support for campaigning
voluntary organizations, which will need to be independent of those
providing services, is another mechanism.

Accountability

> Community care is a poor relation: everybody's distant relative, but
> nobody's baby.... Nothing could be more radical in the public sector
> than to spell out responsibilities, insist on performance and
> accountability and to evidence that action is being taken; and even
> more radical, to match policy with appropriate resources and agreed
> time scales.
>
> (Griffiths Report 1988: paras 9 and 20)

Griffiths' solution to these problems is straightforward: a clear line of
accountability and authority, with the Minister responsible for resources
and policies, the social services authority setting local priorities and
developing management systems, the named care manager accountable
for services to the customer and, in turn, holding service providers to
account. Both the desire and the capacity of these various actors to
conform to that solution have to be questioned.

At the national political level there remains a massive uncertainty
about the balance of responsibility between individuals, families, and
wider society in the face of particular adversities, and no desire to debate
the subject. Equally, it is much more politically convenient to give
general powers and duties to lower-tier authorities, with the leeway to
interpret them according to the level of resources the economy 'can
afford'. Why create hostages to fortune by specifying what can and
cannot be done when a few isolated, short-term, but well-publicized
demonstration projects are usually enough to reduce the clamour for
action? Before Ministers and mandarins feel free to develop clear
comprehensive statements about policies and priorities, they will need
to escape from the shackles of tight Treasury control and supply-side
economics (Walker 1984).

Local authority councillors are likely to be caught in the same trap.
Central controls over planning and resource allocation will be tighter
and more specific than at present. Councils' only scope for raising more
is through increases in a poll tax purpose-built to discourage such
actions, or via increased charges. The temptation will again be to push
down the line uncomfortable choices about whom not to help. One of the
alleged reasons for the latest sacking of the Director of Social Services
in Brent is that he exposed the consequences of political decisions,

whilst refusing to recommend which cuts to make. Griffiths' means of forcing authorities to specify and cost objectives – and to consult widely in the process – is to make this a condition for payment of central government grant (Griffiths Report 1988: para. 6.35). Given the politics surrounding this process and the limited capacity of central government to assess, monitor, and insist on adherence to such plans, this is unlikely to be an effective safeguard. Paradoxically, in a dispersed, decentralized system in which power is devolved to local managers, there is a far greater need for the local authority to specify what are its priorities and its criteria for an acceptable service. Only then can such values as equity be protected.

To ensure such protection, it is also necessary to exercise effective oversight. The capacity of councillors and senior officers to do so is already open to serious question, due to the complexity, scale, and specialized and hidden nature of many services (Day and Klein 1987). Griffiths acknowledges that these problems would be increased in a dispersed, competitive system and calls for the urgent and large-scale development of information systems (Griffiths Report 1988: paras 28, 8.1). These would be closely aligned to clear statements about obligations to various audiences, including users 'as part of the total management process' (Griffiths 1988: 201). The place of elected councillors in this process, be they front-bench or back-bench, is not explored.

We do not share the same faith in a top-down, managerialist and relatively closed system. The process needs to be opened up to a wide range of influences, including the decentralization of political control. Lipsky (1980), among others, shows how social workers and other 'street-level bureaucrats' are placed in a paradoxical position of considerable power in relation to users and considerable weakness in relation to policy-makers. The paradox becomes more acute in the Griffiths model. Social workers are the guardians of access and quality for users. Unlike those above them, they cannot avoid making hard decisions on priorities. Unlike doctors they have neither the background of universal provision, nor the respectable users, nor yet the legitimacy to challenge the position in which they are placed.

What happens when a care manager, having exhausted her budget, is faced with a high-priority need? How often can she ask for more before her managerial abilities are questioned? How feasible is it to renegotiate the contracts for people of lower priority? Or what if she strongly suspects, but has no proof, that someone on her caseload is receiving poor-quality care in an establishment run by a powerful, well-connected voluntary or commercial agency? Does she then remember that the bearer of bad tidings is often punished? Lipsky's analysis suggests that, in such circumstances, officials make life tolerable for themselves at the expense of vulnerable service users. There is evidence that this already happens: difficult, exposed jobs in unsupportive authorities – including directorships – are hard to fill; high-priority cases are left unallocated to avoid overload and its attendant risks; services for unpopular groups are not developed; attempts are made to throw a protective wall around those who are shown to have made mistakes, since the system is thought to be impossible and unfair. The appropriate people will not be held to account unless the process becomes more visible and open to challenge at all levels.

In conclusion

The picture painted in this chapter of the future of the personal social services and the possibilities of user empowerment is one of considerable complexity and conflict. We recognize that this raises more dilemmas and questions than answers.

Ultimately, the resolution of this complexity has to be achieved at national policy level. The various proposals currently receiving national attention are likely to be dangerous to the interests of the majority of service users, and the Griffiths recommendations are no exception. They concentrate power without providing adequate checks and balances. In the present climate – and despite the intentions of their author – they may well produce a more coherent, efficient, and better-managed system for producing specialist, stigmatized services for stigmatized groups. Alongside them will develop services more sensitive to the interests of users, so long as they can pay. This is the consequence of the consumerist model of empowerment.

We advocate a different model of user empowerment and control: one which is based on collective solutions to the kinds of problems we have identified. Throughout this chapter we have tried to give examples of ways of developing and enhancing user control at the various levels of the decision-making and service-delivery structure. Many of these are tentative, inadequately tested, and messy: liable themselves to generate conflict and frustration. They are also generally small in scale. None the less, they represent positive developments, and it is through such developments that we see the potential for a strengthening of the collective voice and capacity for action of social service users. This spread of empowerment at the more local levels – contact between users and workers; within the unit; at service level management and planning – is leading to real changes in the experiences of some service users and ultimately could influence a shift in the structure of power relationships at the national level.

Note

1 The government's initial response to the Griffiths proposals was announced as this book was going to press. The discussion here thus refers only to the original recommendations in the Griffiths Report.

References

Audit Commission (1986) *Making a Reality of Community Care*, London: HMSO.

Bailey, R. and Brake, M. (eds) (1975) *Radical Social Work*, London: Edward Arnold.

Balloch, S. (1985) *Advice and Advocacy in Local Government*, Community Services Topic Paper 1.11, Birmingham: Department of Social Administration, University of Birmingham.

Banks, A. N. (1986) 'Dissertation on Participation by Consumers in the Organization of Mental Health Centres', unpublished M.Soc.Sc. Dissertation, Department of Social Administration, University of Birmingham.

Barnes, M. (1987) 'Editorial', *Social Services Research* 2.

——(in press) 'New perspectives on management information', in D. Pia and J. Tibbett (eds) *Performance Review in Social Work Agencies*, London: Jessica Kingsley Publishers.

Barnes, M., Bowl, R., and Fisher, M. (forthcoming) *Sectioned: Social Services and the Mental Health Act 1983*, London: Routledge.

Barnes, M. and Miller, N. (eds) (1988) 'Performance measurement in personal social services', *Research Policy and Planning* 6 (2).

Bayley, M., Parker, P., Seyd, R., and Tennant, A. (1987) *Practising Community Care*, Sheffield: JUSSR, University of Sheffield.

Bell, L. (1987) 'Survivors speak out', in I. Barker and E. Peck (eds) *Power in Strange Places, User Empowerment in Mental Health Services*, London: Good Practices in Mental Health.

Beresford, P. and Croft, S. (1986) *Whose Welfare? Private Care or Public Services?*, Brighton: Lewis Cohen Urban Studies Centre.

Bosanquet, N. (1987) 'Buying care', in D. Clode, C. Parker, and S. Etherington (eds) *Towards the Sensitive Bureaucracy: Consumers, Welfare and the New Pluralism*, Aldershot: Gower.

Bulmer, M. (1987) *The Social Basis of Community Care*, London: Allen & Unwin.

Burnheim, J. (1985) *Is Democracy Possible? The Alternative to Electoral Politics*, Cambridge: Polity Press.

Butler-Sloss Report (1988), *Report of the Inquiry into Child Abuse in Cleveland*, CMD 413, London: HMSO.

Camden Mental Health Consortium (1986) *Mental Health Priorities in Camden as We See Them. The Consumer Viewpoint*, London.

Challis, D. and Davies, B. (1986) *Case Management in Community Care*, Aldershot: Gower.

Clarke, M. and Stewart, J. (1987) 'The public service orientation: issues and dilemmas', *Public Administration* 65 (2).

Colvin, M. (1984) 'Children, care and the local state', in M. D. A. Freeman (ed.) *State, Law and the Family*, London: Tavistock.

Dartington, T., Miller, E., and Gwynne, G. (1981) *A Life Together*, London: Tavistock.

Davies, B. (1987) *The Development of the BRITSMO Concept*, unpublished discussion paper 519, Personal Social Services Research Unit, University of Kent.

Davis, K. (1986) *Developing our own definitions: draft for discussion*, unpublished, British Council of Organisations of Disabled People.

Davis, L. (1987) 'Involved in making the decisions', *Community Care*, 24 September.

Day, P. and Klein, R. (1987) *Accountabilities in Five Public Services*, London: Tavistock.

Derricourt, N. (1987) 'Where the tenant is boss', *Community Care*, 11 June.

Firth Report (1987) *Public Support for Residential Care*, Report of a joint central and local government working party, London: DHSS.

Fisher, M., Barnes, M., and Bowl, R. (1987) 'Monitoring the Mental Health Act 1983: implications for policy and practice', *Research, Policy and Planning* (5) 1: 1–8.

Fisher, M., Marsh, P., Phillips, D., and Sainsbury, E. (1986) *In and Out of Care*, London: Batsford and BAAF.

Gladstone, F. (1979) *Voluntary Action in a Changing World*, London: Bedford Square Press.

Griffiths, R. (1988) 'Does the public service sector serve?', *Public Administration* 66, Summer.

Griffiths Report (1988) *Community Care: Agenda for Action*, London: HMSO.

Hoggett, P. and Hambleton, R. (1986) 'Emerging patterns of relationship between local authorities and their committees', *Study Paper 1, The Future Role and Organisation of Local Government*, Birmingham: INLOGOV, University of Birmingham.

Hoggett, P. and Hambleton, R. (eds) (1987) *Decentralisation and Democracy*, Occasional Paper 28, Bristol: SAUS, University of Bristol.

Holden, A. (1980) *Children in Care*, Leamington Spa: Comyn.

Hurd, D. (1986) 'Speech to RIPA Conference', *Politics and Administration*.

Jowell, T. and Prior, D. (1989) 'Caring for the carers', *Social Services Insight*, 2 May.

Kline, R. and Mallaber, J. (1986) *Whose Value? Whose Money? How to Assess the Real Value of Council Services*, Birmingham: Local Government Information Unit, Birmingham Trade Union Resource Centre.

Kuh, D., Lawrence, C., and Tripp, J. (1986) 'Disabled young people: making choices for future living options, *Social Services Research* 4/5: 57–86.

Labour Party (1988) Review Group on Consumers and the Community.

Leonard, P. (1984) *Personality and Ideology: Towards a Materialist Understanding of the Individual*, London: Macmillan.

Lewis, N., Seneviratne, M., and Cracknell, S. (1987) *Complaints Procedures in Local Government*, Sheffield: University of Sheffield, Centre for Criminological and Socio-legal Studies.

Lipsky, M. (1980) *Street Level Bureaucracy*, New York: Russell Sage.

Macdonald, R., Qureshi, H., and Walker, A. (1984) 'Sheffield shows the way', *Community Care*, 18 October.

McGloin, P. and Turnbull, A. (1986) *Parent Participation in Child Abuse Review Conferences, a Research Report*, LB of Greenwich, Directorate of Social Services.

Means, R. (1986) 'The development of social services for elderly people: historical perspectives', in P. Phillipson and A. Walker (eds) *Ageing and Social Policy*, Aldershot: Gower.

Miller, N. (1986), 'Management information and performance measurement in the personal social services', *Social Services Research* 4/5: 7–55.

Minford, P. (1987) 'The role of the social services: a view from the New Right', in M. Loney (ed.) *The State of the Market*, London: Sage.

Mitchell, S. (1987) 'Homing in on help', *Social Services Insight* 2 (39), 25 September.

Morrison, C. (1988) 'Consumerism – lessons from community work', *Public Administration* 66, Summer: 205–14.

National Consumer Council/National Institute for Social Work (1988) *Open to Complaint*, London: NCC.

Peace, S. (1986) 'The forgotten female: social policy and older women', in C. Phillipson and A. Walker (eds) *Ageing and Social Policy*, Aldershot: Gower.

Phillipson, C. and Walker, A. (1986) 'Introduction', *Ageing and Social Policy*, Aldershot: Gower.

Potter, J. (1988) 'Consumerism and the public sector: how well does the coat fit?', *Public Administration* 66, Summer: 149–64.

Rhodes, R. (1987) 'Developing the public service orientation', *Local Government Studies* May/June: 63–73.

Richards, S. (1985) 'A right to be heard', *Social Services Research* 4: 49–56.

Saunders, P. (1979) *Urban Politics*, London: Hutchinson.

Shakespeare, R. (1975) *The Psychology of Handicap*, London: Methuen.

Simpkin, M. (1979), *Trapped Within Welfare, Surviving Social Work*, London: Macmillan.

Social Services Inspectorate (1987) *From Home Help to Home Care*, London: DHSS.

Wagner Report (1988) *A Positive Choice: Report of the Independent Review of Residential Care*, London: HMSO.

Walker, A. (1984) *Social Planning*, Oxford: Blackwell.

Warnock, M. (1987) 'Ethics, decision making and social policy', *Community Care*, 5 November.

Webb, A. and Wistow, G. (1987) *Social Work, Social Care and Social Planning, the Personal Social Services since Seebohm*, London: Longman.

Willcocks, D., Peace, S., and Kellaher, L., with Ring, A. (1982) *The Residential Life of Old People*, Vol. 1, Research Report no. 12, London: Polytechnic of North London, Survey Research Unit.

Wootton, B. (1959) *Social Science and Social Pathology*, London: Allen & Unwin.

7

Health

Christine Hogg

The National Health Service, now forty years old, remains the most popular public service. Even the Conservative government of Mrs Thatcher has been reluctant, in public at least, to question the basis of the NHS as a universal service funded out of general taxation and still largely free at the point of use, though it has taken many actions to undermine it. There are traditions of public involvement in health services as volunteers, as fund raisers, and even, through lay membership of health authorities, as managers. However, the NHS has been rightly criticized for its failure to take account of the customer or the consumer in the way services are provided (DHSS 1983). People often feel that they are not treated as customers, for whose benefit the service is run. They are often kept in ignorance about their illness and treatment, kept waiting in unfriendly environments, and not given the information they need to make decisions for themselves. Out-patient clinics and hospital routines are organized for the convenience of staff, not customers.

In western society, health services have been dominated by the medical profession and the way that it looks at disease and the individual. The medical view of health focuses on:

- the individual and individual causes of illness, such as bacteria, genetics, and unhealthy lifestyles, rather than economic, social, or environmental causes of illness
- the organic nature of illness: disease is seen as an autonomous and potentially manageable alien intruder to be expelled; the interaction of physical symptoms and the personality and circumstances of the individual are minimized
- the cure rather than the prevention of disease: the body is a machine to be repaired by technical means; the most appropriate setting for the 'repair' is in hospital (Hart 1985).

The acceptance of the medical model in turn justifies the power of the medical profession in the health service and the way that resources are allocated (Ham 1985). It also justifies the passivity and acceptance expected of patients and lack of public involvement. A further result is that the medical profession has concentrated on new techniques and 'heroic' cures. There is enthusiasm for new miracle techniques and new drugs, which are introduced with much publicity but can often prove to be damaging and costly failures (Jennett 1984). After each failure, hopes are transferred to the next generation of advances.

This optimistic faith in medical advances means that there is no real tradition of scientific evaluation in the NHS (Council for Science and Society 1982). Randomized controlled trials to evaluate new research and techniques are often opposed by clinicians on ethical grounds (Challah and Mays 1986). The perceptions and experiences of users are rarely included in evaluation. 'Success' for medical and surgical techniques tends to be defined in terms of length, not quality, of life following treatment, often without comparison with the length and quality of life which might be expected if no treatment were given. As a result, techniques are introduced which can sometimes have devastating effects on individuals and families.

It is because of this predominance of the medical model of health that acute hospital services have been given priority, while public health, primary health care, community services, and services for elderly, mentally ill, and mentally handicapped people have been, and continue to be, neglected (Hogg 1988). Prevention of disease through environmental measures or national policies has been largely ignored and separated from the NHS. The concentration on treatment has sustained the view that there is potentially unlimited public demand for health services. New techniques and drugs tend to be more expensive than existing ones but mean that more people can be offered some treatment: since spending on the NHS has not increased to meet the demands of new techniques, this underfunding over many years has resulted in the financial crisis of the 1980s.

However, in addition to the escalating costs, the National Health Service has lost a sense of direction in the 1980s. The financial and policy crisis has encouraged consideration of alternative ways of funding health care, including private insurance, income-generation schemes, and charitable donations. Whatever their other consequences, the adoption of such schemes would mean the end of the NHS as a public service, rooted in the principles of equity and universality.

It is argued here that the lack of involvement of users in planning and managing health services has contributed to the problems which the NHS is experiencing. Various proposals are being made for increasing consumer choice. These include the reduction of waiting times, improved quality in 'hotel' services, and increased rights to information.

The proposals of some of these reformers from the political Right culminated in the White Paper, *Working for Patients* (DoH 1989; Pirie and Butler 1988). Though the proposals aspire to give individual users more choice in health care, they may only promote choice between the NHS and private practice. Not only does this approach accept the medical model of illness, and is thereby likely to encourage further priority being given to the 'cures' provided by acute medicine rather than creating a healthier environment; but it will also do nothing to help achieve a balance between the health needs of different groups of patients, or determine proper priorities in health services, or ensure that the interests of vulnerable groups are protected.

Against this background, this chapter considers the role of users in the health service on four dimensions: (i) the relationship between service providers and users; (ii) complaints, audit, and redress; (iii) the NHS and the local community; (iv) the accountability and involvement of users in formulating national policies.

Strengthening the role of users is the way that a vision and sense of direction can return to the NHS, and a rational basis for making priorities and allocating resources be established. Some suggestions for a framework for strengthening the role of users are put forward in conclusion.

The relationship between service providers and users

The individual has a number of basic rights in relation to the NHS. These include rights:

- to be provided with health services appropriate to their needs regardless of financial means or where they live, including the right to be referred to any hospital, regardless of where they live (under the NHS Act, 1977)
- to be treated with reasonable skill and care (under common law)
- to refuse or accept treatment and to leave hospital when s/he wishes (under common law)
- to make a complaint (under Hospital Complaints Act, 1985)
- to seek redress if care or treatment is not provided to a 'reasonable' standard (under common law).

These rights are difficult to enforce in law, mainly because of the difficulties people have in obtaining information before, during, and after treatment. Traditionally the user is seen as the patient, a view which assumes that expertise is with the professional and that the user is passive. Patients are considered not to need information. Information may even be dangerous for them, and responsible staff should withhold it in their best interest. The power in the relationship lies with professional staff, who have expertise which users find difficult to assess or question. Furthermore, when using health services, people are generally ill and this makes them particularly vulnerable.

However, to be successful, health services require the active involvement of the individual. First, those seeking help from the health service are not passive recipients of treatment. For example, it is estimated that up to half of the people prescribed drugs do not take them as instructed. (Evans and Spellman 1983). People have control of their own habits and behaviour. These may have caused or exacerbated their illness, and will clearly affect the results of treatment.

Second, medical diagnosis and treatment are inexact. Even for common diseases such as cancer, whether someone has surgery, drugs, or radiotherapy, or a combination of all three, or no treatment at all, is determined by the judgement of the doctor, which is not necessarily the same as an understanding based on research as to which will achieve the best results. Some treatments are more hazardous and painful than the disease itself. New techniques are sometimes introduced without evaluation and can prove dangerous as well as ineffective. Equally, well-established techniques continue to be used long after it is proved that they are ineffective or unnecessary. For example, it was first established in 1937 that radical mastectomies were no more effective than merely removing the tumour, yet even in the 1980s mastectomies are still commonly undertaken, especially in the USA (Greenberg and Stevens 1986). Fetal heart monitors, which are common in all maternity units, have proved to be no more effective than monitoring with a stethoscope and can give false signs of distress leading to unnecessary Caesarean sections and forceps deliveries. While this is now acknowledged, there are no plans to discontinue their use (Prentice and Lind 1987).

In spite of all this, doctors are often reluctant to share the uncertainty of diagnosis and prognosis with the individual or carers. Bryan Jennett, a leading neuro-surgeon, has described the background to this:

> Like the church from which it had emerged, the medical profession depended much on a combination of authority and mysticism or magic; also on the unquestioning faith of those to whom it ministered. That was no bad thing at a time when few medical interventions had any direct therapeutic benefit and the placebo effect was all important. Placebo, first used as a medical term in 1811, is defined in the *OED* as 'medicine given more to please than to benefit'.

(Jennett 1984: 10)

However, times have changed, and the drugs and techniques available to doctors are powerful, hazardous, and often toxic (which, of course, is why they have an effect on the disease). Now surgery, radiotherapy, and chemotherapy are sometimes given to dying patients as 'palliatives', the modern placebo. They are not always given to relieve pain or suffering but so that the patient, family, and doctor can be sure that everything possible has been done, even at the cost of additional and unnecessary pain and distress.

As a result of this mystical tradition, the information given to the patient still depends on the judgement of the doctor. No one has the right to personal medical information. Medical records and the results of tests are the property of the Secretary of State and are confidential. The British Medical Association has strongly resisted moves to allow people to look at their own medical records. This is in spite of the success of schemes where women receiving antenatal care have held their full notes (Lovel *et al.* 1986).

This lack of information and choice has been heavily criticized and prompted the development of the consumer movement in health. This started with concerns about the quality of services provided in maternity units in the 1970s. Women exercised choice by going to units which gave the sort of service they wanted, even if it meant travelling long distances to have their babies. The *Good Birth Guide* provided them with the information needed to assess services at different hospitals (Kitzinger 1979). 'Market forces' encouraged good units and led others to question the service they were providing.

Thus women having babies questioned the medical model. They wanted childbirth to be treated as a normal event – which can sometimes go wrong – rather than as a hazardous event which requires every possible technology to make it safe. Since then the consumer debate has moved away from questioning the medical model to focus on access to services as well as on their quality. For example, the College of Health publishes waiting times at particular hospitals for different specialisms to enable people to be referred to hospitals where the waiting might be less (College of Health 1987). The Association of Community Health Councils has published a *Patient's Charter*, which outlines basic principles which should underlie all health services in order to make them more consumer-orientated (ACHCEW 1986).

However, there are those (especially on the radical Right) who have pressed for a rather different consumer model of health, with very different consequences. They have focused on two ways of increasing consumer 'choice'. These are to develop an 'internal market' to encourage hospitals to compete with each other for patients; and to encourage private medicine so that some people can choose between private or NHS health care. This has been supported in the 1989 White Paper.

Competition and 'internal markets'

There is an economic principle that competition as a way of allocating resources can ensure that consumers get what they want and that providers do not assume a dominant position. It is now argued that this principle can be applied to the NHS, even though consumers do not pay for services and, for most forms of health care, there are not often enough different providers to make a 'market'. The idea of an 'internal market' was first promoted by an American who undertook a review of the NHS in 1985 (Enthoven 1985). This arrangement would enable health districts to buy and sell services with others and the private sector. It is argued that this would provide an incentive to efficiency and better-quality care.

There are a number of fallacies in this approach. First, some hospitals would flourish and others run down, regardless of the needs of the local residents. People might have to travel much longer distances from where they live, and co-ordination between GP and hospital services would be difficult. It would make more sense to set up systems to monitor and maintain standards in all hospitals.

Second, if 'internal markets' are to increase consumer choice, the consumer must have the information, motivation, and energy to find the best and quickest treatment. At the moment, there is very limited information on which to base such decisions. The system is likely to benefit the advantaged health care users who can make it work for them. Those who are poor or elderly will not benefit so much from this freedom. However, the proposals in the NHS White Paper consider the decisions about which hospitals to use not as matters of individual consumer choice but as management 'best-buy' decisions made on behalf of consumers (DoH 1989). In this form 'internal markets' will reduce rather than increase the choice available to health consumers.

Third, the cost savings for the NHS of 'internal markets' are not at all clear. If a district is not using its services to full capacity, they could sell services to other districts. However, the underuse of beds and operating theatres is generally due to lack of finance and staff rather than lack of demand. Nor it is clear whether it is always cheaper to centralize services, since most costs are for staffing and there is a limit to the savings that can be made (Robinson 1988).

There may be a limited role for 'internal markets', in particular for specialist services, and there is a need to ensure that health authorities are adequately reimbursed for treating people from outside their boundaries (NAHA 1988). However, if a district health authority (DHA) can make profits from concentrating on providing specialist services, high-technology medicine will be encouraged at the cost of other services. The development of 'internal markets', unless it is in the context of health service planning and priorities, will not assist the health service to provide a comprehensive public service.

Encouraging private medicine

The private sector has developed considerably in the 1980s, especially in southern England. It is estimated that one in five of the operations which make up waiting lists (hernias, varicose veins, and hip replacements) are undertaken in the private sector. Less than 10 per cent of the population are privately insured, often through their employers (Higgins 1988).

The private sector supplements the NHS, and depends on it for support services and emergency back-up as well as for consultants (Griffith *et al.* 1985). Costs of treatment must be kept down and premiums low in order to maintain profits. Therefore private hospitals prefer to undertake routine interventions and leave emergency care, more innovative and expensive techniques, and care for chronic illness to the NHS. Some illnesses, such as chronic renal failure and AIDS, are generally specifically excluded.

The development of private hospitals can give those who can afford it choice in facilities and enable them to avoid waiting. It is, however, only a limited choice with the risk that the rich are given treatments they do not need and the poor do not get the treatment they do need. It is well to recall Bernard Shaw's observation in the Preface to *The Doctor's Dilemma*:

> That any sane nation, having observed that you could provide for the supply of bread by giving bakers a pecuniary interest in baking for you, should go on to give a surgeon a pecuniary interest in cutting off your leg is enough to make one despair of political humanity

Unfortunately, the present concern with this kind of consumerism in the NHS does not consider issues of the quality and effectiveness of health care, the most important issues for users. Nor does it question the medical model of health care, promote the individual's access to clinical information, or protect consumers from unnecessary or hazardous treatments. It is not, of course, interested in involving users in planning or monitoring services. It is, therefore, necessary to go beyond 'consumerism' in order to empower health services users, if the intention is also to maintain the public-service basis of health care.

Complaints, audit, and redress

The NHS as a public service should be responsive to its users. A satisfactory public service needs procedures which:

- enable users who have a grievance to express their views about services, make suggestions, and have them investigated
- monitor standards and protect users from inappropriate care, incompetence, and negligence
- enable staff who are not providing adequate standards of care to be identified and disciplined
- provide compensation to the patient who suffers a mishap.

Procedures for making a complaint, monitoring standards, and disciplining staff have different objectives and a procedure developed for one purpose is unlikely to be effective for another. However, in the NHS there is confusion between them all. As a result, all are unsatisfactory and generally ineffective.

Complaints procedures

According to the Health Service Ombudsman:

> What [complainants] want, above all, are: open and full information about what has happened; next, where appropriate, sincerely expressed contrition; and, lastly the reassurance that what has gone wrong for them will not go wrong for someone else in the future. Indeed, if they had got those in the first place, their recourse to the Ombudsman would not have been necessary.
>
> (Health Service Commissioner 1984)

The first problem facing a complainant is the complexity of the different procedures for making a complaint. Complaints may involve different services and different aspects of them. There is no mechanism for investigating complaints across more than one service. The areas and avenues for complaints are:

- hospital staff, where the complaint should be made to the district health authority (DHA)
- the family practitioners (GPs, dentists, pharmacists, and ophthalmic practitioners), where the complaint should be made to the Family Practitioner Committee (FPC)
- nursing staff in the community, where the complaint should be made to the DHA

- professional misconduct, where the complaint should be made to the appropriate professional body
- clinical judgement, where the complaint should be made to the DHA and then to the regional health authority (RHA)
- bad administration, where the complaint should be made to the DHA and, then, the Health Service Commissioner.

The procedures available to users to make complaints against family practitioners and professional misconduct by doctors are primarily intended for discipline. Complaints against family practitioners must be channelled through the Family Practitioner Committee, who hold the practitioner's NHS contracts. The system was set up in 1911, not to investigate or remedy a patient's grievance, but to investigate whether a practitioner was in breach of the terms of service. The FPC may set up a formal hearing where both 'sides' can present their case. The procedures are daunting (even when an informal stage is used) for the complainant who is placed in the role of prosecutor rather than witness. The FPC only pursues individual complaints and not general complaints into the standards of services provided by a practitioner. Even then, unless the complainant is prepared to follow through the procedure, the substance of the complaint may not otherwise be investigated. Even when practitioners are found in breach of their terms of service, their name is kept secret.

As for the General Medical Council (GMC), while it is responsible for maintaining standards of professional conduct, it discourages complaints being channelled its way. It may reject a complaint brought by a member of the public, however serious, unless the doctor has already been found guilty by the FPC or the courts. The same complaint may subsequently be referred to the GMC by the DoH, if the doctor has been found in breach of contract by the Family Practitioner Committee. However, the complainant is not informed of this and the complaints investigated by the FPC specifically exclude most aspects of professional misconduct as defined by the General Medical Council.

Hospital complaints procedures, on the other hand, now have to be established and publicized under the Hospital Complaints Act, 1985. Complainants are required initially to approach the staff concerned or the hospital administration with their complaint. Managers have the responsibility for investigating complaints, but do not necessarily have the authority that goes with this. They are not independent of the service and they often see their role as a defensive one, not least when a serious mishap has occurred and the complainant has a case, though may not know it, for legal action. They do not have specialist knowledge and lack the authority to question medical staff, who may not co-operate. The fear of legal proceedings means that hospital doctors have been advised to refer all complaints to their medical defence organization and check any reply with them. An apology may even be construed as an admission of liability (Capstick 1985). This can prevent the consultant from explaining what happened to the patient or the family.

If the complainant is not satisfied, it is possible to take the case to the Health Service Commissioner (ombudsman). Although independent, its powers are limited to investigating administrative matters and it cannot consider issues of clinical judgement. Furthermore, it has no powers to enforce changes or give redress. Clinical matters can be dealt with by the Regional Medical Officer's clinical review procedure which enables a second opinion to be given. However, such procedures may not be sufficiently independent and there are many variations in the way they operate between regions (Scott 1985).

Independent investigations, by the Health Service Commissioner and the Regional Medical Officer, are only available to people who are willing to state that they are not considering legal proceedings. Moreover, the Special Hospitals, such as Broadmoor, Park Lane, and Moss Side, have particular problems. They are for more disturbed people, and by no means all are referred from prison or have committed any criminal offence. Here the investigation into serious grievances relating to physical ill treatment may be blocked by staff. They can refer all cases of alleged assault to the police, who will investigate, generally in the presence of staff. Complainants may be suspect because they are in a Special Hospital. In cases where police have not brought charges against a nurse, the union has refused to co-operate with any subsequent internal disciplinary inquiry (Mental Health Act Commission 1987).

There are, then, many obstacles in the way of possible complainants. They have to find out the correct procedure, try to get hold of medical information, and, frequently, risk being branded as unstable or a trouble-maker. They may fear that their treatment, or that of their relative, will be adversely affected. Even if the complainant perseveres, the complaint may not be properly and impartially investigated, nor appropriate action be taken to remedy the fault identified.

Protection of patients and monitoring standards

The most important aspect of quality of health services is the clinical competence of staff. In spite of the value placed on professional self-regulation, the medical tradition is strongly against criticism or audit of colleagues. In fact, engaging in it may amount to 'serious professional misconduct', the worst accusation which can be made of a doctor. The General Medical Council advises that: 'the Council regards as capable of amounting to serious professional misconduct the deprecation by a doctor of the professional skill, knowledge, qualifications or services of another doctor' (GMC 1983).

Respect for the professional autonomy of each doctor may not work in the interests of achieving high clinical standards. Once a hospital doctor becomes a consultant, there is no method of supervising or monitoring his or her work. John Yates has described how this autonomy may contribute to waiting lists and deny some people treatment:

> Experts are more often interested in the new and exciting rather than the well established and the mundane. It is highly desirable to develop new techniques which will ultimately reduce morbidity, but sometimes this is done at the expense of providing a routine service. One orthopaedic surgeon who specialises in the treatment of scoliosis operates on 120 such patients a year. He also sees about 10 new outpatients each week who do not suffer from the disease. They are placed on the waiting list and never operated on.
>
> (Yates 1987)

The evidence is that standards between doctors and hospitals vary enormously. One study compared average death rates in different hospitals. While there was little difference in overall death rates between RHAs, there were sharp variations between hospitals which could not be accounted for by differences in age and type of case (Kind 1988).

A confidential inquiry in three regional health authorities into deaths occurring within a month of surgery revealed wide variations and a considerable number of unnecessary operations and avoidable deaths (Buck *et al.* 1988). Surgeons and anaesthetists were asked to fill in questionnaires on the treatment they had given to patients who had died within one month of an operation. There were then assessed independently. Though the inquiry was completely confidential, not all consultants were prepared to co-operate; in one RHA only 55 per cent of the peri-operative deaths in the period were reported to the inquiry. The inquiry was also concerned that only 5 per cent of participating doctors asked for feedback from independent assessors on their cases.

This situation means that there is no formal structure to enable consultants to learn from each other's experiences or, equally important, to work as a multi-disciplinary team with other health professionals who may have a better understanding of the views and experiences of patients and families. Medical audit has relied entirely on the willingness of doctors to participate. The NHS White Paper proposes that all consultants will participate in future. However, there is no provision for the involvement of users or other professionals in medical audit.

District research ethics committees have been set up in most district health authorities to review all proposed research projects and ensure that research procedures do not endanger the safety or well-being of the research subjects. However, there are enormous variations in their membership and the way they operate. Some have lay membership, sometimes through the community health council (CHC), but all are dominated by clinicians, and generally proceedings are confidential. A study by the Institute of Medical Ethics concluded that protection for the subjects of medical research depended on the district where they lived (Nicholson 1987). If the terms of reference of District Ethical Committees were extended to include all new clinical techniques and their membership were strengthened to make them more independent with stronger user representation, they might provide a basis for ensuring that patients' interests were protected throughout the local health service.

Disciplinary procedures

Medical staff are reluctant to criticize or even judge the competence of colleagues, and this attitude pervades disciplinary procedures, which are cumbersome and expensive and inappropriate for all but the most blatant and gross behaviour. Professional standards rely on self-regulation, and this has failed to protect patients from incompetent practitioners. Often when things go wrong, colleagues and other staff are aware of it, but do not support complaints or report malpractice when it occurs. Not all health authorities have procedures for staff to report incidents where they feel that patients are at risk or are not experiencing the standards of service they should expect to receive. A survey by the National Association of Health Authorities revealed that only about one-quarter of health authorities had such a procedure (NAHA 1985).

For GPs the powers of the FPC to monitor standards and protect patients are limited, and disciplinary procedures are normally initiated by complainants. If the FPC considers that a practitioner is not fit to practise, it can refer the matter to the NHS Service Tribunal with a recommendation that his or her name be removed from the FPC's list. It can refer serious professional misconduct to the appropriate professional body, such as the General Medical Council or the Dental Council, but this will only be considered if a hearing has been held and the practitioner has been found in breach of the terms of service. There is no mechanism to suspend a doctor from practising, however serious the charges are, until he or she is found guilty by the protracted procedures of the General Medical Council.

For hospital doctors, the most serious cases can be dealt with under a procedure introduced in a circular in 1961 (HM(61) 112). This enables a dangerous practitioner to be suspended immediately; if the practitioner denies the charges, a lengthy and expensive investigation is carried out. It can often take up to five years to work through the procedure during which time the consultant – guilty or not guilty – is suspended on full pay.

About forty doctors are suspended each year under this procedure. Inquiries are held when there is a dispute about the facts (not, for example, if the suspension is the result of a criminal conviction) and most are not held in public. The procedure is slow and expensive, and the outcome is rarely dismissal. Each inquiry costs about £250,000 and it is estimated that these procedures cost the NHS about £4 million a year. They are sometimes used inappropriately, as when Wendy Savage, a consultant obstetrician, was suspended in 1985. She believed in limiting medical intervention in childbirth and letting women make decisions for themselves. No complaint was made by her patients. The public inquiry centred on only five of the 1,000 births for which she had been responsible. In fact, statistically fewer babies had died in her care than in that of her colleagues. The inquiry alone cost about £250,000, Wendy Savage was suspended on full pay for nineteen months, and many senior medical and managerial staff spent many weeks preparing for and attending the inquiry. In the end she was vindicated. Because of the public uproar and media coverage, the issues behind the inquiry became clear: it was not about protecting patients, it was a dispute between doctors about how childbirth should be managed (Savage 1986).

There is one other mechanism for disciplining medical and dental staff which can be used to prevent harm to patients resulting from physical or mental disability, including addiction (Circular HC(82)13). This enables the health authority to set up Specialist Professional Panels of 'three wise men'. Complaints will normally be brought to the attention of one of the panel who will decide whether and how to investigate. Only when the complaint has been substantiated in some way will the case come to the notice of the managers.

At the moment users have little or no information about the standards or kinds of service provided by hospitals or particular doctors. It is time that clinical performance information became an integral and public part of all performance reviews. This is an essential basis to enable consumers to influence the quality of services.

Compensation and redress

If a mishap occurs, the victim may never know the cause. The fact that the victim has a possible legal claim against the hospital, whether he/she knows it or not, may mean that ordinary channels of communication will be closed. It is easy for the staff involved to tamper with the evidence;

and difficult for the victim to gain access to evidence and witnesses. Even if the victim or relatives can get the information to prove they have a case, legal action is often financially prohibitive, and legal aid difficult to get. Furthermore, proceedings take years to come to court and be resolved. In the case of disability arising from an accident, compensation is needed immediately to help victims reorganize their lives.

It is up to the victim of a medical accident, or of the side-effects of drugs, to prove negligence in order to seek compensation. This is the opposite of what we would expect of a public service. One possible way forward is the introduction of a no-fault compensation scheme which is based on what happened to the patient rather than on why it happened. This would remove the onus from the individual to prove negligence and provide compensation at the time it was needed (Brahams 1988). Similar schemes have been introduced in New Zealand and Sweden, and the British Medical Association supports the establishment of such a fund, largely because the increased costs of litigation, and higher compensation payments now awarded against doctors found to be negligent, are causing medical insurance to escalate.

From this review, it is clear that the present machinery for investigating complaints, providing redress, and generally monitoring standards has serious shortcomings. The procedures do not enable grievances to be investigated or staff to learn from their experiences. As a result the quality of services is not properly monitored or patients' interests properly safeguarded. The procedures can even be used to further limit the involvement of users in the service.

The NHS and the local community

Individual users want a high-quality service when needed, and the information necessary to make their own decisions. Increasing the power of the individual may lead to a more 'user-friendly' service, but will not by itself lead to user control. In fact, the trend towards a more complex and disparate health system of public and commercial providers will confuse and disempower users. Users can only influence the planning or provision of services if they work together.

User involvement at local level in the NHS is split between district health authorities, who manage the health service, and community health councils (CHCs), who have a pressure group (or quasi-representative) function. Family practitioner services are separately administered by Family Practitioner Committees. None of these bodies is elected or is accountable to the local community. DHAs report to RHAs, and RHAs and FPCs to the Department of Health. Under proposals in the White Paper FPCs would be managed by RHAs in future. CHCs have no line of accountability.

Management

The origins of the management structure go back to the establishment of the NHS. When local authorities managed hospitals, management and representation were combined in the locally elected councillors. When the NHS was established, the Hospital Management Committees were responsible for both managing the service and representing users. In 1974 there was an awareness that there had been conflicts of interest between management and representation in the NHS. The system had broken down at times, especially in the management of the long-stay hospitals, where standards of care had given rise to national scandals. So there was a conscious decision to separate management and user representation and community health councils were, therefore, established in the 1974 reorganization.

Regional health authorities plan the development of health services and allocate resources to the DHAs. Each RHA has about twenty members appointed by the Secretary of State after consultation with interested organizations, including professional bodies, trade unions, local authorities, and voluntary organizations. RHA members have no line of accountability.

District health authorities are responsible for managing the local health services. Members are appointed by the regional health authority. They are mainly selected for their 'management' skills and to represent groups with an interest in the management of local health services: hospital consultants, GPs, trade unions, nurses, and local authorities. No member is appointed specifically to represent users or for their close links with the local community. The chair of each authority is not elected from the membership but appointed by the Secretary of State and paid a part-time salary. The DHA chair is therefore, in effect, a DHA officer appointed by the Secretary of State. There is no line of accountability to users or the local community.

Democratic accountability was not a part of the new management structure in 1974 or of the subsequent management reorganizations in 1980, 1983, and 1989. Since 1983 there have been strong moves towards increased central control of RHAs and DHAs by the Department of Health. The NHS Management Board was set up in 1984 to review the performance of health authorities in carrying out central policy. The board is accountable to the NHS Supervisory Board, which the Minister of Health chairs. There has also been increasing intervention in the appointment of senior staff and RHA and DHA members. The Department of Health has tried to ensure the appointment of District General Managers and chairs of FPCs and DHAs who will carry out central government policies.

Health authority meetings are public under the Public Bodies

(Admissions to Meetings) Act, 1960. They are not, however, subject to the Local Government (Access to Information) Act, 1985. There is a great variation among health authorities as to what matters are discussed in the public part of the agenda and what in the confidential part. In some health authorities, matters are discussed in confidence more to avoid political embarrassment than for reasons of public interest.

DHA members have had difficulty in finding their role (Ham 1984). Because they do not have a representative as well as a management function, unlike local authority councillors, they do not necessarily have links with the local community or contact with users. They have no obvious legitimacy and no mechanisms for accounting for themselves. They are appointed as managers, though most have sectional interests. Their responsibilities are also arduous and they are often under pressure to make service cuts to meet financial or priority targets. The proposals in the White Paper would replace present membership with five executive and five non-executive members, with no pretension to local contacts or knowledge.

Some DHAs have attempted to develop mechanisms for involving the community in service planning. This can be done by setting up planning forums for different sections of the community, whose views can be fed into the NHS planning system. This can enable more sensitive planning for groups of the population with particular health needs, and more local consultation in planning. It is very easy for NHS managers, most of whom are based in offices in district general hospitals, to concentrate on the hospital services and overlook the needs of the community services. The first health district to start locality planning was Exeter in 1985, where the DHA funded the CHC to set up local forums to feed information into the planning system.

Family practitioner committees are responsible for planning and administering family practitioner services. They were set up in 1974, to work alongside area health authorities. In 1985 they were given independent status, which further separated them from the mainstream NHS. Family practitioners, even if working wholly for the NHS, are self-employed, and the FPCs have always emphasized administering rather than managing family practitioner services. Half the FPC members are appointed from the various professional groups, specifically to represent their views. The other half are lay representatives appointed by the Secretary of State. Lay members do not necessarily have any local or consumer interest. It was not until 1985 that community health councils were given observer status at FPC meetings and the same rights to consultation as they have with DHAs. They were not, however, given the right to visit premises where NHS family practitioner services are provided, unless the practitioner agrees.

Some GPs, as individuals, have set up Patient Participation Groups to enable local people to monitor and comment on the services they provide. However, the indications are that they have had limited impact and are unlikely to develop further. The groups are not independent and are most likely to work where communication between the GP and patient is already good; they will not develop in the areas where they are most needed (Richardson 1986). In West Lambeth, local advisory groups are being set up attached to particular health service units. The first one was set up for a new day centre for elderly people. The aim of the groups is to give local people and users a say in the way the centres are run. Half the members are health or social service staff and half from the community, with the CHC organizing the elections for the user representatives to the group.

Representation

Community health councils were set up in 1974 to represent the interests of the local community to the management of the health services. CHCs are advisory bodies, with certain statutory rights and duties. These include the right to information, and the right to be consulted on closures and changes of use, to enter and inspect NHS premises, to meet the health authority and receive their comments on their annual report, and to attend health authority meetings as observers. CHC members have no lines of accountability. Half the membership is appointed by local authorities, a third are elected by voluntary groups, and the remainder appointed by the RHA.

CHCs have been successful in opening up the NHS to the public and in strengthening representation of the weakest groups of users, such as elderly, mentally ill, and mentally handicapped people, and ethnic minorities. CHCs were given vague terms of reference, and this has led to enormous variation in the standards of the service provided. Some CHCs act as advocates for complainants, others will merely tell complainants to whom they should write. Some encourage the public to participate in their meetings and activities, others do not. Some have established sophisticated mechanisms for consulting local people about issues, others consider this unnecessary. The major activities of CHCs vary considerably (Hogg 1986). Some act mainly as pressure groups against cuts, others undertake health education and consumer research, provide information and advice to the public, and set up health projects. Many CHCs produce handbooks and leaflets about services available, consumer rights, and even medical information. A few CHCs have extended this to set up advocacy schemes for patients who find it difficult to express their wants and needs, whether because they have a mental handicap or language difficulty, or are socially or culturally disadvantaged. Advocacy is an important way of empowering the more vulnerable users and helping them to gain confidence. In the USA all people with a mental handicap have the right to an advocate to represent their interests on the basis of trust and partnership. In the UK there is no such right and even access to the patient in hospital depends on the institution's co-operation.

However, there are a number of inherent weaknesses which undermine the effectiveness of CHCs:

- there are inevitable tensions in the relationship between NHS managers and CHCs. The terms of reference of CHCs are vague, leaving the details to local agreement between the CHC and managers. Many of the disputes between CHCs and local management have been about procedures for consultation rather than issues of concern to local people
- CHC members have no established lines of accountability or mechanism for reporting to or consulting with the community
- CHCs have very limited resources. Most CHCs have only two members of staff and this restricts the amount of work they can do. In areas affected by many cuts, the CHC can easily devote all its resources to consulting on cuts and closures, an area where it is unlikely to achieve very much. It is too easy for CHCs to be merely reactive bodies and not develop ways of involving users in monitoring health services
- CHCs have no formal status in relation to Regional Health Authority planning, even though RHA decisions are often the most important determinant of what happens to local services. CHCs have formed loose regional associations, but they have too few resources and may represent competing interests (for example, between city and rural areas) to provide an effective input to regional planning
- CHCs only have observer status with FPCs, which limits their involvement in planning and developing primary health care services.

The impact users can have on local services is limited, though some CHCs have been effective and innovative in helping to increase involvement and general public awareness. A few DHAs have attempted to communicate with the public to make services more accessible. However, users are not a homogeneous group and they represent many different interests. The machinery needs to be extended and strengthened to ensure wide public debate about priorities and resource allocation.

Users and national policy

The National Health Service is a national service. Decisions about the services to provide and money to be given to health are determined at national level. Accountability is limited and there is no effective forum for public debate about policy and priorities. As a result the health service continues to be dominated by the medical view of health and its associated view of the role of health services.

Accountability for running the NHS comes through the Secretary of State to *Parliament*. Democratic control comes through parliamentary questions, debates, and the Select Committee. MPs often represent other interests and have other loyalties – for example, to the drug industry, professional groups, and trade unions. The strength of the drug industry, and of food, alcohol, and tobacco lobbies in influencing Treasury policy is well established (Doyle 1979). NHS users are only one of the interests they may represent and are arguably one of the weakest. This is mainly because users' interests are diverse and not well articulated nationally.

The Secretary of State is accountable for the *Department of Health*, which is responsible for advising him or her and acting on his/her behalf in allocating resources, developing policy, and issuing advice to Regional Health Authorities. The department has a number of Advisory Committees on policy, evaluation, and funding specialist services, but users are not represented.

Throughout the history of the NHS the views of the medical profession have determined the structure, priorities, and allocation of resources (Gould 1985). Important compromises had to be made to ensure the co-operation of the British Medical Association when the NHS was established; otherwise there would have been no NHS at all (Ham 1985). The special position achieved by the medical profession at the outset has remained. However, other power groups may have more influence in maintaining the medical view of health services, sometimes even in opposition to the medical profession itself. The pharmaceutical and medical equipment industries as well as private hospitals have a direct interest in NHS policies which allocate the most resources to new drugs and equipment, and which are concerned with cures, not causes or prevention. Those anxious to keep down public expenditure are not interested in recognizing the extent to which disease is caused by pollution, unemployment, bad housing, and lack of amenities.

Since 1980, the lobby for hospitals and high-technology medicine has increased. In the 1970s the DHSS set clear priorities which were to hold back acute hospital services, and develop primary and community care, and services for elderly, mentally ill and mentally handicapped people (DHSS 1976). Yet in the 1980s these priorities have been lost, as the Department of Health pushes new priorities for bone marrow transplants, cardiac surgery, and cancer screening.

One of the most effective ways for a hospital unit on the 'frontiers' to obtain funds is for doctors to publicize through the media that their patients are dying or about to die unnecessarily. This is possible because the NHS does not collect the information to ensure a rational basis for planning and allocating resources. Evaluation of new techniques such as CT scanners is not always undertaken before they are introduced in an *ad hoc* way all over the country (Stocking and Morrison 1978). There is little evaluation of medical techniques in terms of the long-term outcome for patients. Health economists have considered this from an economic perspective. Quality Adjusted Life Years (QALYs) are a new, and as yet crude, way of measuring health outcome. Each treatment is measured in terms of how many years of life the recipient of the treatment can expect and the quality of life it will give (Maynard 1987). This enables consideration of treatments which may seem successful in that they lengthen life but the patient survives in great pain and discomfort. For planners, QALYs are useful in comparing different medical techniques in terms of cost-effectiveness when they need to plan services and allocate scarce resources. However, the data obtained on how patients assess quality of life have yet to be properly collected.

Because the media and politicians are giving so much support to specialist techniques, it is assumed that this reflects public opinion. However, surveys of public opinion have demonstrated that the public are concerned about prevention and caring services. CHC members, who have an excellent opportunity to become informed about health issues, have generally not become involved with calls for more CT scanners, but have consistently supported the need for better primary and community services and better care for mentally ill, handicapped, and elderly people.

However, the public have neither access to information nor a channel to express their views at national level. There is no strong national voice for health service users. Medical research charities spend millions of pounds each year on research, but their policies are generally determined by clinicians, not users. There are self-help groups for sufferers of particular diseases. There are voluntary organizations interested in specific aspects of the NHS, such as MIND and MENCAP, who provide services and also act as pressure groups. But there is no effective pressure group working for users nationally. The Association of CHCs, because it does not represent any one sectional interest, could act as an advocate for users. However, CHCs have tended to concentrate on local issues rather than taking a broader view, and have not confronted clinical issues or questions of priority. There is a vacuum in user representation in national health policy, planning, and evaluation which ought to be filled.

Conclusions

It is clear, then, that users' views have always come a poor second to the views of 'experts' and professionals about the services which should be provided for them and the way the provision should be made. All staff groups claim to represent users' views, yet there are evident conflicts of interest from time to time. The public appears to make 'unlimited demands' on the health service, but this demand is led more by the medical profession and the media than by the public.

If we believe that all abnormalities, whether they cause problems or not, can be made normal by clinical intervention, demand may be unlimited. Politicians and the media stress the high-technology answers. We have tended to assume that the best treatment is the most treatment. This is not always true, and people are sometimes given unnecessary, painful, and costly treatments. If they were better informed, they might have preferred no treatment. The more understanding people have about clinical issues, the less likely they are to demand more treatment. There may be a role here for health education in raising public awareness about clinical matters. In 1984, the public health department in a Swiss canton undertook a media campaign to point out to women that the number of hysterectomies performed there was four times that of the West Midlands Region and eight times that in Norway. The result was an almost immediate 25 per cent reduction in the number of hysterectomies performed, and the gynaecologists in the region established an ethical committee (Domenighetti *et al.* 1986).

However, if we look at the real impact of health care in terms of health outcome, and social and psychological health for the individual patient and his/her carers, the limitations of modern medicine are clearer and there is a more rational basis on which to allocate resources. The wide and continued acceptance of the medical model of illness and health services will maintain the inherent problems of the NHS. It is, therefore, essential to change the way that health policies are decided and the way the service relates to its consumers. The way to do this is to strengthen user involvement in all aspects of the NHS and at all levels. In terms of the discussion here, this suggests a number of practical conclusions.

The relationship of service providers and users

The traditional doctor/patient relationship does not encourage patients to question or think for themselves. User control should be seen as part of a different model of health and health care. The aim must be to develop a partnership, where the professional provides information on which the user can base his/her decision.

Whereas the development of good practices may improve the service for the individual, change should have a foundation in rights which can be enforced in law. This has a number of aspects.

Personal information

If people are to participate actively in their health care, they require information. They must have the right to information on all aspects of their care and to see their medical records, even to retain a copy themselves.

The individual should also have an automatic right to a second opinion. At present this can be arranged on the NHS, but requires the co-operation of the GP and consultant. Since there is little certainty in medical diagnosis and treatment, it is reasonable, even wise, to make sure that all the possibilities have been explored before having any radical or irreversible treatment. A system for providing a second opinion has been set up as part of the procedures for dealing with clinical complaints through regional medical officers. However, it is more important to make the second opinion available before grounds for the complaint arise, and the procedure should therefore be extended.

Public information

A tradition of secrecy pervades the whole of the NHS. All the Advisory Committees of the DHSS, such as the Committee on the Safety of Drugs, are subject to the Official Secrets Act.

Performance indicators have been introduced as a management tool, but they are concerned with management processes, not the quality of services. They provide little information to help users make 'consumer' choices. Information should be publicly available about particular specialist expertise, clinical competence, and 'success' rates, as well as information about waiting times and general amenities.

Established standards

A 'users' charter' should be established to lay down specific standards of service which users have the right to expect. This information should be publicly available and should include waiting times. Where someone has been waiting for an operation for a specified period, the DHA should have the responsibility to arrange treatment in another hospital.

Codes of practice should be established for all aspects of the service, such as dealing with children, stillbirths, or the terminally ill. All clinical specialisms should have a code outlining the procedures staff should follow, the information they are required to give about alternative treatments, and the outcome likely for particular patient groups. These would guide clinicians in good practice and protect the individual from unnecessary interventions. Codes of practice should be based on a consensus developed with patients and their families, and reviewed frequently.

Complaints, audit, and redress

The NHS has confused the role of a complaints procedure with the need to monitor standards, discipline staff, and provide compensation following a mishap. As a result none is carried out to the standards which should be expected of a public service.

Complaints

There is a need for a comprehensive review of the whole system of complaints and redress in order to provide a coherent system across all health services. Complaints procedures need to be established which aim to resolve grievances, and which are independent and without prejudice to any legal proceedings.

The role of the Health Service Commissioner should be extended to include clinical issues, the right to investigate even when an individual complaint has not been made, and the power to insist on remedial action.

Audit and redress

Routine audit of clinical activities of consultants and departments should be established. These need to be multi-disciplinary and to take account of long-term outcome of treatments provided for patients and their families.

All medical accidents and unexpected outcomes should be investigated as a routine in order to enable staff to learn from experience. A no-fault compensation scheme should be set up so that the onus is no longer on the victim and the family to pursue the matter in law, but this should not be seen as a substitute for effective clinical audit and accountability.

The role of District Ethics Committees should be extended to cover all areas of the service, not just new research proposals. They should be involved in monitoring not only to ensure that patients' interests are protected, but also to ensure that the views and experiences of patients are included in all research. Membership should be multi-disciplinary with a strong user representation. Ethical issues are of public, not just professional, concern.

The NHS and the local community

There is a need for both local democratic accountability of health service management and also a mechanism for local people to participate in local health services. This involves making District Health Authorities more accountable and democratic, and community health councils more effective as independent user bodies.

Extending local democracy

In extending democratic control, one option would be to make changes in the methods of selection of DHA members in an attempt to make the present system more user sensitive. However, this would not increase democratic accountability. Because the health service is so important to the local community, the aim should be to work towards democratically elected health authorities and the integration of family practitioner services within the main structure. In terms of planning and management, there is no justification for separate administrative structures for hospital and community services on the one hand and family practitioner services on the other.

The establishment of locally elected health authorities would require decreased control by central government on how money is spent and on priorities for local services. However, central funding would need to continue to ensure that the national character of the NHS is maintained and that there is equal access to specialist services provided on a regional basis.

Two ways of establishing direct elections have been proposed. The most radical proposal is to reintegrate the NHS and local authority services. When the NHS was created, hospitals were transferred from elected local authorities to appointed health authorities or boards. At that time, many hoped that when local authorities were restructured, health services would be transferred back to their control. The opportunity to reintegrate services was not taken in the 1974 reorganization; opposition to it from many different interest groups is now firmly entrenched, and it is not a political possibility in the near future. It would require a massive reorganization of both health and local government, including the redrawing of health or local authority boundaries. A regional structure would also be required to provide a base for planning specialist services.

However, in the long term, such a reintegration may be the only way to provide a structure which would enable collaboration and co-operation between health, social services, and other services which have a direct effect on public health, such as occupational health, leisure facilities, housing, employment, and environment. Local authorities lost control of hospitals in 1947 and community health services in 1974. The post of Medical Officer of Health was transferred to the NHS in 1974 as the District Community Physician (now District Medical Officer); but in practice the District Medical Officer has become a senior NHS manager and few of them have taken on the wider community public health responsibility (DHSS 1988). A number local authorities are increasingly conscious of the health implications of their policies and are involving themselves in public health activities.

The less radical, and perhaps more politically feasible, option is to establish elected health authorities. This is obviously attractive in that it re-establishes the democratic principle and should not involve a major reorganization. However, there are drawbacks to the introduction of direct elections without a more radical restructuring.

First, members might be held responsible and accountable locally for decisions over which they had little control. Unless the basis of the NHS were changed, local health authorities, directly elected or not, would still have no control over resources available or policy directions. They would have no way of raising funds independently of the DoH. Second, if the party system came to dominate, which is all too likely, the pool of potential health authority members would be restricted to the party faithful, and many people who now make a useful contribution as authority members, or could do in the future, would not stand for election. With these reservations in mind, the present situation is clearly unsatisfactory and it is time to move towards directly elected and accountable health authorities.

Empowering the community

Even if health authorities are elected, this will not necessarily bring participation and representation. There will still be a role for a users' council. There might even be advantages in incorporating the functions of CHCs into a wider community council which covered social services, housing, and other ares where collaboration is essential for the smooth running of health services and the promotion of public health.

The role of a users' council might be:

- to encourage participation in the NHS, in particular in the development of local planning forums and ensuring user representation on planning committees
- to provide information and advice to the public, including assisting complainants and setting up and running advocacy projects in hospitals. The councils should have the specific brief to raise public awareness on health issues and on the rights and responsibilities of people in relation to their own health
- to monitor local services by undertaking research and information

collection on local health services and identifying unmet needs and poor-quality service.

There are a number of factors which would be crucial to the success of the new councils. First, the staffing levels and funding must reflect the scope and importance of the activities undertaken. User representatives on expert committees require support and information in order to participate fully. Second, they must have a clear code of practice to ensure greater consistency of standards to the public, and also to regulate the ways that management and users relate to each other in order to avoid the unnecessary misunderstandings which have bedevilled CHCs. Third, procedures for selection and accountability of the membership must be established. Electoral colleges of community organizations and user groups might be set up to nominate and elect representatives. This would bring in a wider range of people than the present method of electing and appointing CHC members.

User councils would provide a framework for people to be involved at community level. Health districts cover an area with populations up to 250,000. There is increasing interest in developing locality planning, which divides each district into, say, patches of about 40,000 people and this might provide a framework within which users' councils could work.

In turn, the regional planning structure established to plan specialist services would require a regional users' council, independently funded, to participate in decisions and represent the views of the local users' councils.

References

Association of Community Health Councils for England and Wales (ACHCEW) (1986) *Patient's Charter*, London.

Brahams, D. (1988) *The Swedish Medical Insurance Schemes: the Way Ahead for the UK*, *The Lancet*, 2/9 January 1988: 43–7.

Buck, N., Devlin, H. B., and Lunn, J. N. (1988) *Confidential Enquiry into Perioperative Death (CEPOD)*, London: Nuffield Provincial Hospitals Trust and King's Fund Publishing Office.

Capstick, B. (1985) *Patient Complaints and Litigation*, Birmingham: National Association of Health Authorities.

Challah, S. and Mays, N. (1986) 'The randomised controlled trial in the evaluation of new technology: a case study', *British Medical Journal* 292: 877–9.

College of Health (1987) *Guide to Hospital Waiting Lists*, London.

Council for Science and Society (1982) *Expensive Medical Techniques*, London.

DHSS (1976) *Priorities for Health and Personal Social Services in England*, London: HMSO.

——(1983) *NHS Management Inquiry* (The Griffiths Report), London: HMSO.
——(1988) *Public Health in England, the Report of the Inquiry into the Future Development of the Public Health Function*, London: HMSO.
DoH (1989) *Working for Patients*, London: HMSO.
Domenighetti, G. (1986) 'Reducing hysterectomies: the mass media', paper given at the Copenhagen Conference on Regional Variations, November.
Doyle, L. (1979) *The Political Economy of Health*, London: Pluto Press.
Enthoven, A. (1985) *Reflections on the Management of the National Health Service: an American Looks at Incentives to Efficiency in Health Service Management in the UK*, London: Nuffield Provincial Hospitals Trust.
Evans, L. and Spellman, M. (1983) 'The problem of non-compliance with drug therapy', *Drugs'* 25: 63–76.
General Medical Council (1983) *Professional Conduct and Discipline: Fitness to Practise*, London.
Gould, Donald (1985) *The Medical Mafia: How Doctors Serve and Fail their Customers*, London: Sphere Books.
Greenberg, E. R. and Stevens, M. (1986) 'Recent trends in breast surgery in the US and the UK', *British Medical Journal* 292: 1487–91.
Griffith, B. and Rayner, G., with Mohan, J. (1985) *Commercial Medicine in London*, London: Greater London Council Industry and Employment Branch.
Ham, C. J. (1984) 'Members in search of an identity', *Health and Social Services Journal*, 23 February: 222–3.
——(1985) *Health Policy in Britain*, (2nd edn), London: Macmillan.
Hart, N. (1985) *The Sociology of Health and Medicine*, Ormskirk: Causeway Books.
Health Service Commissioner (1984) *Annual Report 1983/84*, London: HMSO.
Higgins, J. (1988) 'Private practice in health care', ESRC Newsletter 62, June: 8–10.
Hogg, C. (1986) *The Public and the NHS*, London: Association of Community Health Councils for England and Wales.
——(1988) *New Medical Techniques and the NHS*, Radical Community Medicine, Summer.
House of Lords (1988) *Priorities in Medical Research*, Select Committee on Science and Technology, London.
Jennett, B. (1984) *High Technology Medicine: Benefits and Burdens*, London: Nuffield Provincial Hospitals Trust,
Kind, P. (1988) *Hospital Deaths – the Missing Link*, Discussion Paper 44, York: Centre for Health Economics, University of York.
Kitzinger, S. (1979) *The Good Birth Guide*, London: Fontana.
Lovel, A., Lander, L. I., Foot, S., Swann, A. V., and Reynolds, A. (1986) *St Thomas's Maternity Case Notes Study: Why Not Give Mothers Their Own Case Notes?*, London: Cicely Northcote Trust.
Maynard, Alan (1987) 'Balancing the budget and maintaining standards', *Health and Hygiene* 8: 7–13.
Mental Health Act Commission (1987) *Second Biennial Report 1985–87*, London.

National Association of Health Authorities (1985) *Protecting Patients*, Birmingham.

——(1988) *Funding the NHS: Which Way Forward?* Birmingham.

Nicholson, R. (1987) 'Research ethical committees', *Times Health Supplement* IV (1) January: 3.

Pirie, M. and Butler, E. (1988) *The Health of Nations: Solutions to the Problem of Finance in the Health Care Sector*, London: Adam Smith Institute.

Prentice, A. and Lind, T. (1987) 'Fetal heart rate monitoring during labour – too frequent intervention, too little benefit?' *Lancet*, 12 December: 1375–7.

Richardson, A. (1986) *Promoting Health through Participation? Experiences of Groups for Patent Participation in General Practice*, London: Policy Studies Institute.

Robinson, R. (1988) *Efficiency and the NHS: a Case for Internal Markets*, London: Institute of Economic Affairs.

Savage, W. (1986) *A Savage Enquiry: Who Controls Childbirth?* London: Virago.

Scott, J. A. (1985) 'Complaints arising from the exercise of clinical judgement: a report by the English Regional Medical Officers', *Health Trends* 17: 70–2.

Stocking, B. and Morrison, S. L. (1978) *The Image and the Reality*, London: Nuffield Provincial Hospitals Trust.

Yates, J. (1987) *Why Are We Waiting?* Oxford: Oxford University Press.

8

Education

Stewart Ranson

Strong moral and political purposes have underpinned the development of the post-war government of education. These purposes have centred upon the importance of education in providing the conditions for citizenship in a democratic society. What has changed is the conception of those conditions. For much of the period following the 1944 Education Act the emphasis was upon professional planning to develop the individual powers and capacities of all young people. From the mid-1970s this professional domination was challenged: education had to become more accountable to the society which resourced it, and the learning process more responsive to the needs of employers and wealth production. The 1980s has seen a more radical attack upon 'the producers' of education. Because, it is claimed, professional control has created dependent, rather than active and autonomous, citizens, the organization of the government of education has undermined, rather than supported, its expressed purpose. The solution is to contract the bureaucracy and to extend public choice and accountability to users and consumers of the service.

This prevailing conception of a consumer democracy in education is critically analysed in terms of the criteria of public service outlined in the Introduction to this volume: accountability, representation, access, choice, and so on. I shall argue[1] that the vision of creating citizenship through a more responsive education service can only be realized by integrating some of the ostensibly disparate values and conditions developed within the post-war government of education. The chapter begins, however, by clarifying the dominant order and the challenge to make it more accountable to an active public.

The 1944 settlement: justice as fairness

Before the 1944 Education Act most young people only received an elementary schooling. The Act realized for the first time Tawney's ideal of universal free secondary education for all directed to the needs and capacities of youngsters rather than dependent upon the material well-being, status, and power of their parents. The Act established the universal right to personal development through education.

If these radical ideas for the expansion of educational opportunities are to be fully understood, however, they have to be located within a broader context of social reconstruction and reform which began during the Second World War. There was a groundswell of social and political opinion that there could be no returning to the social order of the 1930s: idleness, poverty, disease, ignorance, and squalor had to give way to employment, income, personal dignity, health, and opportunity. The unity which had won the war could recreate a new, more just, open, and modern society. While Keynes offered the design for economic planning and Beveridge shaped the blueprint for universal welfare support, Butler provided the framework for educational opportunity and the possibility of social mobility that could dissolve a rigid, outmoded, class-divided society: 'The state came to be seen as something vaster and more beneficent ... as the real guarantor of reform and reconstruction' (Middlemas 1979).

The state was constituting the institutional conditions for citizenship: common membership and the dignity which derives from contributing to the wealth production of the community in which one lives; the universal right to health and welfare services in times of need; the equality of educational opportunity to fulfil personal powers and capacities; and the right to franchise and representation within the polity. Archbishop Temple articulated the importance of the 1944 reforms to the creation of an educated democracy of citizens who would form the only safeguard against the memories of encroaching fascism in the 1930s:

Until education has done far more than it has had the opportunity of doing, it cannot have society organised on the basis of justice: for this reason there will always be a strain ... between what is due to a man in view of his humanity with all his powers and capacity and what is due to him at the moment as a member of society with all his faculties underdeveloped, with many of his tastes warped and with his powers largely crushed. Are you going to treat a man as what he is or what he might be? That is the whole work of education. Give [the man] the full development of his powers and there will no longer be conflict between the claim of the man as he is and of the man he might become. And so you cannot have justice as the basis of your social life until education has done its full work ... and you cannot have political freedom any more than you can have moral freedom until people's powers have developed, for the simple reason that over and over again we find that men with a cause which is just are unable to state it in a way which might enable it to prevail.... There exists a mental form of slavery that is as real as any economic form. We are pledged to destroy it.... If you want human liberty you must have educated people.

(quoted in Butler 1982)

Yet the unity which framed the post-war educational and social reconstruction was a political settlement, a contract between the estates of the realm: capital, labour, and the state (Middlemas 1979). Bullock (1960) recalls the belligerence of Bevin in forging a social and political partnership for peace: 'Why should the working class lend the government money for war with no guarantee of employment or improvement after?' Kogan (1978) and Maclure (1985) as well as Middlemas (1979) have recalled the great radical move to create a social and political order that would afford justice and opportunity. As Butler described it in his *The Conservatives*: 'Our contribution flanked by the Workers' Charter, attempted to give capitalism an human look.'[2] This was the orthodoxy of the wise and the good in the immediate post-war years.

This post-war partnership had widespread political appeal and formed a cross-party consensus for a generation. A state, a system of rule, had been constituted which endured. Its organizing of power and task were legitimated by a moral and political order whose primary value was justice as fairness: the foundation stone of common citizenship.

If the 'contract' had received a philosopher's seal it would, in retrospect, have been Rawls' (1972). If men and women were to decide the foundation charter of their society – that is, the basic institutional structure of rights and duties, of advantage and disadvantage – they would, in the 'original position ' where none knows his or her advantage or how society will turn out, choose to create a fair society. They would constitute a just structure which would provide the conditions for equal citizenship and the inviolability of each person. Individual freedom and well-being for all require agreement about the basic constitutive rules that would ensure a society based upon justice as fairness. Those contracting a foundation charter would choose a just structure in order to secure freedom. Freedom requires justice, argued Rawls.

Dividing power and responsibility

The system of education embodied in the 1944 Education Act was constituted to implement these radical changes in educational purpose and value. Power and responsibilities were distributed amongst the parties to education so as to form, as Briaults (1976) has called it, 'a triangle of tension, of checks and balances'. Legislators held beliefs about the importance of diffusing power over educational decision-making not just so as to prevent unwarranted concentration of control over such a vital service, but also so as to organize power in a way that was appropriate to the task. Thus the Education Ministers and their department were to control education but through clarifying and promoting broad policy objectives and by securing the appropriate volume of national resources. The local education authority (LEA) was the 'providing' authority, building, staffing, and maintaining schools, and planning a local function in relation to local needs and demands and statutory responsibilities: 'it shall be the duty of the LEA for every area, so far as their powers extend, to contribute towards the spiritual, moral, mental and physical development of the community' (Section 7, 1944 Education Act).

The development of the curriculum and appropriate teaching methods were regarded as largely the professional responsibilities of teachers in schools guided by university syllabuses. Parents had a duty to send their children to school although the LEA had a duty to make schooling responsive to parents: 'pupils are to be educated in accordance with the wishes of their parents' (s.76). In short, Whitehall was to promote education, town or county hall was to plan and provide, teachers were to nurture the learning process so as to meet the needs of children and the wishes of parents.

The constitutive system of government of education formed a complex 'polycentred'[3] division of power and responsibility appropriate to differentiated tasks. Divided power was designed to ensure partnership between necessary and equal parties to the government of education.

It was nevertheless a decentralized system constituted in a way which reflected dominant beliefs about the significant relationship between teacher and child. Centre, locality, and profession were accorded the necessary authority to support that relationship because: 'The keynote of the new system will be that the child is the centre of education and that, so far as is humanly possible, all children should receive the type of education to which they are best adapted' (White Paper 1943). The school and its professional community of teachers provided the key to the educational development of the child.

Nurturing young citizens

Education expanded to meet the birth bulge; also because it was believed to be an essential vehicle for a modern – and just – society. By the 1960s education policy began to develop fully the expectations expressed in the Butler legislation. A consensus grew for sweeping away the institutional principles of selection and segregation, and establishing comprehensive schools which provided equal opportunities for all to develop their powers and capacities. The expansion of higher education opened up opportunities previously restricted to an elite. At primary level, the Plowden Report in 1967 celebrated a process of learning which laid 'special stress on individual discovery, on first-hand experience and on opportunities for creative work'. Schools sought to develop the personal qualities and capacities of each individual. To educate according to this perspective is to bring out, to unfold, to foster the development of each young person's inner potential.

The emphasis upon the education of each individual pupil reinforced the original bias to decentralization within the system. Only the professional judgment of the teachers in the classroom could identify the learning needs of each pupil and release his or her talents and capacities. Other partners were needed to support that fragile relationship. Young citizens had to be nurtured in a caring environment by professionals dedicated to public service.

Education like other services, though more reluctantly, began to reach out to its public and consult them about proposals for comprehensive reorganization. It was often, however, at the level of informing the public, and by the mid-1970s the view was gaining ground that teachers and educational professionals had become too powerful: they had to become more accountable to society and public.

From the mid-1970s: accountability to economy and society

The economic crisis of the 1970s created steering problems for government. To maintain control and integration, governments progressively extended their boundaries of intervention. The 'corporate state' strove to achieve national unity and order by increasingly concentrating and rationalising its control. In education from the mid-1970s, government challenged the dominant ethos of personal development and promoted in its place the vocational preparation of young people for their future economic roles on the grounds that:

> the school system is ... prejudiced against work in productive industry and trade; that teachers lack experience, knowledge and understanding of trade and industry; that curricula are not related to the realities of most pupils' work after leaving school; and that pupils leave school with little or no understanding of the workings, or the importance, of the wealth producing sector of our economy.
>
> (Green Paper 1977)

Education, in future, had to be answerable to the society which paid for it: 'there was growing recognition of the need for schools to demonstrate their accountability to the society which they serve' (ibid.). In this way education could play a vital role in 'improving industrial performance and thereby increasing national wealth' (ibid.).

The service had neglected employers and society as legitimate users of education. In curriculum development for ('average ability') 17-year-olds this new injunction meant courses in vocational preparation that would help 'them understand what employers will expect from them [and] what they should expect from employment' (Keohane Report 1979). The Certificate of Pre-Vocational Education (CPVE), Training and Vocational Education Initiative (TVEI) in schools, together with the Youth Opportunities Programme (YOP) and the Youth Training Scheme (YTS) within colleges and industry, reflected the pattern of curriculum development in this period which sought to prepare young citizens for their working lives. The curriculum should:

> serve to develop the potential of every pupil and to equip all for the responsibilities of citizenship and for the formidable challenge of employment in the world of tomorrow. It is vital that schools should always remember that preparation for working life is one of their principal functions.
>
> (DES, 1985: para. 46)

Power shifted rapidly to the centre as Whitehall administrators extended their control of curriculum development and institutional organization at the expense of the local authorities and the teachers. The struggle focused upon whether the Manpower Services Commission or the DES would prevail.

The 1980s: consumer rights and accountability

The transformed context had generated a review of the purposes and practices of the education service as well as the roles and relationships between the education partners. There was growing agreement about the need for change and redirection of the service. For some (Hargreaves Report 1984), the emphasis was upon reforming and developing existing practice: celebrating more diverse aims of learning, broadening the curriculum, and reforming assessment. For others (Adam Smith Institute 1984; Hillgate Group 1986; Sexton 1987), the reform of education required a rejection of the whole post-war scheme of things. For them the original 'charter' was misguided. It is this second critique which has come to dominate the polity and which informed the preparation of the 1988 Education Reform Act.

This critique of post-war education focuses upon falling standards, inadequate and distorted curricula, and a failure to educate children

187

according to their parents' wishes (according to s.76 of the 1944 Act). These failures of education, it is argued, derive from professionals and (local) politicians appropriating control of the service from its proper source – the parents. The most important users of the service, its customers, had been neglected. The Adam Smith Institute's *Omega File on Education* generalizes the problems facing education in common with other state monopolies as those of 'producer capture': 'whereby the service comes to be organised more to suit the needs of producers than consumers'. The professionals create a technical language which serves only to bamboozle ordinary people and they organize the system for their own convenience rather than to respond to the demands of its consumers. The result is inertia and resistance to change.

The education system, it is argued, must be rebuilt upon the principles of public choice and accountability. Individual parents have an inalienable right to choose the education which their children receive. These values articulate beliefs about educational standards which assert that a system which is accountable and responsive to the choices of individual consumers of the service will improve in quality as a necessary consequence. As in other forms of market exchange, the products which thrive can only do so because they have the support of the consumers. Those products which fail the test of the market-place go out of business. The astringent experience of the market can be the test of quality in schooling as much as in the production of chocolate bars.

For consumers to fulfil their allotted role as quality controllers in the market-place, they require some diversity of product and information about the scope of choice and the quality of performance, as well as the opportunity to choose.

If schools were made to respond to the market 'there would be a built-in mechanism to raise standards and change forms and types of education in accordance with that market demand':

> In short, it supposes that the wisdom of parents separately and individually exercised, but taken together becoming the collective wisdom is more likely to achieve higher standards more quickly and more acceptably to the public than the collective wisdom of the present bureaucrats, no matter how well meaning those bureaucrats may be.
>
> (Sexton 1987)

Creating this direct accountability between consumer and producer is the secret, it is argued, of renewal in education. To shift from a producer- to a consumer-led system will take time, but placing public choice at the heart of the system will release the quality which is at present alleged to be submerged under the weight of administration.

Radical reforms are proposed to the government of education in order to reconstitute it according to these new organizing principles and values. The LEAs should be stripped of their powers and reduced to an administrative role. In time it is proposed that the ownership of all schools and the management of teachers should be transferred to independent trusts or boards. This would create self-governing institutions under the control of parent governors and subject to consumer pressures in the market-place. The survival of schools

> should depend on their ability to satisfy their customers. And their principal customers are parents, who should therefore be free to place their custom where they wish in order that educational institutions should be shaped, controlled and nourished by their demand.
>
> (Hillgate Group 1986)

Strengthening the rights of individual consumers is the secret of improved education quality.

From pamphlets to legislation: the 1988 Education Act

The 1988 Education Reform Act can be seen as the culmination of a decade's campaigning to strengthen the rights of parents in the government of education. Introducing the legislation in Parliament, the Secretary of State said:

> The Bill will galvanise parental involvement in schools. Parents will have more choice. They will have greater variety of schools to choose from. We will create new types of schools. Parents will be far better placed to know what their children are being taught and what they are learning.... And the Bill will introduce competition into the public provision of education. This competition will introduce a new dynamic into our schools system which will stimulate better standards all round.
>
> (DES 1987d)

Parents are brought centre-stage in the establishment of an education market-place. Parents are accorded choice, influence over governing bodies, and control – if they choose – of new grant-maintained schools. 'Open' enrolment is designed to end the LEAs' capacity hitherto to place artificial limits on admission to schools. 'The government is committed to securing wider parental choice within the system of state schools.' To this end schools will be allowed to recruit up to their available capacity defined as physical capacity or 'the standard number' admitted in 1979 (when schools were largely full) or, if it is higher, the number admitted in the year before the legislation takes effect. If a governing body decides it wishes to accept a larger number of pupils, it can apply to the Secretary of State. Moreover, local electors can object to the Education Secretary if they believe an LEA has set the limit too low.

Parents acquire a determining influence over school governing bodies. The 1986 Education (No. 2) Act gave parents an equal representation with the LEA on governing bodies. Now the Reform Act gives governors responsibilities for school budgets and the appointment and dismissal of staff, as well as the ability to overrule an LEA on redeployment of staff. The Act extends such proposals to the governing bodies of colleges. The representation of college consumers – for example, business and commerce – is increased 'to ensure that the governing body is, and is seen to be, properly independent of the maintaining LEA'. Parents are granted the capacity to acquire control of schools if they choose:

> The Government is taking action to increase the autonomy of schools and their responsiveness to parental wishes.... The Government considers that it should ... respond to the numerous indications it has received that groups of parents want the responsibility of running their schools as individual institutions. It proposes to provide an additional route to autonomy by introducing legislation ... to enable governors of county and voluntary maintained schools, with the support of parents, to apply to the Secretary of State for maintenance by grant from central government, instead of maintenance by LEAs. The Government believes that this proposal ... will add a new and powerful dimension to the ability of parents to exercise choice within the publicly provided sector of education. The greater diversity of provision which will result should enhance the prospect of improving education standards in all schools. Parents and local communities would have new opportunities to secure the development of their schools in ways appropriate to the needs of their children and in accordance with their wishes, within the legal framework of a national curriculum.
>
> (DES 1987b)

These schools will receive grant directly from the Secretary of State and form a new type of independent school within the maintained sector; initially at least, they will retain their existing form (for example, a comprehensive cannot opt out and immediately become a grammar school). Governors of the larger primary schools as well as of all county and voluntary secondary schools can apply to opt out but only if they already have the support of 20 per cent of parents in a secret postal ballot. Parents, if necessary, can override the opposition of governors and pursue their own application according to the same rules. Parents will have a determining influence on the governing bodies of newly formed grant-maintained (GM) schools.

Other independent schools, known as city technology colleges (CTCs), will accompany GM schools in creating much greater variety of institutions for parents to choose from in the market-place. CTCs will be established by the Secretary of State who 'may enter into agreement with any person' to provide such urban schools. They will offer free education for pupils of different abilities within a broad curriculum emphasizing science and technology. CTCs have more discretion in relation to the national curriculum than other LEA schools although they must broadly adhere to it as a condition of receiving grant.

Schools and colleges are to be granted more autonomy so that they can become more responsive and accountable to their consumers. The Act proposes to delegate financial responsibilities to school governors:

i   to ensure that parents and the community know on what basis the available resources are distributed in their area and how much is spent on each school;

ii to give the governors of all county and voluntary secondary schools and of larger primary schools freedom to take expenditure decisions which match their own priorities and the guarantee that their own school will benefit if they achieve efficiency savings.

(DES 1987a)

LEAs are required to submit to the Secretary of State 'schemes' which will describe how they propose to delegate financial resources to schools including the allocation formula to be used. Parents will be able to assess the efficiency of each school because:

at the end of each year the LEA would be required to publish information on actual expenditure at each school which could be compared to the original plans. This information together with that required of governors relating to the achievement of the national curriculum would provide the basis on which parents could evaluate whether best use had been made of the resources available to the governors.

(ibid.)

Colleges, also, are to be governed by equivalent formula-funding arrangements, and performance indicators are to be used to assess their efficiency. In the past, the allocation of resources has been a closed professional affair. Now it is likely that the criteria as well as the distribution of resources will become a subject of public debate as consumers enquire why one institution received more than another or was more efficient than another.

191

If consumers are to express their preferences in the market-place then their choices need to be informed. Strategic direction is given to a new system through proposals for the Education Secretary to prepare a National Curriculum that will make explicit the goals pupils are to pursue, the curriculum followed, and the learning levels which have been achieved against national targets. Thus: 'Parents will be able to judge their children's progress against agreed national targets for attainment and will also be able to judge the effectiveness of their school' (DES 1987c). Clarity of purpose, process, and achievement will make schools accountable to their consumers, and as a result reinforce standards of learning and teaching.

Thus the working of the market-place is not to be left entirely to the hidden hand of competitive self-interest. Rather, it is to be interpreted and guided by the 'public' hand of the Secretary of State who will be granted an extraordinary new range of regulatory powers that will more reflect Bentham's panopticon than Nozick's minimal state. The market will be monitored by Ministers. Schools may be 'privatized' progressively but their reproduction of culture (the curriculum) will be nationalized (or anglicized). (The pamphlet from Hillgate has been more influential than those from the Adam Smith Institute or the Institute of Economic Affairs.)

Between the emerging forces of market and hierarchy[4] is finally suffocated the centre piece of the 1944 legislation – the local education authority, and the local government of education. The LEA's former powers and responsibilities are largely dissolved or redistributed. The way the education profession often liked to describe education – as a national service locally administered – was mistaken then but becomes a reality now.

Towards education for citizenship

The organizing principles which inform the Education Reform Act value public choice and accountability. This is underpinned by an extraordinary extension of state regulatory power. Indeed, it is the juxtaposition of 'consumer sovereignty' with 'ministerial power' which forms an intriguing tension in the development of the new government of education. Here, however, I wish to focus upon the conception of active public participation embodied in the Act and whether it can achieve its intended objective of accountable public choice.

The principles of public choice and accountability are to be welcomed as a strengthening of government. The Act reasserts the basic principle of government as grounded in the consent of society. Authority resides with the public and is held in trust by officials and elected representatives on condition that they account to the public on the use of their power. Accountable government routinely tests and reaffirms that public consent. The traditional form of holding to account and of testing consent has been the periodic election. Across the political spectrum there appears to be a growing consensus about the need for a more active public participation and accountability to complement election by involving users, consumers, and citizens in creating services that respond to the needs of the public.

The debate is now about how the public is to be conceived and involved. What is contested is whether the public is an aggregate of individual consumers or a community of active citizens. The new Education Reform Act is a centrepiece in the constituting of a new moral and political order of individual rights and public accountability of government to consumer choice in the market- place. It is a moral order of individual self-interest in a market society. It is flawed in means and conception.

Can consumers realize public choice?

The moral and political order informing the Act proposes competitive self-interest in the market-place as the best means of realizing both individual choice and quality in the provision of goods and services.

Yet it needs to be examined whether the market-place is an appropriate mechanism for every purpose. The assumption can exist that all goods and services are discrete products which can be purchased in the market. Yet the market can actually change certain goods. If I purchase a chocolate bar or take an Austen novel out of the library my 'purchase' has no effect on the product although pressure may be placed upon production or delivery. But my preference for a school, privately expressed, together with the unwitting choices of others, will transform the product. A small school grows in scale with inevitable consequences for learning style and administrative process. The distinctive ethos which was the reason for the choice may be altered by the choice. Some of the most important writing[5] in the human sciences is preoccupied with the unintended public consequences of private decision-making: with the growing realization, especially in many public services, that self-interest can be self-defeating. It is likely in education, moreover, that choice will not only change the product but eliminate it. Choice implies surplus places, but if market forces fill some schools and close others then choice evaporates leaving only a hierarchy of esteem with little actual choice for many. But assuming that choice is a continuing reality, is education a 'product' which can be marketed?

If education is no more than acquiring a social status which schools can readily confer then it may be a discrete product which can be purchased in the market-place. If education, however, is regarded more as an unfolding learning process which is adapted continuously to suit the needs of particular individuals then it is neither a product nor a process which is appropriate to the market-place. The changing needs of individuals cannot be packaged and marketed, nor can the institution which is a vehicle for their realization because it is changed and damaged by the market. Let the market-place be supported wherever it is appropriate but its limits be understood.

Whatever the product exchanged in the market, however, it is its unique social functions which are of fundamental importance. The market is formally neutral but substantively interested. Individuals come together in competitive exchange to acquire possession of scarce goods and services. Within the market-place all are free and equal, only differentiated by their capacity to calculate their self-interest. Yet, of course, the market masks its social bias. It elides, but reproduces, the inequalities which consumers bring to the market-place. Under the guise of neutrality, the institution of the market actively confirms and reinforces the pre-existing social order of wealth and privilege. The market is a crude mechanism of social selection. It can provide a more effective social engineering than anything we have previously witnessed in the post-war period.

How are we, therefore, to evaluate the quality of public service provided by the consumer democracy of the 1988 Reform Act? Deakin and Wright's seven criteria offer a helpful framework of analysis:

(i) Information: schools are required to publish information about their educational prospectus and achievement and they will be encouraged to market their distinctive ethos. But the public will need to look to their LEA to be more completely informed and to receive a more dispassionate analysis of institutional performance.

(ii) Representation: parents will be represented by the parent governors they have elected, but the influence of the representatives of the public as a whole – the elected councillors – will be considerably weakened. There is also concern that the 'first governors' of opted-out schools will become, over their five-to-seven-year term of office, very unrepresentative of existing parents as well as the wider community.

(iii) Participation: having made their consumer choice there is no guarantee that (non-governing) parents will be encouraged to participate with teachers as complementary educators in the learning process or in the management of the school.

(iv) Access: nor is there any guarantee that the school will be used for the community as a whole, so that adult learners and community groups can have access to it as an educational resource.

(v)   Redress: parents will be able to complain to their governors as well as to their elected councillors. Much, however, will depend upon the LEA developing a new role of 'quality assurance' in relation to its schools and colleges.

(vi) Choice: although the organizing principles of the new legislation stress the importance of public choice, in reality, as the discussion has suggested, choice will depend upon pre-existing social and economic characteristics of parents.

(vii) Accountability: market accountability to individual consumers is a significant change and in many ways an improvement because it enhances the status of the public and, radically, regards the individual consumers as agents, as active participants in the process of managing services effectively. Yet there are important internal contradictions in this model of consumer accountability. Responding to choices of some consumers may, as we have seen, frustrate the choice of the public as a whole.

But individual consumerism in education is not only flawed as an instrument for achieving its purported objectives, it is misconceived in its conception of public choice. By defining the public as an aggregate of individual consumers in the market-place, it fragments and undermines the idea of the public as a collective whole. Individuals cannot alone achieve a 'public choice'. Can consumerism, moreover, achieve citizenship? A consumer expresses self-interest registered privately and with uncertain (though often malign) public consequences. A citizen, however, has a concern for the well-being of others as well as for the health of society, and believes that both should become the subject of public debate in order to constitute a public choice. The challenge for more public participation and accountability requires different vehicles to support the objective of securing active citizenship.

The conditions for citizenship

Reforming education to improve public choice and accountability is timely. In a period of change there is need to establish a more active democracy. This requires opportunities for members of the public to participate as citizens. The citizen is both an individual and a member of the collectivity. Indeed, the citizen has to be understood as 'individual-as-a-member-of' the public as a political community (Ranson and Stewart 1989).

Citizens need to be involved in education because it is a public good: a good, that is, in which we are all interested due to its pervasive significance. It is a good which, because of its public characteristics, cannot be determined by individuals acting in isolation from each other. Education, therefore, is a good which should be the subject of public choice which is accountable to the public as a whole. This public choice will be accountable if it reflects the interests of the public as a whole: if it relates to the common good. Public choice which secures wide public agreement will acquire legitimate authority because it is grounded in the consent of the public.

What institutional conditions are required to support the development of active citizenship that can shape a more accountable public choice? This requires an attempt to integrate the strengths of government from different periods since the Second World War.

Just government

Just government is needed to protect and support the basic preconditions for personal development and citizenship: the rights and duties that define common membership, work and earned income, health, and equal educational opportunities that are not dependent upon wealth, status, or power. These conditions formed the post-war settlement and are as valid today if we still seek to constitute a fair society. They form Rawls's foundation contract, or charter, for a just society based upon the understanding that one cannot be a person or take advantage of liberty unless there is justice. Even Dworkin (1977, 1984) who wants us to 'take rights seriously' argues for the inescapable importance of a just distribution that can enable all to contribute equally in a market society.

The enabling authority (LEA)

The LEA has lost direct control of its institutions. Nevertheless, the LEA can create a role of strategic influence in enhancing learning quality and public accountability.

Working within the national framework their role can be to serve schools and colleges: advising on educational leadership and progress; encouraging clear and consistent thinking; enabling policy planning in schools; helping them to set standards and disseminate good practice; managing progression between the stages of learning; making staff development suit the needs of schools and encouraging good management at institutional level. In this way the LEA can ensure the achievement of quality in the learning process.

Yet this reinforcing of learning quality will only improve public confidence if the LEA continually seeks to involve the public at every stage and become accountable to it. The role of the LEA is to facilitate public accountability by presenting information, evaluating performance, and enabling public discussion about achievement and educational purpose. It requires, for many LEAs, a radical change in their attitude to the public and a new commitment to involve the public as partners.

Schools and colleges in partnership with the public

The post-war contract for a liberal democratic society of equal opportunities for all was delegated to skilled professionals to provide for the rest of the people. Services have sometimes, however, been perceived as those of the profession rather than the people. A balance needs to be restored. A new perspective of the enabling professional offering and negotiating specialist skills in partnership with the public can provide a necessary condition for releasing the potential of citizens. Schools and colleges have a vital role to play.

Even HM Inspectorate, the priesthood of professional knowledge, increasingly urges schools to form a partnership with parents, governors, local employers, and the community in order to develop the quality of education: 'schools cannot afford to be insular; they are part of society and accountable for their performance'. Evidence of the benefit of involving parents and the community as 'complementary educators' grows year by year: in nursery and infant classes (Tizard *et al.* 1981); in home–school reading schemes (Haringey 1982; Widlake and Macleod 1984); in primary schools (from Plowden Report 1967 to Mortimore *et al.* 1988); in secondary-school tutor group parent associations and home–school councils (Hargreaves Report 1987); and in members of the community becoming 'coaches' to young adults making the transition from school to work (Bazalgette 1976). Through such strategies and many more, parents and the community can develop understanding of schools and their work. The government paper *Better Schools* stressed the important role of parents in the learning process and encouraged schools to 'reach out and support ... parents' as 'partners in a shared task for the benefit of the child'. The reason for forging closer links of this kind is that 'parents can become familiar with the school and its aims' (DES 1985: 59–60).

The careers and further education services have in many parts of the country developed imaginative strategies for involving employers and communities: providing outreach counselling services and courses in the community; designing courses which more directly meet the needs of industry and commerce; and working more closely with employers and the training agencies as partners of the service. It should also be remembered that the adult education service in its various forms has been distinguished by its responsiveness to users.

Active citizens

If choice is to be public it requires the opportunity for citizens to express their views, for their voices to be heard, so that the inescapably diverse constituencies of education are enabled to present, discuss, and negotiate their account. Public choice presupposes public participation and mutual accountability.

These organizing principles and values for an active citizenship presuppose arenas in which citizens can become involved and form the partnership which is a precondition for public choice and agreement about education. An important condition is extensive consultation that uses surveys, the outreach staff of an authority in the community, and, perhaps, community polling which could be developed as a form of listening to the views of the public. There is also a major role for adult continuing education in providing the educational underpinnings of active citizenship.

A constitutive condition, however, for an active democracy is to provide arenas for public participation. A model in the recent past has been the creation of local youth councils which have enabled young people to debate and make decisions about youth policy and provision. Some schools have developed councils which involved a much broader representation from the community in the attempt to make the life of the schools wherever possible serve the needs of the community.

Some colleges have sought to play an enabling role with community businesses by providing the community with the skills, advice, and resources to deploy as they choose. The role of the educator is to encourage community groups to take responsibility and ownership for their own learning enterprise.

An education service which seeks actively to involve citizens in its policy-making and to become accountable to the community as a whole needs to constitute local community forums or councils. These would enable the several interests – including women's groups, the black and ethnic minorities, and the disabled – within a community to participate, articulate needs, and contribute to decision-making.

Where an authority has formed a pool of resources – perhaps from urban aid funds, EEC grants, or local grants – to support community groups, decision-making about distribution could be delegated to these forums. In this way the citizens within the community are being enfranchised to influence and take responsibility for their own learning environment. They can negotiate with the providers to use educational resources so as to meet the needs of the community: in access courses, back-to-work classes for women, health courses, community language learning, and so on.

The institutional conditions for active citizenship, I suggest, more clearly meet the criteria established at the outset of this book for democratic control of public services. Citizens will be able to participate directly, as well as be represented, in decision-making about educational services. Members of the community as well as parents and employers will be informed about provision and encouraged to have access to educational institutions to benefit from, as well as to shape, their services. The channels for redress of grievances would be more extensive and public than in the past or in the consumerist model discussed earlier. Most significantly, the relationship between the active politics of community forums and the collective decision-making of local government can allow the possibility of public choice that reflects the expressed interests and needs of the whole and is accountable to the public as a whole.

A learning democracy therefore is one which listens, enables expression, and strives for understanding. Its conditions are a charter for justice, an enabling profession, and an active citizenship involved in and shaping public choice.

Notes

1   This chapter develops a discussion begun in my 'From 1944 to 1988: education, citizenship and democracy', *Local Government Studies* 14 (1), January 1988: 1–19.
2   Quoted in *The Times Literary Supplement*, 13 March 1987.
3   A term used by David Regan.
4   Beginning since the early 1980s. See Ranson, S., Jones, G., and Walsh, K. (eds) (1985) *Between Centre and Locality: the Politics of Public Policy*, London: Allen & Unwin.
5   See Sen, A. (1984) *Choice, Welfare and Measurement*, Oxford: Blackwell; Parfit, D. (1984) *Reasons and Persons*, Oxford: Oxford University Press; Elster, J. (1983) *Sour Grapes*, Cambridge: Cambridge University Press; and Elster, J. (1979) *Ulysses and the Sirens*, Cambridge: Cambridge University Press.

References

Adam Smith Institute (1984) *The Omega File on Education*, London: Adam Smith Institute,

Bazalgette, J. (1976) *School Life and Working Life*, London: Hutchinson.

Briault, E. (1976) 'A distributed system of educational administration: an international viewpoint', *International Review of Education* 22 (4).

Bullock, A. (1960) *The Life and Times of Ernest Bevin*, London: Hodder & Stoughton.

Butler, R. A. (1982) *The Art of Memory*, London: Hodder & Stoughton.

DES (1985) *Better Schools*, London: HMSO, para. 46, p. 19.

——(1987a) *Financial Delegation to Schools, a Consultative Paper*, London.

——(1987b) *Grant Maintained Schools, a Consultative Paper*, London.

——(1987c) *The National Curriculum 5–16: a Consultative Document*, London.

——(1987d) Press release, 20 November.

Dworkin, R. (1977) *Taking Rights Seriously*, London: Duckworth.
——(1984) 'Liberalism', in M. Sandel (ed.) *Liberalism and its Critics*, Oxford: Blackwell.
Green Paper (1977) *Education in Schools: a Consultative Document*, London: HMSO.
Hargreaves Report (1984) *Improving Secondary Education*, London: ILEA.
Haringey Local Education Authority (1982) *The Thomas Coram Home Reading Scheme*, Haringey.
Hillgate Group (1986) *Whose Schools: a Radical Manifesto*, London: The Hillgate Group.
Keohane Report (1979) *Proposals for a Certificate of Extended Education*, London: HMSO.
Kogan, M. (1978) *The Politics of Educational Change*, Glasgow: Fontana.
Maclure, S. (1985) 'Forty years on', *British Journal of Educational Studies* 33 (2) June.
Middlemas, K. (1979) *Politics in Industrial Society*, London: André Deutsch.
Mortimore, P., Sammons, P., Stoll, L., Lewis, D., and Ecob, R. (1988) *School Matters, the Junior Years*, Wells: Open Books.
Nozick, R. (1974) *Anarchy, State and Utopia*, Oxford: Blackwell.
Plowden Report (1967) *Children and their Primary Schools,* London: HMSO.
Ranson, S. and Stewart, J. D. (1989) 'Citizenship and government: the challenge for management in the public domain', *Political Studies* 37 (1).
Rawls, J. (1972) *A Theory of Justice*, Oxford: Oxford University Press.
Sexton, S. (1987) *Our Schools – a Radical Policy*, London: Institute of Economic Affairs.
Tizard, B., Mortimore, J., and Burchell, B. (1981) *Involving Parents in Nursery and Infant Schools*, London: Grant MacIntyre.
White Paper (1943) *Educational Reconstruction*, Cmnd. 6458, London: HMSO.
Widlake, P. and Macleod, F. (1984) *Parental Involvement Programmes and the Language Performance of Children*, Coventry: Community Education Development Centre.

9

Conclusions

Nicholas Deakin and Anthony Wright

Towards new forms of public services

Our opening editorial assertion (which also formed the starting point for this collection of essays as a whole) was that there is an urgent need for informed debate about the future role of the public sector in social policy and the different ways in which it could change. In our view, the individual contributions by our colleagues strongly reinforce that assertion. They show that a wide range of issues are emerging which should now take their place on the policy agenda; and a whole series of new ideas about increasing the effectiveness and responsiveness of public provision are being evolved and tested out. The variety of form and context in which these ideas are appearing makes it next to impossible to pull them together into a neat and tidy pattern. However, there are a number of general themes that have emerged with particular force in all the individual service areas which have been examined. These are that the principal characteristics of a citizen- and user-controlled service are that it should: (a) function under some form of democratic control; (b) be organized on a human scale; and (c) be a high-quality service.

These general characteristics incorporate the user-control criteria (accountability, representation, information, access, choice, and redress) identified in our Introduction – in the sense, for example, that access requires a manageable scale of service, or choice is a component of quality. They also integrate them with wider considerations about the kind of public service that greater user control is wanted for and to which it could be expected to contribute.

Taking each of these characteristics in turn, it is clear that democracy should be a key characteristic of a service in which user control is taken seriously. Elected representation in the government of the service provides the simplest form of accountability – one that is universally understood and generally well recognized: so much so, in fact, that it is tempting to gloss over the difficulties and take the means as well as the end for granted. In fact, some form of democratic accountability has always been contemplated for the public services. For example, in his introduction to the pre-war New Fabian Research Bureau's review of public enterprise William Robson (1937), arguing for an extension of 'social ownership' (the term has a distinguished pedigree), emphasized the importance of retaining control by 'the instruments of public government'. By this, though, he meant control by the Cabinet and a Minister answerable to Parliament for the policies and performance of public boards and commissions (for day-to-day supervision he foresaw the creation of an Audit Commission). Similarly, Aneurin Bevan vested ultimate responsibility for the Health Service in a Minister accountable to Parliament for each and every detail of the administration of the service.

There can be no dispute that, once the principle of democratic control is conceded, Parliament must have a role in the process; but experience has shown that direct concern with the detail of service delivery is cumbersome and ultimately inefficient. A hospital service in which (to take Bevan's own example) a bedpan cannot be dropped without a parliamentary question being asked is not accountable in the real meaning of the term. The case for parliamentary oversight of policy, on the other hand, has been greatly strengthened by the creation of the new Select Committees. For example, the work done by the Health and Social Services Committee has provided a valuable check on the performance of Ministers in that department; the proposal by Enid Wistrich (Chapter 3) for the creation of a similar committee for transport policy reflects this increase in effective parliamentary scrutiny.

However, that still leaves the question of detailed review and control to be resolved. Elected local authorities are the natural focus for these responsibilities; but that approach raises difficulties both of principle and practice. Both Right and Left have agendas for fundamental change in local government, ranging from a basic shift of emphasis in operation from service provision to resourcing and co-ordination through to a pruning so drastic as to amount virtually to abolition. Even if we make the assumption (which would be highly unwise) that local government will continue in broadly its present form, there is the question of its representative legitimacy in view of the very low turn-out in local government elections and disputes about the validity of any 'local mandate' arising from them.

Next, there is the role of parties; and the tendency (on both sides of politics) to use the official machinery of government to impose party priorities, often determined nationally, not locally. The actions of some local authorities (both Labour and Conservative controlled) in excluding opposition party representatives from school governing bodies is an example of a mentality that seeks to monopolize the whole political system at every point. There are also questions about the style in which local authority business is conducted and the ways in which this excludes outsiders (what Beresford and Croft (1985), who have been persistent critics of the system, call 'committeebabble'). The willingness of elected members to modify these procedures, share information, and provide direct access to technical advice is also often problematic, in large part because it modifies their traditional (and still important) role of acting as the first point of reference for complaints by dissatisfied users of public services.

These deficiencies suggest that a pure representative model, in the way in which it functions at the moment, will not suffice. But if representative systems are reinforced by participative devices, other difficulties arise. Who is to determine which groups are represented, and how? The experience that the Greater London Council had with its Women's Committee is instructive here: an attempt to create a body which would be fully representative of all women in London collectively ran into serious difficulties in trying to construct appropriate forms of representation. Nevertheless, a mixture of different techniques can enable progress to be made: participation based on the locality can incorporate identifiable interest groups as well as interested individuals in local forums; use of particular facilities can be the basis for users' groups (surgeries, day centres, leisure facilities); and special roles can be allocated to specific bodies (tenants' groups are one helpful example and self-help groups in the health field, sometimes organized around specific illnesses, are another). The emergence of user groups in the social services (of which the National Association of Young People in Care (NAYPIC) is a particularly good example) provides further opportunities for users to be involved in setting objectives and in implementation (see Chapters 4 and 6). More ambitiously still, the Community Care Special Action Project (CCSAP) in Birmingham, established by the City Council, is attempting to establish an inter-corporate approach, involving a range of different agencies in the city and based on consumer involvement in service planning, as well as delivery (Jowell and Wistow, forthcoming).

All this goes beyond the traditional device of co-option on to council committees and can help to open up fresh channels of communication, even if there are restrictions on how far participants may be able to exercise ultimate control over the processes with which they are involved. The government has recently introduced legislation to address the practice of using cross membership between authorities to bring political influence to bear within the administrative process: much the same issue arises with officers becoming involved in participation exercises as users or members of voluntary groups. A more serious difficulty, in many ways, is the introduction of producer interests into consultative and participative processes in such a way as to squeeze out consumers or restrict their opportunities to criticize the quality of services.

The opposite danger, much canvassed in the literature on participation, is the risk of domination of the process by the articulate middle class. Certainly, it is essential to provide that the 'inverse law of participation – that those with the greatest need to push their own interests have the least capacity to do so effectively' (Klein 1984: 25) does not work against the minorities and the poor. At the same time, we would not want to be dismissive about the progress that has been made by many consumer groups whose activities have been based on traditional middle-class styles of lobbying though established networks and bringing other pressures to bear – for example through undertaking consumer research and securing wide publicity for the results. The problem about such an approach is that it tends to be fragmented; the collective interest becomes nothing more than the sum of individual concerns. It can also be politically naïve. In her recent review of 'consumerism and the public sector', Jenny Potter comments that:

> the apolitical nature of consumerism, and the fact that it is grounded in economic theory, means that it is not equipped itself to develop this kind of swapping of roles between the governors and the governed, the administrators and the administered. Consumerism's primary role is to place consumers' preferences on the agenda, rather than to encourage consumers to take account of the preferences of others.
>
> (Potter 1988: 156)

In other words, there is no clear engagement with the question of power. The consumer army is a guerrilla army, adept at hit and run and picking off some public-sector stragglers. But it is less well equipped to undertake a long march through institutions to permanent change.

Yet, when all these difficulties are stated, and due account taken of changing circumstances in local government and its highly restricted (or in some cases barely existent) role in some service areas at present, the argument for some form of strengthened democratic control at local level still seems to us clear. But it is not going to provide magic short cuts to accountability. Day and Klein's comparative study of services under the control of directly elected members and those (the health and water services) where members were nominated reached the dispiriting conclusion that 'the widespread assumption that direct election can somehow be equated with the effective practice of accountability does not hold water' (sic) (1987). Indeed, the bland assumption that it does can bestow a false legitimacy that is less conducive to concern about accountability than in non-elected bodies.

In other words, we will need to work at it; and one way of doing so is through changing the scale at which services are provided. Although small may not invariably be beautiful, it has incontestable merits in helping to bring the consumers closer both to the source of delivery of services and to those with responsibility for them. One of the most convincing criticisms of the major reforms that took place in the public sector in the course of the early 1970s is that they adopted the principle of larger units to secure economies of scale without reference to the consequences in terms of the lack of responsiveness and flexibility in large institutions.

This brings us to decentralization – the favourite device of the 1980s, just as participation was the favourite slogan of the 1960s. The growth of monolithic bureaucracies can be arrested by breaking them down in a number of ways, by function as well as by territorial unit. Smaller-scale services should, in principle, both improve accessibility and provide new opportunities to participate in determining priorities (the costs of participation will be smaller and the benefits correspondingly greater).

However, there can be serious problems about the nature and purposes of decentralization. In some cases, it has clearly been employed as an administrative device, and the main purpose has been to bring services closer to the people in the most economical and efficient way. This, it is hoped in turn, will help to humanize the service in question and restore the agency's image as a responsive and caring organization. This approach has been criticized as excessively management-centred both in its objectives and in its outcomes (Beresford and Croft 1985).

Alternatively, decentralization has been seen as a political mechanism, bringing power nearer to the people (in the sense of providing a greater degree of accountability) and encouraging their participation in decision-taking at local level as a means of sharing its exercise. Attempts to introduce participatory devices like community forums and users' committees should be seen in this light; and the problems already identified in the context of participatory democracy are exposed with particular clarity by such initiatives. In such schemes, who determines which issues reach the agenda and where the limits of public involvement and responsibility for decisions are drawn? On what side of the line does the employment of staff, their promotion and, if necessary, disciplining (and even dismissal) fall?

In addition, there are serious conceptual and practical problems about the potential conflict between, on the one hand, introducing participation into service delivery and breaking service units down to the local level and, on the other hand, the goals of effectiveness, equity, and maintaining common standards, across local or health authority areas as a whole. How much diversity is tolerable if these other standards are to be met?

This leads to the third crucial characteristic, high quality of services. As we indicated at the outset, the major problem facing the Left is the widespread assumption that public services are by definition poor-quality services, and the substantial (though not overwhelming) body of evidence suggesting that this has in the past been true. One common answer has been that many of the inadequacies in public services have been deliberately generated by the present government, which – by starving the public sector of resources – has provided a ready-made justification for criticism leading to structural changes and in some cases transfer into the private sector.

While there may be some truth in these assertions, they are not a sufficient answer. Given that the public sector does have distinctive characteristics, as we have already indicated, can it none the less perform at a level of effectiveness at least the equal of market-based organizations providing comparable services? This is a crucial question, which must not be dodged or fudged.

In the period between the two world wars when the case for the creation of new public-sector agencies to implement the Left's social and economic policies was first being made, the importance of confronting this challenge was clearly recognized. The much-maligned Herbert Morrison devoted part of his study of the subject to this issue; concluding that the systematic measurement of performance coupled with publicity for outcomes (the devices proposed for this purpose by the Webbs in their earlier writing on the subject) offered the best guarantees of securing and maintaining high standards in public-sector enterprises. To these, he added recruitment and retention of high-quality staff and the identification of suitable (non-financial) rewards to motivate them (Morrison: 1933).

The authors of the recent Local Government Training Board (LGTB) manuals referred to in our Introduction have developed the case in a far more elaborate and sophisticated form, but essentially along the same lines. The movement for performance measurement has gained substantial impetus lately and has been taken up and developed by diverse agencies like the Audit Commission and the National Consumer Council. However, warning has properly been issued that the bandwagon may be hijacked by service providers for their own purposes if the objectives of measurement are not kept clearly in view (Day and Klein 1987; Pollitt 1988).

Furthermore, the new information technology has vastly increased the extent to which relevant data can be gathered and analysed, though, here again, the objectives of collection and the availability of the outcome in readily assimilable and accessible form are crucial. The VDU on the counter is an invaluable tool for the official behind the desk; but is it capable of being swivelled so that the user of the service can share its usefulness? Without such guarantees, a service based on new technology risks becoming (re)centralized and impersonal.

There may be some trade-offs to make here, too. Impersonality is not in itself always a bad thing – indeed, there is some evidence to show that in certain circumstances some consumers prefer it. But where the new technology is used to distance consumers from the service in a way that seems to threaten their interests, the losses will outweigh any gains in efficiency. Similarly, attempts to secure and maintain quality ('quality assurance' in the new jargon) which draw on the experience of the commercial sector in a variety of ways (speed, presentation of choice, improved efficiency in customer relations, consumer research) are fully justified if they are set in the context of the strategic objectives of the agency, and do not confuse the McDonald's effect (satisfying slickly and efficiently superficial short-term demand) with the complex and longer-term issues arising from consumers' more fundamental needs. Similarly, the very proper emphasis on better communications and securing favourable publicity for new enterprises in the public sector will be more effective if it draws on best – rather than worst – practices in the commercial sector, sharpening awareness and improving access rather than image-building for its own sake (or that of the advertising agency involved).

The question of sustaining staff motivation in order to secure and maintain high standards of service is also crucial. Few people are any longer likely to be satisfied with the Morrisonian answer that service to the public brings its own reward. Puritanism about monetary rewards can be as self-defeating as crass appeals to greed, especially when it is coupled with blatant inequalities of outcome in status and salary terms, as between black and white, and men and women. But the satisfaction of a job well done for a user with whom human contact is not momentary but sustained (as services provided through a neighbourhood office are likely to be) should not be brushed aside; nor should the *esprit de corps* deriving from membership of an efficient organization in which performance is generally accepted as excellent.

Nevertheless, there are questions to be asked about whether the search for quality and choice in all aspects of public service does not imply that the traditional model of public services as public monopolies is no longer appropriate. Does the evidence suggest that public monopoly is a guarantee of quality or an impediment to it? Is it possible to enlarge choice by consumerist borrowings applied *within* public services (for example, free availability of information about performance) or the buttressing of individual rights (for example, to choose schools or go elsewhere for medical care)? Or does real choice involve a more radical break with the model of the monopoly supplier?

If it is the case, as Bosanquet suggests (and some of our own collaborators take sharp issue with him) that 'choice can only develop where there is a variety of suppliers and a variety of suppliers can only develop where there is a pricing system which allows providers to operate long term without subsidy' (Bosanquet 1987: 27), then it becomes rather urgent to develop a model in which the principles and objectives of public service are maintained (or even enhanced), but not necessarily in the form of a public monopoly.

Among several difficulties that such a project will have to address is that of simultaneously being competitive in the market by offering value for money, and providing a distinctive style and approach. Among the assets, perhaps still not sufficiently recognized, is the relatively poor performance of the public utilities that have been transferred into the private sector as a result of the government's privatization programme. In particular, the unsatisfactory record of British Telecom in the early stages of its new incarnation and the ineffectiveness of the regulatory agency created by the government, Oftel, in defending consumer interests during this period underlines the particular disadvantages, in these terms, of the creation of private-sector monopolies or near-monopolies.

Finally, accountability and redress, even within a high-quality public-service system, present their own particular difficulties. The potential for conflict between user and producer interests has already been referred to: the marginalization of community health councils, despite some heroic local struggles, in the face of exceptionally powerful producer interests, is a case in point. More broadly, is movement towards a greater degree of workers' control, which might be desirable for other reasons, compatible with users' control, and, if so, on what terms? More power for service users will inevitably mean less power for other groups, and will lead to sharp conflicts of interest. Who will resolve these conflicts, given that powerful professional lobbies with strong incentives to defend well-entrenched positions are likely to be involved? This leads on to a whole series of issues associated with professionalism, and the need to define a version that is neither self-regarding nor paternalistic. There are a number of risks here that need to be defined: promoting accountability in adversarial style may simply lead to frustrations all round.

Openness and informality in operation are rightly seen as desirable characteristics in a high-quality public service: responsiveness to user complaints is another. The past failure of local authorities to develop effective and open mechanisms for dealing with complaints is a longstanding problem which is only now slowly being put right (Birkinshaw 1985; Senerivatne and Cracknell 1988). It has to be added, however, that the commercial model of reliance on customer complaints has been shown to be barely – if at all – superior. A recent survey indicated that the passion for excellence in meeting customer demands proclaimed as a fundamental characteristic of market-based organizations is often not followed through down to the essential levels of staff training and motivation of local managers. Perhaps more significant still, it showed an overwhelming tendency on the part of the public to steer clear altogether of the complaints mechanisms on which senior managers rely to monitor customer satisfaction (Ernst and Witney *Independent* 9 August 1988).

In learning how to respond constructively to grievances, it is important not to side-step the issue of more structured and fundamental forms of redress, from the different variants of ombudsmen to the courts in their assorted manifestations. Compared with their American opposite numbers, British consumers of public services have often been strangely slow to seek legal remedies. This may be partly explicable in terms of the way in which the British system functions, providing some remedies for individuals but none for the collectivity when the courts' role in public policy is so restricted – as Lord Scarman has put it, 'literally no more than peripheral' (Birkinshaw 1985: 176). Nevertheless, a theory and practice of welfare rights have developed over the past decade and have done much to alert us to the potentialities – and problems – of legal action in this area. This issue is currently the focus of much interest and controversy in the health service (Chapter 7).

In sum, we seek to press for public services that exhibit all three characteristics – high-quality services delivered under democratic control on a human scale – while recognizing that sometimes these characteristics may cut against each other and that experience in particular service areas may lead to one rather than the other being given priority in different circumstances.

Sustaining a new public-sector initiative

How can a new approach be defined and sustained, and the potential conflicts referred to in the previous section resolved constructively? We do not think that a single omni-purpose 'user's charter' is necessarily the best way of approaching the job of producing long-term change in the public sector. Rather, we believe that the concept of a set of principles that are accepted by both users and providers as basic ground rules is what matters; and that action needs to be taken in parallel in each service area, the form and content of the action being determined by their particular circumstances. As the LGTB rightly observe in *Getting Closer to the Public*: 'the politics, politicians, problems and public, as well as culture of each authority are different, and to prescribe a single route would be to go against the whole tenor of this book' (1987: 74).

And if this comment is true of an approach confined to local government, it must be all the more valid if all the different agencies that deliver public services are to be taken into account.

Nevertheless, as we have also shown in the preceding section, there are important general issues, and these have been identified in the main body of the book. These common themes help to bring into focus the question of implementation – ensuring that 'empowering users' is not merely a piety but an objective that has been brought within reach in all services.

Our proposals for further action are therefore organized around the six criteria set down in our Introduction. They are not meant to be exhaustive, but to help provide the basis for a consistent approach which could in future evolve into something more formal.

On accountability, we believe that there is an urgent need to explore ways in which the electoral system can be made to function more effectively. The argument for democratic control at local level is constantly undercut by low participation rates and the unrepresentative character of bodies formed as a result of first-past-the-post elections. With Stewart and Stoker (1988) we believe that early consideration needs to be given to electoral reform; but that the question of users' involvement needs to be a central feature in that process. As part of any review, we would also wish to see the question of selective referenda considered. The past history at local level has not been altogether happy (witness the Coventry example, reported in *Public Administration* (1988)) but there is a potential there which is worth further exploration.

This obviously links closely with the issue of representation. If there are to be reforms intended to reinforce the role of service users, careful consideration will have to be given to the form in which this is achieved. Stewart and Stoker argue that 'it is not clear that direct user democracy will do much to help previously disadvantaged groups' (1988: 17). We accept that it may be preferable to create specific structures for user representation and would point to the model of the Scottish Community Councils as one device which offers a form of direct representation. However, if such bodies are created it is imperative that they possess both the powers and the resources to enable them to make an effective contribution to the planning as well as the running of services. The experience of the community health councils is instructive here; but they have achieved enough to suggest that there may be merit in exploring the possibility of creating similar bodies in other service areas. A series of proposals for such bodies for the social services have been floated at various points but never implemented; the absence of an independent body of this kind in a situation like Cleveland arguably contributed to the sequence of events that took place there, following diagnoses of widespread child abuse (Butler-Sloss Report 1988). Indeed, there is a case worth further examination for establishing user councils for all public services where they do not already exist (irrespective of whether the service currently has formal electoral accountability), and plenty of scope for exploring different combinations of representational devices in the composition of such bodies. Finally, where effective local organizations exist to articulate the views of groups of users – for example tenants' organizations – they should be given resources and responsibilities to enable them to enlarge their role (the Sheffield model (see Chapter 4) of a levy on tenants with the right to opt out is one way of achieving this).

Enough has perhaps already been said about information. The technology exists; what is needed now are the decisions that will make it freely available. It is unlikely, given the present government's general attitude towards freedom of information, that a constructive lead will come from the centre, where the emphasis on financial disciplines has meant that the information so far required to be made available has been related chiefly to expenditure, in the form of output measures. What is needed is a broader range of material that will help both individuals and local organizations to make better choices about services.

This connects with access and the willingness of local agencies in the public sector to move closer to the public not merely in the physical sense of implementing decentralization schemes, where these improve the quality and responsiveness of the service, but also in terms of attitudes. That new technology should be user-friendly is a cliché that is not merely tired but almost exhausted; but it takes on a new meaning in this context, where it provides a device that potentially gives the user (and users' groups) direct access to the material on which they can base their own decisions. Not all this information will be straightforward for them to interpret – which is where well-briefed and adequately funded consumer groups have an important part to play. Perhaps even more important, experience in the planning field ever since the heady days of participation shows how local authority professionals (architects and planners as well as those with specific skills like community development workers) can perform a valuable – and often personally satisfying – role by placing their skills at the disposal of users.

Choice opens up a whole series of issues about the form in which services are provided. We are in sympathy with those who argue that like it or not, developments in the last decade have tended to discredit the old model of public-sector agencies as monopoly providers, the only alternative to which is leaving the system. Hiving off various services to new executive agencies or consortia, subcontracting to voluntary organizations, placing services out to tender in the market, creating new co-operative agencies, and empowering self-help groups are all techniques that have a legitimate place, provided that the key imperatives of democratic control, human scale, and high quality are not compromised. The precise organizational form adopted should depend on the particular circumstances of the particular agency and area: we would not wish to be dogmatic on this score. As with much else, it should be a matter for local discretion, not a ukase from the Department of the Environment.

However, if control is to be exercised and quality secured, some kind of national scrutiny is required. We have already referred to the role of the Audit Commission (and its lineage). In the first round of its policy review in 1988, the Labour Party argued for the replacement of the Audit Commission with a quality commission, designed to 'change the culture of local government, as well as addressing the problem posed by local authorities reluctant or unable to provide decent levels of service' (*Guardian*, 8 November 1988). Our view is that quality issues should not be treated separately. The role of the Audit Commission should be extended to questions of quality of service delivery and the title of the commission should be changed to 'audit and quality commission' in order to reflect that change, with appropriate arrangements for user representation. In addition, the role of inspectorates needs a full review, in order to explore their possible contribution to the general approach proposed here. In service areas where they already exist (education and social services are two key examples) their role in sustaining a new model of public services with appropriate user involvement is potentially of great importance. Consideration should be given to the formal inclusion of this responsibility in their terms of reference. In service areas where they do not exist or are inadequate (as in health) there is an urgent need to examine the possibility of creating them.

Finally, redress. We have made it clear that we consider that present means of securing redress are inadequate. The political system does not provide sufficient scope (chiefly, the occasional and often inadequate sanction of the ballot box); the failure of local authorities to develop effective mechanisms for dealing with complaints needs to be urgently addressed. Other means for redress of grievances do exist, notably the ombudsman procedures which have been gradually extended from central government to local government and the health service (and are now being voluntarily applied in some private service areas, for example insurance and banking); but they are underpublicized, underpowered, and underused. As we have seen, the law provides inadequate and over-elaborate remedies, not suited to immediate user needs. A thorough overhaul of this whole area is needed, which ensures that comprehensive, swift, and effective grievance procedures are in place for all public service activities (whether or not they are performed by public-sector agencies). We would see the new audit and quality commission as having the responsibility for ensuring that this takes place. Complaints systems should be seen as positive instruments of quality assurance. There is a further point here. Redress only has meaning in relation to a framework of rights, standards of performance, and legitimate expectations. We believe that this framework should be made explicit (and, of course, public) in each public service. Its adequacy should be debated and it should be strengthened where necessary. Such a statement of rights, performance standards, and legitimate user expectations should be seen as an integral part of the kind of approach to an eventual codification in a users' charter for which we are preparing the ground here.

Envoi

Some of these proposals are related to particular services, some are not. Some are for implementation locally and some depend upon a framework for action set nationally. Some are politically feasible in the short term; others will require a change of government (which still remained a distant prospect at the time of writing, late 1988). What is also crucially important is that space should be created for new initiatives generated locally which may be capable of extension beyond the locality in which they were first devised. Some of the most interesting developments in public services over the past decade have begun in this way, and it would be paradoxical to attempt to devise a user-sensitive approach so elaborate and rigid as to screen them out.

We do not seek to set aside all the changes that have taken place in the past decade, even if that were possible (and it is not). An uncritical exercise in turning the clock back would be neither sensible nor constructive. As John Willman points out, the role of the state is bound to be different in 'a world where most people will be able to afford to buy themselves services and benefits that 20 or 30 years ago they could only have obtained through universal state provision' (*Guardian*, 21 November 1988). Not all the policy changes that have been imposed, or new devices that are part of this changed environment, are necessarily inimical to the kind of approach that we wish to see adopted. Even those changes that are clearly not now in the best interests of all users may none the less turn out to have created spaces into which better alternatives can in future be fitted.

But there are clear limits to what should be accepted, in terms of what has been done to (rather than for) our major public services during the present government's period in office. The attack on the whole concept of public services as an expression of the collective interests of the community runs wholly contrary to the spirit and substance of what we believe their purpose to be. That purpose is still best expressed by Tawney who, taking up Burke's remark that all men have equal rights

Nicholas Deakin and Anthony Wright

but not to equal things, pointed out that:

> unfortunately, Nature, with her lamentable indifference to the maxims of philosophers, has arranged that certain things... shall be equally necessary to all her children, with the result that, unless they have equal access to them, they can hardly be said to have equal rights, since some of them will die before the rights can be exercised, and others will be too enfeebled to exercise them effectively.
>
> (Tawney 1931: 136)

This answers those philosophers of the New Right whose nostrums require erosion of public services and the principles of communal provision on which they rest, and who are disdainful of any concern with the consequences of what they propose, in terms of 'irrelevances' like social justice. However, that answer now has to be supplemented, and fortified, by offering a new model of how a public service could, and should, be organized.

Our contention is that movement towards greater user control – potential and achieved – charted in the contributions to this volume is an essential, not a peripheral, element in creating responsive and effective public services. These developments help to define ways in which commitment to quality of services can be combined with greater sensitivity to individual and collective preferences and choices. We present them, together with our own proposals here, as part of an attempt to revive political commitment to the concept of public services as an indispensable element in the structure and values of our society.

References

Beresford, P. and Croft, S. (1985) *Whose Welfare?*, Brighton: Lewis Cohen Centre.

Birkinshaw, P. (1985) *Grievances, Remedies and the State*, London: Sweet & Maxwell.

Bosanquet, N. (1987) 'Buying care', in D. Clode, C. Parker, and S. Etherington (eds) *Towards the Sensitive Bureaucracy*, London: Gower.

Butler-Sloss Report (1988) *Report of Inquiry into Cases of Child Abuse in Cleveland*, London: HMSO

Clode, D., Parker, C., and Etherington, S. (eds) (1987) *Towards the Sensitive Bureaucracy*, London: Gower.

Day, P. and Klein, R. (1987) *Accountabilities: Five Public Services*, London: Tavistock.

Ernst and Witney (1988) *Independent*, 9 August.

Jowell, T. and Wistow, G. (forthcoming) 'Corporate community care', *Social Services Insight*.

Klein, R. (1984) 'The politics of participation', in R. Maxwell and N. Weaver (eds) *Public Participation in Health*, London: King's Fund.

Labour Party (1988) *Consumers and Community*, Policy Review Group.

Local Government Training Board (LGTB) (1987) *Getting Closer to the Public*, London.

Morrison, H. (1933) *Socialism and Transport*, London: Constable.

Pollitt, C. (1988) 'Bringing consumers into performance measurement: concepts, consequences and constraints', *Policy and Politics* 16 (2).

Potter, J. (1988) 'Consumerism and the public sector: how well does the coat fit?' *Public Administration* 66 (2).

Robson, W. (ed.) (1937) *Public Enterprise*, London: Allen & Unwin.

Seneviratne, M. and Cracknell, S. (1988) 'Consumer complaints in public sector services', *Public Administration* 66 (2).

Stewart, J. and Stoker, G. (1988) *From Local Administration to Community Government*, London: Fabian Society.

Tawney, R. (1931) *Equality*, London: Allen & Unwin.

Willman, John (1988) 'Labour's lumber-room of old ideas', *Guardian*, 21 November.

Index

216